Smart Questions for Successful _____

plaining a new strategy for getting ahead that has received wide media coverage throughout the world. It offers a technique which will help you to become a more effective manager, climb the corporate ladder or find a better job.

The book is aimed at managers at every level, from trainees to managing directors. It starts with three quizzes which help test your overall questioning approach, assess your ability for getting maximum productivity from your staff, and evaluate the way you use questions to get ahead. Using anecdotes, case histories and lists of possible questions, *Smart Questions for Successful Managers* covers such topics as training, problem-solving, negotiating, getting a rise, delegating and interviewing.

   The author is the President of a US management consultancy firm and she also develops and conducts management and sales seminars.

SMART QUESTIONS FOR SUCCESSFUL MANAGERS

A New Technique for Effective Communication

Dorothy Leeds

SPHERE BOOKS LIMITED

SPHERE BOOKS LTD

Published by the Penguin Group
27 Wrights Lane, London w8 5tz, England
Viking Penguin Inc., 40 West 23rd Street, New York, New York 10010, USA
Penguin Books Australia Ltd, Ringwood, Victoria, Australia
Penguin Books Canada Ltd, 2801 John Street, Markham, Ontario, Canada l3r 1b4
Penguin Books (NZ) Ltd, 182 190 Wairau Road, Auckland 10, New Zealand

Penguin Books Ltd, Registered Offices: Harmondsworth, Middlesex, England

First published in Great Britain by Judy Piatkus (Publishers) Ltd 1988
Published by Sphere Books Ltd 1989
1 3 5 7 9 10 8 6 4 2

Printed and bound in Great Britain by
Richard Clay Ltd, Bungay, Suffolk

For Nonny,
Laura,
and Ian,
with love

Contents

Part Three: Getting Ahead

Acknowledgments

In my seminars and speeches, I always say that there is nothing new under the sun—I am just the lucky catalyst to bring it out. In writing *Smart Questions*, I was the catalyst again. *Smart Questions* was definitely a team effort.

This book would not have been possible without the support, hard work, and involvement of so many people. Thank you to:

Tom Miller, my editor. This book would not be in its present state without his expert advice, persistence, and ability to conquer all obstacles.

Barbara Lowenstein, my agent. Without her original belief in *Smart Questions*, the concept would not have become a reality.

Gerry Miller, Bill Lee, Ed Weihenmayer, Allen Murray, Helen Galliand, Alan Barratt, Shel Caras, Harvey Schein, and Bill Granville, who have so graciously added their wisdom and time.

Anne Dalton for her encouragement and direction; when I struck out, she came to bat.

Judy Schwartz and Florence Levitt for their exceptional editing assistance.

Kathie Ness for her superior copy editing and knack of tying it all together.

Sanja Kabalin and Raquel Altreche, whose devoted administrative assistance have helped so much.

All the managers and supervisors at Mobil Oil, Duke Power, and Prudential-Bache who gave of their time to be interviewed and added so much through their participation in my questionnaires.

All the participants in my seminars and workshops, from whom I continue to learn the value of asking smart questions.

And to my other teams: my family and friends, who have been so lovingly involved and who have always tried to answer all my questions. Onward and upward!

Introduction

One much-sought-after production chief in a high-tech industry told me, "Only 20 percent of my job is spent working with the computers; the other 80 percent is solving people problems."

As technology permeates every facet of the business world today, a manager's people skills often become his or her most valuable commodity. We are smack in the midst of what futurist John Naisbitt calls the "high-tech high-touch" society, when to get the most out of our machines we have to pay more attention than ever to people. At the same time, it's harder than ever to understand human feelings and motivations. Competition is keener, everything moves faster, machinery grows more complex.

Ultimately the day will come when the same technology that threatens to dull our humanity will actually enhance and even extend our own mental abilities. For now there is an uneasy alliance between the two. If human relationships break down, the machinery stops turning.

Now, I don't pretend to be the first management consultant to discover this basic truth. In fact, I add my voice to that of every expert writing in the field of business management today. The issue isn't recognizing the importance of human relationships in business, it's finding effective ways to improve these relationships.

Managers on all levels are searching out tools for building excellence

1

through people productivity, as well as through their own efforts. That's what *Smart Questions* does for you: it provides a tool for building excellence. And it does something else as well. Asking the right questions—of the right person and at the right time—gives the young manager a way to stand out.

Despite the trends of "new humanism" and "participative management," it's not easy to make yourself visible within a corporation. As good as a young executive may be, there are always others as good—or better. How can a newcomer stand out among so much talent? For a high-level executive in the upper reaches of management the problem might be somewhat different: how can he control the action and fast-moving events of modern business? The manager who knows how to ask smart questions can stand out in a crowd of giants and can also reduce much of the pressure that radiates from the centers of power.

Lee Iacocca, undoubtedly the most visible CEO in the nation, comments, "I've seen a lot of guys who are smarter than I am and a lot who know more about cars. And yet I've lost them in the smoke. Why? Because I'm tough? No. You don't succeed for very long by kicking people around. You've got to know how to talk to them, plain and simple."

Knowing how to "talk to them, plain and simple" involves knowing how to ask smart questions. Once you learn to ask the right questions, career success is the response you'll get.

Smart Questions offers a simple technique to help you reach your career goals. You don't have to adopt a special high-powered diet or get up at the crack of dawn to work out three times a week. Forget about dressing for success, meditating, or learning how to nab the right table at the best restaurants. No need to go back to school and collect professional degrees. And don't concern yourself with finding a lifetime mentor.

In fact, you don't need to do anything you haven't been doing all your life—you just have to do more of it, and in the right way. *Smart Questions* shows you how to turn an ordinary conversational skill—the art of asking questions—into a formidable business tool.

Does it sound as though I've discovered a secret code or a magic formula? Well, in a sense that's true. *Smart Questions* holds the secret to success the way a hieroglyph holds the key to a prehistoric civilization: once you understand the symbols, the story unfolds before you. Years of observing communication among executives has given me enough insight to break the code.

As a management consultant I have participated in hundreds of staff meetings, board meetings, coaching sessions, sales calls, job hirings—not to mention firings—and performance appraisals. As time went on, I noticed that the most successful leaders invariably asked the best questions. Effective questioners demonstrated both mastery over their jobs and consideration for other people, a highly desirable combination in modern business.

To test this observation, I devised a three-part questionnaire to measure the quantity and quality of questions asked by managers in various companies. Of more than five hundred managers from several large and small corporations, those considered by upper management to have the greatest potential for leadership all scored in the ninetieth percentile on each part of the questionnaire.

You may have a question about this theory. No, it's not enough to turn yourself loose and assault everyone you know with scores of questions. Shining up to your boss with "And how are you feeling today?" isn't going to do it. Dale Carnegie has always said that you win friends when you ask people about themselves. But good management is not a popularity contest. Good managers know how to use questions to get the most from other people, as well as to win allies.

They also know how to ask *themselves* smart questions. Routinely, the best managers ask themselves what they're doing and why, and what result they expect to achieve. Asking questions is an introspective process. The value of the system lies not only in what you ask other people but in how willing you are to question your own motivations and goals.

In a recent in-house newsletter Donald Petersen, chairman of Ford Motor Company, described his company's mission. One of the four guiding principles Petersen emphasized was this: "Asking more of the right questions and reducing the need to have all the answers. Having more discussions about how to make things happen instead of focusing on why they don't work."

In an interview for this book, Allen E. Murray, Chairman of Mobil Oil Corporation, told me, "In the final analysis, management is a skill of communication. Conveying ideas, work assignments, and priorities is based on communication. So is the ability to command loyalty and good performance." At Mobil one of the top priorities on each employee's annual performance appraisal is "communication skills."

As both Petersen and Murray so emphatically point out, communicating with people is essential for success. Executives who fill upper management positions are always reaching, and a crucial part of their jobs is reaching out to those they work with, trying to help them do their jobs better. At the same time, they're reaching upwards—trying to create footholds for climbing towards their own future in top management. Successful managers must also reach deep inside themselves to find positive and creative answers. Questions can help you reach out in all of these crucial directions.

Smart Questions is addressed to managers at every level, from trainees to vice presidents. All managers—even CEOs who must report to a board of directors—work in two directions. They strive to get maximum performance from their staff people. And they also strive to impress upper management with their own performance and to get ahead within the organization. Because of the bidirectional quality of their professional lives, we've divided *Smart Questions* into three sections.

Part One concentrates on the basic system of asking smart questions: why questions are powerful, how to pose good questions, and how to avoid questions that backfire. At the end of Part One we'll talk about targeting your questions to different personality types and using the special Smart Questions System in virtually any situation.

With the basics spelled out, you can begin to apply Smart Questions to the two primary aspects of every manager's life. In Part Two you will see how questions help you get the most from your staff. This section begins by describing questions that help you hire the best people. Once you have a high-quality staff, however, your job as a manager is just beginning. The following chapters show you how to use smart questions to keep your staff motivated: by delegating, by training and coaching to get your people through trouble spots, by counseling staff people who have special problems. Finally, we'll show how—by using questions—you can turn the ubiquitous performance appraisal into a prime motivating tool.

In Part Three we turn the Smart Questions System upwards, to show managers how to climb the corporate ladder by asking the right questions of the right people. Here we'll talk about using questions, particularly self questions, to solve business problems and make good decisions, and to become a sharper negotiator, especially when it comes to negotiating your own raise. We'll also talk about what to do if your career stalls out—how to use questions to find a new job with a big future—and about creating the special image that will let you pick out a career path in your organization. Finally, in an exclusive roundup of advice from top-level executives who were interviewed especially for this book, we're going to give you an overview of the star qualities that today's young managers must possess—or develop—to get ahead.

The best way to reach out to people, those who work for you and those who control your future, is with questions. People—clients, employees, bosses—will be moved not by how much you know but by how much you care, and how you show that you care. Smart questions demonstrate not only your intelligence but also the depth of your attention and concern. When you know how to ask the right questions you can make anything happen.

PART ONE
The System

"It is better to know some of the questions than to know all of the answers."

—James Thurber

1

The Quiz: Part One

Asking questions is a good thing, right? Right. It's productive, positive, creative, and helpful. Knowing how to ask a smart question can get you almost anything you want, anytime. So why don't we all do it? In fact, most of us think we do. We're certain that we ask plenty of questions, particularly in those situations known to require skillful probing.

I recall one of my clients, Barry, a senior vice president who was having a hard time building his staff; every new person he brought on board turned out to be a dud. He was convinced that his staffing problem stemmed from an inferior employee market.

Barry prided himself on his interviewing technique and told me that he always asked questions to uncover an applicant's potential. He readily agreed when I asked to sit in on one of his interview sessions. I was surprised to observe that, contrary to Barry's own impression, he talked throughout the entire interview, mostly from nervousness, and asked only the most rudimentary questions.

Looking for a convincing way to reveal to him his interviewing style, I suggested that we videotape his next interview. When he saw the videotape he was astounded: he couldn't believe that even though he *knew* he should be asking questions, he seldom did.

The truth is that most of us make statements most of the time. Even when we know better, impatience or nervousness or a need to get our point across pushes us into telling rather than asking, talking rather than listening. Ninety percent of us are talking 90 percent of the time.

The quizzes in *Smart Questions* are designed to help you change your basic communication approach, to put you in a questioning mode, so that by end of book you'll be thinking differently and responding differently. To get the greatest benefit from the questions in the quiz, do not ponder them; go with your first, automatic response. Before you can make smart questions a habit, you must look at your current style.

If you are honest, the quizzes will give you feedback in terms of how you use both self questions and direct questions. Learning to question yourself is as valuable as asking questions of others. Try to imagine each situation as if it were really happening to you, and then check the answer that comes closest to your immediate response. Remember, this quiz is for your own personal evaluation, and brutal honesty will give you the best information.

When you have answered all the questions, add up the points and read about the implications of your score.

Do You Use Questions Enough?

1. When a departmental report is criticized, you say:
   a. "I'm sorry, it's my fault."
   b. "What went wrong?"
   c. "Why does this always happen to me?"
   d. "My people never check their work."

2. When someone you call is "in a meeting," you:
   a. Say "I'll call back."
   b. Leave your name and hope he'll call back.
   c. Ask "When is the best time for me to call back?"
   d. Ask "Can you help me get through to your boss?"

3. You've been turned down for a raise. You:
   a. Quit, and start job hunting.
   b. Ask yourself "What's wrong with me?"
   c. Ask yourself "What can I do to get a yes?"

    d.   Stick with it, even though you feel demoralized and de-energized.

4.   Toward the end of a busy day your boss asks, "What are you doing tonight?" You answer:

    a.   "I have an important appointment."

    b.   "Nothing."

    c.   "Why do you ask?"

    d.   "I was looking forward to having some time to myself."

5.   In the space of one morning your boss gives you three top-priority projects, then brings in a fourth. You:

    a.   Plunge into all four assignments; you want to show that your boss can count on you, no matter what.

    b.   Accept the work load but feel furious inside because your boss has so little consideration.

    c.   Tell her straight out that there is no way all four jobs can be done at once.

    d.   Remind her of the four assignments and ask which she needs first.

6.   When introduced to a new associate, in the first three minutes you:

    a.   Talk about yourself and try to make a good impression.

    b.   Ask questions to gain the advantage but resist revealing anything about yourself.

    c.   Draw the other person out by asking questions and talk about yourself when asked.

    d.   Don't say much and let the other person carry the ball.

7.   The chairperson of a meeting of department heads says that your department should be more cooperative. You:

    a.   Ask the chairperson for specific suggestions after the meeting.

    b.   Say nothing, but later complain to your associates.

    c.   Immediately confront the meeting chairperson and ask how you can accomplish the change.

    d.   Nod your head in agreement.

8. Your boss has criticized you severely for a simple error. You:

    a.   Worry for days because he doesn't like you.

    b.   Ask your boss to tell you more about what he expects from you.

    c.   Deny the criticism and loudly defend yourself.

    d.   At a calmer moment ask your boss how he would feel in the same situation.

9. You are notified by mail that you have lost a major contract. You:

    a.   Accept the letter.

    b.   Plan to try again at the next bidding period.

    c.   Call up and ask why.

    d.   Register at the next sales seminar.

10. You are asked by a high-level executive to volunteer for a project you do not want to do. You:

    a.   Agree reluctantly.

    b.   Say, "Can you tell me more about it?"

    c.   Refuse with a lengthy excuse.

    d.   Ask, "How important is this to you?"

11. Without warning, you are asked to move to a smaller, less advantageous office. You:

    a.   Start packing.

    b.   Start looking for another job.

    c.   Tell the office manager "I'm on my way to a meeting; can we talk about this later?"

    d.   Ask your boss what's going on.

12. You schedule a one-on-one meeting with a tough negotiator with whom you hope to do long-term business. To begin, you:

    a.   Ask a direct and leading question to gain control ("What's your bottom line?").

    b.   Ask a nonthreatening question to establish rapport ("What do you feel is the best way to start this?").

    c.   Let him start off.

    d.   Bring along a support person to set the stage.

13. When you have to make a work scheduling decision that will affect your staff, you usually:

    a.   Ask your boss's opinion.

    b.   Call a staff meeting and make a joint decision.

    c.   Weigh all the facts and decide for yourself.

    d.   Ask your staff to work it out among themselves.

14. When you are trying to show strength within a group, you usually:

    a.   Talk louder and longer.

    b.   Ask probing questions.

    c.   Listen.

    d.   Come well prepared with questions and statements.

15. Your CEO has just called and given you some instructions you don't understand. You:

    a.   Take notes and hope you'll eventually be able to figure them out.

    b.   Ask someone else to explain the instructions.

    c.   Say "I don't fully understand. Can you explain further?"

    d.   Ask "Can I call you back for further clarification after I digest this?"

16. A vice president from strategic planning gives you some advice regarding your projected move to another city. You:

    a.   Don't listen because you've already decided in favor of the move.

    b.   Ask why she's sharing this information with you.

    c.   Take in the information and mull it over later.

    d.   Listen, then later feel upset because you've made the wrong decision.

17. At an interview for a top position the interviewer opens with "Tell me about yourself." You answer:

a. "My first job was in the mail room at ABC; after I finished college I moved up to administrative assistant. Then I was office service manager for two years, and promoted to vice president of administrative services."

b. "That's a difficult question; I'm not sure where to begin."

c. "What specifically do you want to know?"

d. "I was born in Cleveland, but my folks moved to California when I was six."

18. At an important conference you make a poor presentation. You:

a. Vow never to make another public speech.

b. Go over and over all the things you did wrong.

c. Ask yourself "How can I improve the next time?"

d. Ask a more experienced, higher-level executive for constructive criticism.

19. As a job seeker, you are told after an interview, "We'll get back to you." You:

a. Ask "When can I expect to hear from you?"

b. Smile and say thank you.

c. Ask "When can I have an answer—I have other offers."

d. Ask, "When in the next ten days can I call you for an answer?"

20. At an important meeting the chairperson suddenly asks you, "Jim, what did you think of Elaine's point?" Your mind was wandering and you weren't listening to Elaine. You:

a. Try to change the subject.

b. Claim that you were still thinking about the preceding speaker's point.

c. Ask, "Could Elaine give an application of her point so I can answer more effectively?"

d. Admit with humor that you weren't listening.

21. When someone asks your advice about a problem, you:

a. Ask "Where do you hope to end up?"

    b. Ask "What would you like to do?"

    c. Ask "How can I specifically help?"

    d. Ask "Whom else have you asked for advice?"

22. In your opinion, the best way for a manager to use questions is to:

    a. Gain information.

    b. Gain commitment.

    c. Control communications.

    d. Gain the upper hand.

23. During your three-week vacation you turn over your department to a highly power-oriented employee. You:

    a. Ask the employee to clearly state the directives you've given.

    b. Hope for the best.

    c. Ask for a written statement of responsibilities and related authority.

    d. Ask the employee to clearly define the limits of his or her authority.

24. When dealing with a confrontational person, do you:

    a. Feel uncomfortable?

    b. Take the offensive?

    c. Get angry, but acquiese?

    d. Ask "Why do you say that?"

25. An unresponsive person has been assigned to your team. You:

    a. Ask "Why are you so quiet?"

    b. Ask "What do I have to do to get you to respond?"

    c. Leave him alone temporarily.

    d. Ask "What projects are you working on now?"

Answers

1.   a = 2   b = 5   c = 1   d = 0

Automatically accepting the blame (*a*) when work is criticized is not a good answer, but at least it shows that you're not trying to pass the buck.

It's better than a woebegone "Why does this always happen to me?" (c) and certainly better than "My people never check their work" (d), which shows a lack of maturity on your part. Obviously, "What went wrong?" (b) is the best all-round answer.

2. a = 2   b = 1   c = 4   d = 5

When someone you call is "in a meeting," the most normal—and least effective—response is to leave your name and hope the person will call back (b), unless you're Lee Iacocca or the President of the United States. "I'll call back" (a) gives you a little more control; "When is the best time for me to call back?" (c) is good, but leads to a lot of calls. "Can you help me get through to your boss?" (d) is the best possible answer because you get a commitment from someone else to help you.

3. a = 0   b = 2   c = 5   d = 0

Only defensive, insecure people quit when they don't get what they want (a); and yet sticking it out (d) is also bad response, because you aren't any value to your company or yourself when you feel demoralized and de-energized. Blaming yourself (b) by asking "What's wrong with me?" is not very good either, but at least it means you are willing to take a look at yourself. Asking "What can I do to get a yes?" (c) is the most productive kind of self-questioning.

4. a = 2   b = 0   c = 5   d = 3

When your boss asks "What are you doing tonight?" he or she has put you on the spot. If you're just trying to ward off another request to work overtime, "I have an important appointment" (a) is not a very good answer; you could miss out on something that might be more important. Answering "nothing" (b) leaves you open for a lot of work. "I was looking forward to having some time to myself" (d) is a pretty good answer, particularly if you sense that your boss is going to ask you to work overtime again. At least you're being honest and assertive. But the best possible answer is (c): "Why do you ask?" will give you all the information you need to make a choice.

5. a = 1   b = 0   c = 3   d = 5

When your boss thoughtlessly piles on assignments, you can knock yourself out trying to do everything at once (a); at least it shows that you're eager and willing. It's better than accepting the workload while seething with anger (*b*). Telling your boss that you can't do all the jobs at once (*c*) is a pretty good answer; you're being assertive, but you're not offering any constructive solution. The best answer is (*d*): setting priorities helps your boss focus and helps you work efficiently.

6.   a = 1   b = 2   c = 5   d = 0

When introduced to a new associate, it's important to show sincere interest. Trying to make a good impression by talking about yourself (*a*) is not the worst thing you can do, but you're not learning much; (*b*) is a little better, although trying to gain the advantage is asking questions for the wrong reasons; letting the other person carry the ball (*d*) is the worst response because good managers should be actively involved in communication. The best response is (*c*): Ask questions and also talk about yourself; it's even better when you volunteer a little bit about yourself without being asked.

7.   a = 4   b = 0   c = 5   d = 1

When a meeting chairperson says your department should be cooperative, you have two good choices: asking for specific suggestions after the meeting (*a*) is a good response if it's a high-level meeting; but in most situations immediately confronting the chair (*c*) is the best response. Saying nothing (*b*) or nodding your head (*d*) doesn't help at all.

8.   a = 0   b = 5   c = 2   d = 4

Your boss has criticized you severely. Worrying for days (*a*) isn't going to help at all; nor will denying the criticism (*c*). A lot depends on what kind of relationship you have with your boss. If your boss criticizes you severely for a simple error, something else is probably bothering him. In this case (*b*) is the best response; asking your boss to tell you more about what he expects will help you get to the bottom of the problem. Waiting for your boss to cool down (*d*) and asking how he would feel in a similar situation is helpful, especially if this behavior is a pattern that you would like to avoid in the future.

9.   a = 0   b = 2   c = 5   d = 3

You've lost a major contract. Accepting it (*a*) after putting a lot of time and effort into it is not appropriate; people who want to get ahead have to be persistent. Planning to try again (*b*) isn't going to help too much either, but at least it shows some persistence. Registering at the next sales seminar (*d*) is not a bad idea, because learning is always helpful and it may give you some clues as to why you lost the contract. But the best answer is to call up and find out why (*c*). Then you know specifically what to do the next time.

10.   a = 2   b = 4   c = 0   d = 5

We're all asked to do things we don't want to do. Agreeing reluctantly (*a*) is not bad; "Can you tell me more about it?" (*b*) might help, because the assignment may be better than you think; refusing (*c*) isn't going to do you much good if you're upwardly mobile. "How important is this to you?" (*d*) is the best answer because the response may affect your decision: if it's not important, you may safely refuse; if it is very important, you may gain extra points for doing it.

11.   a = 0   b = 2   c = 5   d = 3

Unexpectedly being asked to move to a smaller office has happened to many people I know. It comes as a shock, and I've gotten more calls for advice about this situation than almost any other. My advice is, stall for time so you can think about the best way to deal with it. When you act immediately, you inevitably do the wrong thing. You don't want to start packing (*a*); there's no point in looking for another job yet (*b*). Stall for time (*c*), and ask them not to do anything until you can talk further. Asking your boss what's going on (*d*) couldn't hurt.

12.   a = 2   b = 5   c = 4   d = 0

The obvious answer when going one-on-one with a tough negotiator is (*a*)—try to gain control. But gaining control at the beginning is not always wise, even with a tough negotiator, especially when it concerns a long-term project. It's better to gain support. The best answer is (*b*)—establish rapport to gain trust over the long run. The next best answer is (*c*)—letting the other person start off builds trust. If you need a support person present with a tough negotiator (*d*), you'll lose Brownie points.

13.   a = 1   b = 5   c = 2   d = 3

Anytime you have to make a decision involving your staff, let them participate (*b*). If they can solve the issue without you, by all means let them do it and bring you the solution (*d*). It's all right to ask your boss's opinion, but not at the expense of involving your staff (*a*). There are some situations where you will want to make a solo decision (*c*), but for the most part, look for opportunities to involve your staff.

14.   a = 1   b = 4   c = 3   d = 5

It's hard to answer this question about yourself objectively. Ask someone to observe you in a group and to tell you honestly how you show strength. Talking louder and longer (*a*) doesn't help. Asking probing questions (*b*) is good; listening (*c*) is also good. But being well prepared with questions and statements (*d*) is obviously the best answer—especially if it's your style to talk a lot.

15.   a = 0   b = 1   c = 4   d = 5

Your CEO has just given you instructions you don't understand. Neither (*a*) nor (*b*) is a good response: faking your way through it or asking someone else for help is a dangerous way to go. Saying you don't understand and asking for further explanation (*c*) is not a bad response, but (*d*) is best: although you may not need to call back, always leave yourself an opening. Few people digest everything all at once, and it shows you're thinking ahead.

16.   a = 0   b = 5   c = 4   d = 1

You're about to move to a new location, and someone else sticks their nose in with advice. If you're too hotheaded to listen (*a*), you're not going to learn anything. To listen and mull it over later (*c*) is not bad, but you still don't know why the person is offering the advice. If you chose answer (*d*), at least you're willing to listen, although feeling upset isn't going to help. The best response is (*b*): "Why are you sharing this with me?" The person may have some valuable insight, but before you can judge the quality of the advice you need to know her motivation.

17.   a = 1   b = 3   c = 5   d = 0

"Tell me about yourself" is one of those awful questions that people ask all the time. The best possible answer is (*c*): "What specifically did you want to know?" Anything else and you're wandering off track.

18.   a = 0   b = 2   c = 4   d = 5

Never making another speech in public (*a*) is a sure way to put the brakes on your career. Going over all the things you did wrong (*b*) may help, if you also list all the things you did right. The best way to correct any mistake is to ask yourself "How can I improve the next time?" (*c*). But in this situation the very best thing to do is to ask a more experienced executive for constructive criticism (*d*): not only will you get the help you need, but you'll also develop that person's interest in you.

19.   a = 3   b = 0   c = 4   d = 5

When someone vaguely says "We'll get back to you," it's better, from your point of view, to nail down the specifics. As much as possible you want to be in control of the action. Therefore smiling and saying thank you (*b*) is a polite but useless response. "When can I expect to hear from you?" (*a*) is a good response. "When can I have an answer—I have other offers" (*c*) is better, if you feel confrontal on a given day; it lets the person know you're valued. But the best response is (*d*), "When in the next ten days can I call for an answer?" It is both specific and polite.

20.   a = 0   b = 1   c = 5   d = 3

When you're caught off guard, admitting with humor that you weren't listening (*d*) can sometimes pay off. If you do it right, it shows confidence. But since this is an important meeting, the best answer is "Could Elaine give an application of her point so I can answer more effectively" (*c*). It gives you the information you need in order to respond without revealing a lapse of attention on your part.

21.   a = 5   b = 4   c = 4   d = 2

We all like to be asked for advice, but to be useful to the other person— particularly if it's someone doing a job for you—the best answer is (*a*), "Where do you hope to end up?" because before you can help someone solve a problem you have to know their objective. "What would you like to do?" (*b*) is a good answer; it gets the person thinking for himself. "How can I specifically help?" (*c*) gets him to focus on what he really expects from you. "Whom else have you asked for advice?" (*d*) is a good question if you follow it with "What did they say?"

22.   a = 5   b = 5   c = 4   d = 1

For a manager the best use of questions is to gain information (a) and gain commitment (b). If you use questions to control communication in a positive sense, then (c) is also a good answer. I'd like to think that managers don't use questions to gain the upper hand (d), but questions are like any other skill—once you learn how to do it, you can use it any way you wish.

23.   a = 3   b = 1   c = 5   d = 3

When you have a power-oriented employee, you have to give clear guidelines as to what they can and can't do. If you sit back and hope for the best (b), that person is going to take over your job while you're away. You need a written statement of both responsibilities and extent of authority (c). Asking the employee to verbally state limits and directives (a and d) will help, but putting it in writing (c) encompasses everything.

24.   a = 1   b = 5   c = 1   d = 5

This is a question that you must answer in terms of your immediate reaction: what is your initial response when faced with a confrontal person? When dealing with confrontal people, taking the offensive in some way is the best strategy (b and d). "Why do you say that?" (d) is the best answer because it's a specific question.

25.   a = 1   b = 1   c = 3   d = 5

The worst thing you can ask an unresponsive person is "Why are you so quiet?" or "What do I have to do to get you to respond?" (a and b). You can leave the person alone temporarily and see what happens (c). But the best answer is to start asking about unthreatening subjects (d) to draw the person out.

Scoring

100–125 Points

You're self-confident and feel comfortable asking questions. You seek information and take action, no matter how difficult it may be. You are assertive, yet still able to establish long-term, supportive relationships with employees, colleagues, and clients. You take time to plan carefully and are persistent. Because you are secure you don't hesitate to ask others for help and advice. According to current business indicators, you possess the qualities of the manager of the 1980s.

90–100 Points

You are comfortable asking questions, but you don't seek the help and advice of others as often as you could. You feel that the best way to get more power is through your own achievement and recognition. You can take the lead and are visible within the company. You are ambitious, but to guarantee ultimate success you need to listen more and to tune in to new styles of people management.

75–90 Points

You are ambitious and want to get ahead, but you believe asking for help is a sign of weakness. When something goes wrong you tend to blame circumstances or other people. Asking questions will reduce some of your anxiety, help avoid costly mistakes, and let you develop a more people-oriented approach to your career.

Less than 75 Points

To make it to the top you will have to become more assertive. You tend to accept the blame for foul-ups, and you give up too easily. You are a hard worker and probably are overworked and under stress. You avoid confrontations at all costs. Asking questions in nonthreatening situations will bolster confidence and give you a way to assert yourself without anxiety.

You can see from the quiz that the art of asking smart questions is not always as easy as it sounds. There are few absolutely right or wrong answers. Nor is there a perfect response for every complex situation that crops up in day-to-day working and living. This book will help you develop a technique that allows you to deal with most situations in an intelligent and productive manner. To begin the journey into Smart Questions we're going to analyze the mysterious power that questions have over us all.

2

The Power of Questions

"If you could have three wishes at this moment, what would you wish?" Think about it. A question like that would make the most obstinate, closed-off, difficult person in the world open up. Like most smart questions, it's irresistible.

The main reason questions are so effective is that most people love to answer them. Questions stimulate the mind and offer people an opportunity to use their brains constructively. How else can you explain the continued popularity of question-and-answer quiz shows on radio and television? (What's a group of bears called? [A sleuth.] Where is it bad luck to say "Macbeth?" [The theater.])

One of the axioms of human communication is that most people prefer talking to listening. When you ask for someone's thoughts and opinions, you give him an opportunity to talk. For example, a manager who asks to hear an employee's ideas gains great measures of loyalty—and information—in return.

The impulse to answer a question—any question—is as automatic as the "fight or flight" response. Everyone, including that rare individual who refuses to answer, pays more attention to a question than to a statement. "This department is falling apart" is a statement that achieves nothing. Turned into a question—"If you were in my place, what would you do to turn things around?"—it invites innovation.

Hearing a question puts the listener on the alert. The phrasing and cadence instantly let him know he's expected to do more than listen: he's expected to respond. Even questions we really don't want to answer are compelling ("What are you doing tonight?" "How much rent do you pay?" "Why did you do that?" "What salary are you looking for?").

This answering reflex is fundamental to the Smart Questions system. And you can turn it to your advantage in a multiplicity of business situations.

When I was starting out in the advertising business, I worked with a staff of other junior account executives, photographers, copywriters, salespeople, and consultants. Our boss, the marketing director, was a harried, stressed person who would much rather deal with clients than with us. He was always lecturing us about how we should do a better job, develop better attitudes, work more closely with our customers. His comments, so generally phrased and so negative in tone, made me feel uncomfortable and inadequate. As a team we felt off balance because although our boss seemed so totally dissatisfied with our performance, we didn't know how to improve. Every day gloom permeated the atmosphere in the office.

I would often walk all the way home at night, mulling over the situation; I recognized that I would never be happy in the job unless I could find a way to relieve the constant frustration. Since it was clear that things were not going to change magically, I wondered what I could do to improve my circumstances. And one evening during one of my long walks I had an idea, but it involved taking a risk.

The next afternoon my boss came into the office and started giving us his standard lecture about client relations, ending with "You've just got to spend more time with your clients."

As we all shifted from one foot to the other, I looked him in the eye and said, "You approved my schedule and you know where I spend my time. Could you specifically say how I should change that?"

He looked at me, startled. Then he mumbled something like "Well, you'll just have to find a way," shuffled the papers he was holding, and walked out of the room.

That was a turning point in our relationship. He never lectured again, and he addressed me with new respect. We all began to talk over problems and work on ideas for improvement. I can't say he changed radically, but his behavior altered enough to make the work atmosphere more comfortable.

A Boon to Managers

Lee Iacocca, that wizard of the automobile industry, has said: "I've seen too many guys come along who are smart and talented . . . the go-getters who followed a plan, went to school, got a good job, worked hard—and then nothing came of it. Certainly luck plays a part. But a major reason capable people fail to advance is that they don't work well with their colleagues."

If the definition of management is getting things done through other people, then clearly working well with people is the best way to achieve success. And working well with people is 100 percent communication. Or, as Iacocca says, "talking to them plain and simple." Yet today's managers are expected to do even more than "get the job done." They are expected to help their employees make their own decisions and solve their own problems, thereby devising more imaginative solutions and achieving maximum excellence for both the company and themselves.

"Talking" now takes on even more import. A new communication style is needed to make this extra leap. Nothing can get people to take on and solve their own problems faster than a good question ("How would you do it?").

Managers today are also expected to function well in a wide range of circumstances and situations. When you know how to ask the right questions, you can talk to anyone about anything. You can be at ease in a conversation with a count or a cabdriver, an artist or an accountant. You can work smoothly with technical people and outside suppliers, with clients as well as upper management.

Asking questions doesn't require that you change yourself or try to be something you're not. You can work with anyone, or for anyone, whatever your basic nature.

When to Use Smart Questions

Knowing how to ask smart questions gives you the edge in virtually any situation. Did you know that questions help you:

- Persuade people
- Gain information
- Plant your own ideas

- Clear up fuzzy thinking
- Motivate employees
- Solve problems
- Take the sting out of criticism
- Open lines of communication among diverse peoples and departments
- Reduce mistakes
- Overcome objections
- Get cooperation
- Clarify instructions
- Reduce anxiety
- Defuse volatile situations
- Gain control in risky situations

Persuading People

No matter what your job, sooner or later you'll be in a situation where you want to sell someone something. It may be an idea, or a plan, or a pair of shoes. You may want to persuade someone to your point of view to gain their support. No matter what you're selling, questions will help you.

With a smart question you can find out what worries the other person and what would ease his doubts. A good question establishes rapport, gives the other person the sense that you care, and also gives you a more powerful forum for your pitch than you'd get by handing over gratuitous information.

No matter what you're selling, the same philosophy applies. Says Allen E. Murray, Chairman of the Mobil Oil Corporation, "Sometimes just a 'What do you think?' or 'How does it strike you?' or 'What's wrong with it?' can give me a sense of whether I'm succeeding."

When you want to persuade, you'll always get further by asking a question than by making a statement. In my business a good question will give me ammunition I can use in selling. I will often ask a client, "What are the benefits you'd like to see as a result of our working together?" Then I keep the answers in mind as I develop my proposal.

Getting Information

The most obvious use of questions is to gather information. Being well informed is essential to success in any field, and questions allow you to learn. Good managers need all the information they can absorb, and incomplete information or instructions can be costly.

I work with a client whose assistant vice president is a stickler for getting things right. After receiving any assignment, she invariably asks these questions: "Is there anything else I should know? Can I go over it with you one more time and clarify any miscommunication on my part? When can I call you if I have any questions?"

This manager is only 25 years old, and she is the fastest-rising vice president in her firm because she has a reputation for always turning in work that is virtually flawless.

No one can hope to know everything in this "information age." It's the ability to tap into the most accessible sources of information that's important. For example, the ability to listen to and cull the best ideas from staff people is the sign of a top manager. As humorist James Thurber said, "It is better to know some of the questions than to know all of the answers."

Planting Ideas

Often when you tell someone what you want, they fail to hear you: "Here's the plan—if you follow it everything will work out." Somehow they never quite follow the plan the way you described, because people naturally follow their own ideas better than they do someone else's. A clever use of questions is to plant your own idea in someone else's mind and then let them develop it as their own. William S. Lee, Chairman and CEO of Duke Power Company, describes how he uses the technique: "At a meeting, for example, ask, 'What do you think about incorporating Plan A and Plan B?' When the other person starts talking about it, once they've said it themselves, they own the idea—and I give them the credit for it."

Clearing up Thinking

For me, the most valuable use of questions is to clear up fuzzy or ambiguous thinking. Posing a question requires more concentration than making a statement. Asking questions means that you have to think things through more fully, and your thoughts become clearer as you shape each question. You must delve deeper into your own mind. For this reason alone asking questions immediately puts you a jump ahead of those managers who merely make statements.

For example, when I sit down with my staff to go over the week's priorities, we usually list what each of us hopes to accomplish during the week. Naturally I ask, "What has to be done?" But I also ask this question: "How specifically are you going to handle it?" That way, there are fewer misunderstandings and fewer unpleasant surprises.

A smart question organizes the problem—for yourself and for the person with whom you're speaking—and offers an opportunity to find a solution. When you ask a question you force the other person to think more clearly before answering. To answer you, he must organize his own thoughts and put them into words. Expressing thoughts aloud clarifies ideas, exposes any lapses in logic, and reinforces the strong points. So, as a two-way channel, questions create clearer, more direct communication.

We were involved in an especially busy time in our office when an unexpected direct-mail project turned up. Our marketing director felt swamped. I asked this simple question: "What do you think is the best way to work it out?" She stopped worrying, sat down, and developed a workable plan.

Often a person trying to express his ideas will say "I know what I mean and I just can't explain it." A well-turned question will help him clear things up: "What would you do first?" "How do you see the end result?"

Motivating Employees

One of the best ways to motivate employees is to encourage them to solve their own problems. For example, an employee tells you about an idea he has. After thinking it over a moment, you have your doubts. You might say:

"It will take too much time."

· "It will be too costly."

"It's based on false assumptions."

What did you accomplish? You dealt with the idea swiftly, gave your staff person the benefit of your wisdom, and saved him from wasting his time on a chancy project. Or did you? What if instead you had said:

"How much time do you think it will take?"

"What do you estimate it will cost?"

"Does that equation seem profitable to you?"

What did you accomplish this time? By posing your thoughts as questions, you gave your employee your point of view in a more compelling way by allowing him to come to the same conclusion himself. Without creating ill will, you gave him the means to assess his idea, to see the flaws or strong points, and to make an independent judgment. And your receptiveness ensures that he will contribute his ideas again.

Problem Solving

Asking questions helps you get to the bottom of problems and make decisions that are fair to everyone concerned. Gerard A. Miller, Vice President Director of Finance, Merrill Lynch, Pierce, Fenner & Smith, Inc., says: "I use questions to locate pressure points and weak spots. It's important to get out and talk to your people; ask them what's going on. It's the only way you can discover problems before they mushroom."

I once observed two managers who solved problems in completely different ways. When one manager saw his people having difficulties he would say, "Oh, that's easy. I know you can take care of it." He believed that by taking a positive attitude he was building their confidence.

In similar situations, however, the second manager would ask, "What seems to be the problem?" He listened, then asked, "What solutions do you see?"

In the first instance, the staff had little respect for their manager; they felt he didn't care about their problems and that they had to struggle towards a solution alone. It always took them a lot of time to work things out.

In the second situation, the staff thought their manager was the best executive in the company. His simple questions showed interest and helped them think more clearly. As a result, they solved problems faster and more efficiently.

The most interesting aspect of these two examples is that both managers spent exactly the same amount of time and effort helping their staff. Yet one had a terrible time getting his people to solve problems and the other got them solved easily.

Taking the Sting out of Criticism

When you state an opinion, especially a critical one, the other person's hearing turns off and his guard goes up. Whether the person is your friend or your employee, your spouse or your child, direct criticism will put him or her on the defensive. Prefacing negative remarks with "Don't take this personally" doesn't help. Once aimed towards someone, criticism becomes personal. The only way to take the sting out of a negative appraisal is to get the person to see it—and say it—for himself.

A manager can use a question to take the sting out of criticism and at the same time secure a commitment for change. "You're always late" and "You are wrong" are statements that achieve nothing. Turned into questions—"How do you think lateness affects the department?" and "Why do you feel that way?"—they arouse thinking and encourage action. They involve the other person instead of alienating him.

Opening Communication between Diverse Groups

We've all heard about technical wizards who can solve the riddles of the universe but can't carry on a simple conversation with their next-door neighbor. As technological change speeds on, communication between technical and nontechnical people becomes more necessary, and more difficult, than ever.

In my consulting work I find that technicians suddenly promoted into managerial ranks often have trouble getting their ideas across to co-workers who don't speak their language. A nonverbal technical whiz will find he can talk to many different kinds of people, including his superiors, more easily once he learns to ask questions. A questioning approach makes him seem less aloof, more accessible and concerned. Asking questions lets the technical person talk less, listen more, and still establish rapport with co-workers.

Reducing Mistakes

One basic premise of communication is that your perception of a problem determines how you act on it. We go wrong not so much in what we do as in how we originally perceived the problem. Upon assigning a task, a manager will often ask an employee, "Do you understand?" The employee invariably nods affirmatively. To say he doesn't understand is tantamount to admitting that he's slow-witted.

Two weeks later the employee submits a report on the delegated task. The manager explodes. "This isn't what I wanted! I thought you said you understood!" The employee did indeed understand, but what he understood and what the manager understood were two completely different interpretations.

The manager asked the wrong question. Instead of "Do you understand?" he could have asked a smart feedback question: "To eliminate the guesswork, can you sum up what you're going to do as a result of this meeting?" He could then listen to the reply, correct any missteps, and clarify any vague instructions. Smart questions are a foolproof means of generating feedback and reducing mistakes.

When you establish an atmosphere of give-and-take, you can learn a great deal from such smart questions as "Is there anything more I can do to clarify the assignment before you begin?" or "Why don't you give it some thought and get back to me with any questions before you begin?"

Overcoming Objections

We all get into those binds where whatever we say is countered with a series of objections. "Yes, but . . ." is the most frequently heard. You can go on and on like this, offering one option after another, never getting anywhere. The solution? Stop . . . think . . . and ask.

"What are your major concerns about this [project, idea, product]?"

"What other choices do you see?"

"How can I help you?"

Getting Cooperation

Sometimes you get into a situation where you're trying to solve a business problem but can't seem to get attention or cooperation from anyone.

Charles, the head of a new publishing company, was trying to get permission to allow mail-order customers to charge their orders to a bank card. Charles spoke to eight different banks and from each received the same reply: no mail-order accounts because of previous bank losses. In desperation, he asked one bank officer in merchant sales, "Have you ever made an exception?" To Charles's surprise, the merchant saleswoman paused. "I'm not sure," she told him. "I think there was one instance . . . but I can't remember the details."

Charles became alert. "Would it be possible for you to find out for me? Maybe there's something else I can do."

The merchant saleswoman said she would try to find exceptions to the ruling. While waiting for a call back, Charles called five more bank officers in merchant sales and after being turned down, asked each the same question: "Have you ever made an exception?" In every case, the salesperson sought the exceptions, quoted the circumstances, and gave Charles something to go on.

By accumulating enough "exceptions," Charles was able to put together a passable application form and was eventually rewarded with permission to use a bank card. Many difficult legal cases are won in precisely this manner: accumulating the exceptions and building a case.

When faced with a blank wall, remember Charles: "Have you ever made an exception?" is one of the all-time great questions.

Clarifying Statements

The most immediate use of smart questions is to clarify statements of any kind. A new secretary once told me that she would reorganize my files so that I could more easily find things. I took for granted that this would be a positive maneuver. Lesson No. 1: Never assume. Naturally I came back to find that she had organized the files in a manner that was completely incomprehensible to me. The smart question I failed to ask: "How do you plan to do it?"

I remember another instance where an executive vice president of operations, in a state of frustration, addressed his staff with this statement: "What this organization needs is better communication."

He was totally shocked when he wound up with a new telephone system. No one asked him what he meant by "communication."

Stemming Anxiety

Most psychologists agree that anxiety arises from loss of control. Asking a smart question puts you in the driver's seat. Because the other person is compelled to answer, the power goes to the asker. Just watch the power shift when someone asks you, "Where are you going?" and you answer, "Why do you ask?"

With a question you choose the subject to be discussed, and you establish the tone of the exchange. The conversation continues along the lines of your questioning. The moment you feel the conversation turn in the wrong direction you can change the subject simply by shifting the focus of your questions.

It pays to be assertive. Terry's boss was a frantic workaholic, racing in and out of his office all morning with one assignment after another. Terry controlled the action and reduced his own tension with a smart question: "Which of these is most important to you, and what are the time limits?" Because smart questions put him in control, his anxiety abated.

Asking a question also forces you to think before you speak, and the better prepared you are, the more confident and in command you feel.

Defusing Volatile Encounters

Most of us shy away from direct confrontation with others because it threatens to set off an uncontrollable chain reaction of attack and counterattack. Asking questions gives you a way to confront people with minimal conflict. When you begin a confrontation with a question— "Can you tell me more about what you're feeling?"—you reduce the other person's defensiveness and open up the chance for communication.

Reducing Risks

To get to the top you often have to take risks. Melissa, an energetic and outgoing young project manager, was vying to handle an important new project for her company. Yet her boss couldn't seem to decide who would get the job. Melissa decided to take a calculated risk. She approached her boss:

"What are the key qualities I would need to do this job?" she asked.

"Tact, analytical thinking, follow-through, and good public-speaking abilities."

"Do you feel I have what it takes?"

"Yes and no."

"Can you clarify that?"

"You're good on your feet, you're an objective thinker, and you get the job done, but you also irritate a lot of people. You push too hard, and it puts people off."

"How important is that to you?"

"In this case, it's important. The client company has a complex inner structure, with lots of competitive departments and several people in authority who require subtle handling."

"Is that all that's holding me back from the job?"

"That's it."

"Let's say I got Vincent, the departmental diplomat, to handle the outside communication; would that satisfy you?"

"It's an interesting possibility. It might work. I'd be willing to give it a try."

In this case Melissa risked an outright rejection from her boss, which might have left a scar on their working relationship. It also could have confirmed his view of her as being too pushy and aggressive. If the situation had turned out that way, however, Melissa could have gained an important insight.

Her style might hold her back indefinitely in this particular company. It's possible, of course, that this situation might be an isolated case. To make certain, Melissa would need to probe further to see if the only people who get ahead in her company are indeed the diplomats. Were this the case she might get much further if she switched to a different job where her no-nonsense approach was considered an asset rather than a liability.

An Immediate Effect

These are some of the multitude of ways questions can work for you in business—both with your staff and with upper management. If you want to coach your employees, if you want to gain attention and respect from your boss, if you want to persuade, learn to ask questions. The best part about it is that you don't have to be a tactical genius to benefit from a questioning style. You learn how to do it simply by doing it. For one day, concentrate on asking questions. See for yourself how well you can make yourself understood by using questions instead of statements.

Many ordinary statements can be turned into questions. In your conversations, get into the habit of questioning—not just to get facts but to stimulate the other person's thinking, as well as your own. When you do make a statement, don't consider it complete unless you also ask for a reaction. If you try, you can quickly learn to restructure the way you communicate with people. You will become a better persuader almost immediately.

As you get into the habit of asking questions, you will find that your conversations are richer in information and more engaging to both the other person and yourself.

Now, obviously, going around asking questions willy-nilly of everyone you meet isn't going to turn you into an overnight success. The whole point of the Smart Questions technique is to ask the *right question*, at the *right time*, of the *right person*. And that's where skill, intuition, and good sense will make or break your success.

3

The Right Way to Ask

I remember two customer-service managers at a long-distance telephone company who used questions in different ways. The first manager answered customer complaints with this question: "Do you have a problem?" The response invariably was "You bet I have." The manager's ears burned with every telephone problem the customer had ever had. Customers ranted and raved, reliving every injustice ever perpetrated by telephone companies past and present. After all the grievances had been aired, the manager would eventually discover the immediate problem he was expected to solve.

The second manager avoided these long and exhausting encounters by using a different opening question. She would ask, "In what way may I help you?" Her question quickly got the customer off his gripes and got him thinking about a solution.

Even though smart questions have a broad application in almost every profession, they have to be used in the right way. Asking a smart question and asking it in the right way is an art. A thoughtlessly phrased question is like a loose cannon—it can set off wild repercussions. Likewise, too many questions, thoughtlessly phrased, make the questioner look and sound silly. But a thought-out, concise, and stimulating question shows that the questioner is intelligent and discerning. Fortunately it's fairly easy to arrive at this position.

The Two Types of Questions

There are many different types of questions, but most fall into two broad categories: the *closed question*, one that extracts a piece of information but precludes further discussion, and the *open question*, one that stimulates thought and encourages continued conversation. Smart questions invariably fall into the second category, but there are times when the closed question is useful.

Closed questions can be answered with a yes or no, or with a simple statement of fact. They are good for getting information in a hurry. Here are some examples:

"How many forms do you need?"

"Who is responsible for quality control?"

"What is our starting time?"

"Do you want to get ahead in this organization?"

"Is this the entire report?"

"Did the supplies come in on time?"

"Have we received all the payment invoices?"

"When is the meeting scheduled?"

"Did you phone for reservations?"

Closed questions usually get the sought-after information, and they can be useful for capturing someone's attention. William Granville, Manager of Technology Transfer at Mobil Oil Corporation, likes closed questions because "they save time and keep conversations properly directed." Interjecting a yes-or-no question into the stream of a conversation also can steer an undirected discussion back on course ("Didn't you tell me that the only really feasible course of action was to change the contract?").

You can also use a closed question to confirm an agreement: "Are we agreed then? Can we shake on it?"

But closed questions do not always serve a manager's needs, because they don't lead anywhere. The questions most valuable to managers—the questions that get results and encourage growth and development in virtually any situation—are like open roads, inviting exploration. At the same time they have purpose and intent.

The beauty of open questions is that they allow the other person to become involved, to participate in the exchange and come up with solutions of his or her own.

Open questions require a more in-depth response than a yes or no or a simple statement of fact. Some examples:

"How would *you* handle this situation?"

"What kind of people get ahead in this company?"

"What feedback are you getting from your people in the field?"

"How do you feel about this?"

"What is most important to you?"

"What is it you don't like about Brand X?"

"What are your priorities for this assignment?"

Open questions create a conversational tone. They eliminate the sense of interrogation typically associated with closed questions. In fact, the other person may not even be aware that questions are being asked. Open questions also encourage the other person to think about his answer. If he doesn't have the answer on the tip of his tongue, the natural pause that follows the question gives him a chance to think about it. If he does have an answer ready, you've given him an opportunity to express himself. By asking the question, you have invited the other person to offer his view.

An advertising man can earn points with a prospective client if he uses the open question technique:

"What would you like to see happen as a result of a new campaign?"

"Where do you think your previous agency fell short?"

"What's the message that you most want to get across to the public?"

"What do you think are the benefits of your product?"

"Why do you think someone should buy your product instead of the competing brand?"

With open questions you gain more than factual information, you get a good take on thoughts, attitudes, and emotions that influence the other person's actions. Open questions also help the other person clarify his thinking as he states his needs in his own words.

Open questions are prime motivating and coaching tools. We're going to talk more about this in Part Two. In a nutshell: The way to get employees past a problem is to get them involved in the solution. And the way to get them involved is to encourage them to verbalize the problem themselves. Instead of stating "I think your work would improve if you spent more time organizing yourself," ask "How do you think you could plan your time more efficiently?" or "In what way can you use your staff more productively?"

Knowing this, does it surprise you to learn that with all of these advantages, only one out of every twenty questions managers ask is phrased in an open style?

Open questions are vastly underused for two reasons. The first is sheer ignorance. Because questions are generally not part of the standard business communication repertoire, most people are unfamiliar with the technique and therefore don't know how to use it. The second reason is that it takes more effort to think up open questions and to pay the necessary close attention to the responses.

As a consultant working with a variety of corporations I have had plenty of opportunity to observe the difference between approaching my own clients with closed questions and with open questions. While it usually takes more time to think of an open question, ultimately I save much grinding, tedious effort. Here's an example of a management consultant using closed questions to elicit information from a potential client:

Consultant: Is your company involved in executive development?

Client: Yes.

Consultant: Who attends these sessions?

Client: First-line through middle managers.

Consultant: Do you use outside trainers?

Client: No.

Consultant: How often are these classes run?

Client: About once a month, or as needed.

Consultant: How long are they?

Client: One day each.

Consultant: What results do you see?

Client: Fair to good.

The consultant in this example garnered specific information with a series of six closed questions, but the conversation was rudimentary, and he is still a long way from landing the job. Suppose instead he had asked one smart open question:

Consultant: Can you tell me something about the kind of executive training you do?

Client: We have a limited menu of training and our managers are required to take five days of training each year. The courses usually last one day. They can select from the menu of courses, and their bosses okay the training. With cutbacks in budgets we'd like to do more, but we can't.

The word "limited" was a signal to the consultant that there was an opening. So was the information that the company confined itself to one-day courses. One day is not sufficient for many types of managerial training.

From the one question in this example the consultant acquired much valuable information. Also, the client was invited into the situation. Out of the client's own mouth came the answers that allowed the consultant to go on to make a strong case for his own employment.

Creating Smart Questions

A closed question is easily turned into an open question by adding one or two important words. "What," "how," and "could" are perfect examples.

Closed: Do you use word-processing equipment?

Open: To what extent do you use word-processing equipment?

Closed: Do you have any problems with that machine?

Open: What has been your experience with that machine?

Closed: Do you like to travel?

Open: How do you feel about traveling?

Closed: Can the department improve?

Open: How can the department improve?

Closed: Why did you do that?

Open: What could have been done differently?

Closed: Which idea is best?

Open: Could you describe several other options?

Closed: What do you use this for?

Open: Are there any other applications?

Ten Smart Open Questions

Tuck these ten smart and versatile open questions into your mind for future use in almost any situation.

1. "What can I do to help you?"
2. "What has to be done?"
3. "Can you explain the process?"
4. "How do you feel about it?"
5. "Can you explain that further?"
6. "From what standpoint are you asking?"
7. "What are some of the reasons this didn't work as well as we had hoped?"
8. "What can we change to make this work better?"
9. "What key results are we looking for?"
10. "From what standpoint do you ask?"

"Feeling" Questions

"Feeling" questions are wonderful for most people. (There is one important exception—a certain type of person of whom you should seldom ask a feeling question—which we will discuss in Chapter 5.)

For the most part, "How do you feel about that?" will generate a more in-depth response than "What do you think about that?" It's easy for someone to give you an offhand response to "What do you think?" They can hand you a quick opinion, or if they have no opinion, answer "I don't know." But whether or not you know anything about a topic, you can *feel* something about it. Exploring feelings also requires more personal commitment and, ultimately, deeper thinking.

This type of question, by the way, is the favorite of newscasters and reporters. The next time you watch the six o'clock news, listen to the reporters interviewing a subject.

Combine Questions with Third-Party Endorsements

Promoters, public-relations people, and marketers use a familiar persuasive device called "third-party endorsement." The premise here is that most people respond better to stories about other people than to abstract concepts. A promoter, for example, tells his listener a story about someone who struggled with a problem until the promoter's product provided the solution. By identifying with the third party, the listener is persuaded that the product can solve his problem too.

The same technique, combined with a question, works for managers. For example, you might help an employee grappling with a serious problem by saying "Joan once had a similar situation, which she solved this way." You proceed to describe the problem and how Joan coped with it. But that isn't enough. To make a third-party endorsement work as a managerial tool, you need to combine it with a smart question. When you finish Joan's story, ask an open question such as "How do you think that solution would work in this instance?"

A more subtle version of the third-person technique is used skillfully by interviewers when they discuss sensitive issues with celebrities. Let's say you want to get someone to level with you about his or her drinking problem, as Betty Rollin described in her book *Am I Getting Paid for This?*: "If you ask about it flat out," says Rollin, "they'll usually deny it. But if you say, 'A lot of people think it's easy to stop drinking, that all you need is a little willpower—what do you think?' Then you'll hear how it's not easy. And that's probably not all you'll hear. . . . Most people, even stars, seem to *want* to tell you about their true selves."

Questions Are Socially Appealing

You can learn a great deal about others by listening to the way they use—or don't use—questions. A very smart, attractive friend of mine says, "I wouldn't go out with a man who didn't ask me some questions about myself within the first five or ten minutes of our meeting. If he doesn't ask me anything about myself, I figure he's a self-centered sort of person. If he does ask me a few questions, it tells me that he's interested."

Questions are an enlivening conversational tool to help you breeze through any social situation. You needn't restrict your questions to the ordinary ("How do you feel?" "What have you been up to lately?"). Impersonal, imaginative questions can make for stimulating social conversation:

"If you were stranded on an island, what ten books [tapes, videocassettes] would you want? What man [woman] would you most want to be with?"

"If you could live during any period in history, which would you choose?"

"If you could marry any famous person in history, who would it be?"

"If you were suddenly given a million dollars and told that you had to spend it just on yourself, what is the first thing you would buy?"

This is Barbara Walters's favorite conversation stimulator: "If you were hospitalized for three months but not really too sick, whom—and it can't be a relative—would you want in the next bed?"

Johnny Carson shot back: "The best damn doctor in town."

But Chet Huntley picked Charles de Gaulle. And Liberace chose Greta Garbo (so he could do all the talking). Whom would you choose?

Practice Makes It Happen

Creating smart questions is a skill that has to be developed. The next time you have a closed question or a statement on the tip of your tongue, stop and turn it into an open question. You will immediately notice the difference in personal response and communication. Like any other skill, however, your questioning technique will improve with practice. And don't limit your practice to the workplace. Get in the habit of asking questions in your personal interactions as well. In social situations make an effort to cast a few original questions towards other people. With friends, family, and colleagues, consciously try using open questions.

Like anything else, you're not going to get a hit every time. Questions are a wonderful tool, but you have to be careful about the way you use them. In the following chapters we're going to talk about staying out of questioning trouble and avoiding the real clinkers.

4

Questions That Backfire

My favorite dumb question was posed by Jimmy Durante in the movie *Jumbo*. As Durante tried to sneak his enormous circus elephant, Jumbo, out of the fairgrounds he was confronted by the sheriff and his deputies. "Where are you going with that elephant?" demanded the sheriff.

Standing in front of the elephant like a gnat trying to hide an airplane, Durante spread out his arms, looked inquiringly to either side, and innocently asked, "What elephant?"

Can questions ever lead you astray? They certainly can. Silly questions can make you look dumb. And smug questions, like smug statements, can make you wish you had a hole to fall through.

You've heard the story of the snappy young salesman who picked up his client at the airport and jauntily ushered him into a sparkling new Rolls Royce. "Is this your first time in one of these?" asked the salesman.

"My first time in the front seat," answered his amused client.

Everyone's entitled to make a fool of himself or herself occasionally. And questions that make you look foolish are not nearly as bad as questions that sound unfriendly, or even threatening. "May I be frank?," for example, is intimidating and almost always signals unpleasant criticism. Other questions can raise doubts or be aggravating.

I remember once asking a client, "What are some problems you're having with your staff?"

"Who said I was having any problems?" she shot back. She was so indignant that I was unable to steer the conversation back onto a neutral track. Although I had used this question dozens of times with other clients, it triggered a bad reaction in this particular person. For her, a less direct question would have worked better ("What are some of the things you're doing in that particular department?").

Certain questions generate a bad response in certain people, and it's not easy to know in advance how someone will respond. Permanently embedded in everyone's memory are parents and teachers:

"Where have you been?"

"How many times do I have to tell you . . . ?"

"When are you going to shape up?"

"How could you do such a thing?"

The wrong questions posed to the adult can trigger all these old feelings of guilt, inadequacy, and rejection.

Dangerous Questions

Of all the potentially dangerous questions you can ask, "Why?" may be the most harmful. Children use it to drive adults crazy. They eventually learn to stop asking "why" because it generates impatience in mothers, fathers, and teachers.

On an adult level, "Why?" frequently cuts off communication when it sounds judgmental or condescending ("Why are you doing it that way?" "Why do you feel that way?" "Why do you think that's a good idea?" "Why did you tell the client we'd send him an advance copy?").

"Why" is useful only when it is fully stripped of its negative connotations. It must be a sincere question, one that cannot be misread. A disapproving attitude can be expressed through your tone of voice, a gesture, even a raised eyebrow. If you accompany the question "Why?" with any of these signals, the other person automatically goes on the defensive.

Overall, "Why?" is one question that you can virtually eliminate from your stock of smart questions. Occasionally you'll be tempted to ask "why" to clarify an instruction, but even then you should take care. I recently overheard a man dining in a French restaurant make this request of the waiter:

"Would you bring me a new serving of butter? This one looks as if it's been used."

The waiter examined the pats of butter in the butter dish, which he had just brought out, and replied, "It's fresh, sir. It just looks ragged."

"Will you please bring me a new serving anyway?"

"Why?"

The customer lost his temper. "Because I asked you, that's why."

The waiter left in a huff and returned with a new plate of butter, which he promptly slammed on the table.

The customer grumbled to himself, and I could almost see him mentally cut the waiter's tip in half.

If you must ask "why" for information, remove the sting by rephrasing the question ("Could you tell me what the problem is?").

"Why?" can almost always be rephrased into "What," "how," and "could" questions. Consider these alternatives:

"Can you explain more fully?"

"What do you have in mind?"

"How do you feel about this?"

"Can you tell me more about why you want to do it this way?"

"How did you come to your decision?"

"If I knew what factors determined your decision, I could be more specific. Could you tell me?"

"Can you elaborate on that?"

"Can you give me some examples?"

"Why" works in some cases ("Why do you suppose that happened?"), but in general, think twice before you ask "why," and see if another question wouldn't get you a better result.

Manipulative Devices

Some people think they can use questions to gain the upper hand. Indirect questions fall into this category. My former boss used to ask,

"Wouldn't you like to get this for me?" or "Wouldn't you like to do this for me?" The whole point of such questions is to shift responsibility onto the other person, and that other person is bound to resent it. If you have to manipulate someone in order to be in control, you're already working from a tenuous position. People are much more willing to help if you ask straight out: "Please do this for me."

One of the most irritating indirect questions is this one: You're putting on your hat and coat and your boss (or colleague, or mother, or spouse) asks, "Are you going out?" What they really want to know is "Where are you going?" but they insist on taking the long way round.

Some people use questions to make it appear as if they are deeply interested in someone. They ask a string of questions to avoid revealing anything about themselves in the course of the conversation ("If I keep the chatter going, the other person will be happy and I won't have to volunteer a thing"). This assumes that people are so easily fooled that they're satisfied just running on and on about themselves ("How's your mom? Glad to hear it—how's your Dad? What about your little sister Amy? And your cousin who lives in Dubuque? What do you hear from Louie, that fellow you used to room with when you lived in Seattle?").

Some people ask questions because they're lazy or tired and don't have the energy to carry on a conversation. But communication means give-and-take. To make questions work, you have to be willing to talk about yourself.

At a medical convention Richard, a new advertising executive anxious to make contacts, meets a product manager of a pharmaceutical company. Richard has learned that a good conversationalist asks questions.

Richard: What sort of work do you do, Brad?

Brad: I'm in pharmaceutical marketing.

Richard: What company are you with?

Brad: Ross and Tompkins.

Richard: What kinds of products do you handle?

Brad: My division is devoted to over-the-counter drugs—we have the leading cold remedy. Some skin-care products, too.

Richard: Where is your office?

Brad: At Sixth Avenue and Fifty-first Street. It's not too far from Grand Central.

Richard: Do you commute?

Brad:	Every day. We moved up to New Rochelle a few years ago. It's not too bad, though. My wife and I both take the train.
Richard:	How long does the trip take?
Brad:	About an hour and ten minutes, door to door. It used to take me twenty minutes ...
Richard:	How many children do you have?
Brad:	Two boys and a girl.
Richard:	How old are they?
Brad:	The boys are twelve and seven. Penney is five.

With each question Brad, gamely trying to develop the conversation, is feeling increasingly more irritated. All he can think about is how to get away from Richard and escape his verbal assault.

What does Richard think he's doing? He thinks he's being engaging. He has read that good social skills consist of drawing people out by asking them questions. But while Richard is patting himself on the back for being a diplomatic giant, Brad is getting ready to throttle him.

Hurling questions at people gives them the distinct impression that you're oblivious to their feelings. Lawyers are masters at this cross-examination technique, but what works in the courtroom may be a disaster in daily life.

How could this conversation have been different?

Richard:	What sort of work do you do, Brad?
Brad:	I'm in pharmaceutical marketing.
Richard:	That's interesting. Your job must be a tough one right now, with all the new regulations. Do you handle over-the-counter or prescription?
Brad:	OTC—and you're right. Nowadays, trying to sell any drug over the counter without saying anything out of line is a challenge. I'm temperamentally more suited to lying in the sun in Bermuda, but who can afford it?
Richard:	I sympathize—I'm one of the guys who try to help you guys come up with new ways to say the same old things.
Brad:	You must be in advertising. Creative or client side?

Richard: I'm an account executive. And from the looks of my bank balance I believe in my products. I guess I fall into the pattern of conspicuous consumption that everyone identifies with suburbanites. Are you one of us?

Brad: Oh yes, I'm on the run to New Rochelle. Whenever I have a nightmare there's always a commuter train in it. Actually, I like it pretty well. My wife and I both commute in the mornings and it gives us some time to talk without the kids around. I just complain because everyone else does.

In this version, even though Richard holds the initiative because he is the primary questioner, both men have talked about themselves, and both have enjoyed the conversation. Richard responded fully, rather than just collecting Brad's remarks like index cards and filing them away.

Richard has accomplished his purpose: he made a contact. He wasn't looking for a confirmed client or a best friend. He was looking to meet people and make a positive impression within his industry.

Showing Off with Questions

Some people use questions as a sneaky way to look smart. It's a good ploy, but it requires finesse. Recently I attended a seminar on diet and heart disease. The speaker was inexperienced and did not appear to be well informed. A knowledgeable show-off asked, "What about the study on how Type A behavior affects the development of atherosclerosis?" The asker was just showing off that he had as much knowledge as the speaker, and possibly more.

Too Curious

Prying questions are usually beyond the pale, but there are some exceptions. There are different kinds of prying—curious and nosy. You can often get away with being curious, but it's easy to go too far. (In New York you can ask "What rent do you pay?" In the South that might be out of line.) Curious questions fall somewhere into the gulf between needing to know and wanting to know. If you're asking a question because you want to satisfy your curiosity and really don't need the information, in certain situations it might be better to pass it up. You never want to make the other person feel uncomfortable.

Asking at the Wrong Time

In corporate life there's always a right time and a wrong time to ask questions. Stopping someone on his way out of the office is almost always the wrong time. Even if all times seem wrong—if, for example, your office is perpetually fighting a deadline—some moments are more wrong than others.

Before you ask anyone a question make sure you consider what the other person is doing. For instance, let's say you want to talk to your boss about a raise. You've spent a week working up your nerve, and you feel that it's now or never. You stride purposefully into his office:

"Have you got a minute?"

Your boss is obviously buried in paperwork, and both telephones are ringing. He looks up, harried and annoyed. "Sure. What do you need?"

Because you're so eager to make your pitch, you don't hear the warning bell go off. You don't hear the strain in his response. But you should have: clearly it's the wrong time.

Telephone callers, too, need to be aware of timing. "Is this a good time to call?" is a basic telephone question. As obvious as this is, most callers still plunge ahead, without consideration for the person on the other end of the line.

Recently a smart telephone solicitor called to ask me to contribute money to an alumni fund. She first asked, "Is this a good time to call? I only need one or two minutes of your time." Because of her courtesy, I took the time to listen, and she got the contribution.

Too Many Questions

One of the worst things you can do is to ask too many questions. If you go around your organization asking everyone questions all the time, you will get a backlash reaction. "Don't be in the business of asking questions like a child," advises Ed Weihenmayer, Vice President of Human Resources at Kidder, Peabody & Co. "Why, why, why—it's annoying and you might as well light it up on a marquee that you lack intelligence and initiative. To look smart, ask judicious questions, smart questions."

Answering a Question with Another Question

This can be effective when you're looking for clarification or when you don't have an answer to a difficult question. But to do it routinely ("Why are you asking?") makes people furious.

Say a customer asks, "How much will it cost me?" and you answer, "How much do you think it should cost you?" or, "What if I said it will cost you $500?" Well, kiss your good intentions good-bye. When a friend asks "Who wrote *The Managerial Practices of Nomadic Tribes*?" and you answer "You mean you don't know?" you have gone too far. Your questions have served merely to irritate, aggravate, and ridicule.

Dumb Question Rating Scale

Everyone is capable of asking stupid questions (but some of us are more incapable than others). And often it's self-serving or sophomoric motivations that prompt ill-advised queries. Think about your questioning style, and answer yes or no to the questions in both columns . . . honestly.

Column A:

You often use questions because you want to:

- Avoid talking to someone
- Put yourself in a power position
- Intimidate your subordinates
- Be clever by answering one question with another
- Get attention
- Show off
- Waste time
- Hide the fact that you can't think of anything else to say
- Disguise your emotions
- Aggravate or irritate someone

Column B:

You often ask questions because you want to:

- Hear and understand the answer
- Gather news, facts, or other information
- Form an opinion or reach a decision
- Learn someone else's opinion
- Obtain feedback
- Clarify a misunderstanding
- Encourage someone
- Discover hidden information
- Become an interested, helpful manager

Column A:

You often ask questions because you want to:

Get a reaction
Delay a solution or agreement
Add more stumbling blocks
Worm your way out of an uncomfortable spot
Be just plain ornery

Column B:

You often ask questions because you want to:

Solve the problem
Gain commitment
Encourage participation
Stay on track
Stay in control of a communication

If you answered yes to six or more questions in Column A, you're asking too many wrongheaded questions. Think about the circumstances that prompt such questions, and analyze your motives.

If you answered yes to eight or more questions in Column B, your questioning motivation is on the money.

More Stupid Questions

Some people are famous for using stupid questions to make you feel inadequate, unattractive, ignorant, and otherwise at your wit's end—usually to get you to do something you don't want to do. Mothers and fathers, bosses and best friends, spouses and your Aunt Millie can all get away with murderous manipulation. And if you complain, they say "I was only asking." Here are some classics:

"You're not leaving before you're done, are you?"

"You didn't have anything really important to do Sunday, did you?"

"How can you say that?"

"How come a pretty girl like you wants to be an engineer?"

"So, what do you think? You haven't said a thing all day."

"Have you considered the consequences?"

"You look so sad. Is something wrong?"

"Am I interrupting something?"

"Is this all?"

"Do you have a few minutes?"

"Give me a call, OK?"

"May I be frank?"

"Don't you think you should change [your clothes, shoes, hair, personality]?"

"You're not going to do that, are you?"

"Have you been putting on a little weight lately?"

"Are you going to eat all of that?"

"Don't you think you're playing that too loud?"

"Isn't your deadline today?"

Sometimes asking a dumb question is unavoidable. We're only human, after all, and talking is the most human of our attributes. It's bound to go wrong once in a while. One of the best ways to avoid asking dumb questions is to understand the special characteristics of the person with whom you're speaking. Different people respond well to different kinds of questions. Let's see who these different people are, and what kinds of questions appeal to them.

5

Making the Question Fit the Person

I once observed a convention planner at a national organization open a staff meeting with this mild, unthreatening question: "What did you think about the great feedback we got from our last convention?"

She expected an enthusiastic response. Instead, she got five completely different reactions. Joanne merely asked, "So what else is new?" She was already well into planning the next convention. Steve was eager to rehash the whole thing, and the manager had to cut him short. Harry jokingly asked, "Are we getting raises?" But she knew he meant it. And Sara was suspicious that the manager had an angle: "Why are you asking?" she said. And Jan didn't even respond. She was daydreaming about the new graphics for the next convention.

These are some of the frustrating differences in individual behavior that managers must deal with every day. Although there are obvious dangers in jumping to conclusions about people, there are advantages in gaining insight into the people you work with—what turns them on and what turns them off, what attracts some people and repels others, what some people find challenging and others find threatening.

It's clear that every question will not have the same effect on every person. Yet creating categories in which to slip something as prickly and awkward as the human psyche isn't easy. (But it's fun to try.)

Modern psychologists trace the systematic grouping of personality types to Hippocrates, who said that generally people fell into one of four categories: Choleric, people who take the lead; Sanguine, those who have a good time; Phlegmatic, the easygoing and group-oriented; and Melancholic, the analytical perfectionists. Later Carl Jung identified the Feeler, the Sensor, the Thinker, and the Intuitor.

Psychologists today often use tests, such as the Minnesota Multiphasic Personality Inventory (MMPI), and the Rorschach, or inkblot, to identify an individual's stress pattern. One of the things such personality surveys have suggested is that while we are all different, we aren't as different as we think we are. Most people fall into defined patterns of personality—with certain tendencies exaggerated or diminished.

A more practical survey for business—one that distinguishes how different personalities respond to questions—is a five-part system that I've developed, which I call "The Five C's."

The Five C's provide a modern version of Hippocrates' categories: The Choleric is called the Commander; the Sanguine, the Convincer; the Phlegmatic, the Carer-Nurturer; and the Melancholic, the Calculator. In addition, there is a fifth category which has always been an integral part of society in general, and today is more and more vital in business—that of the Creator.

I use the Five C's to help corporations discover the strengths of staff people, put together sales teams that can better relate to specific customers, and help build inter-company teams that promise maximum productivity and harmony. Managers can also discover why certain employees are in conflict with each other, and look for ways to resolve interpersonal problems. Above all, identifying personalities can help managers ask better questions.

Identifying Personalities

In terms of the five basic categories, we all tend to be a mixed bag. And yet knowing a person's personality tendencies gives you a valuable clue about how to communicate with him. Specifically, it tells you what approach and what kinds of questions that person will respond to most positively. Ask the right person the wrong question and you might as well wave a red flag at a bull. Ask the same person the right question and you win him to your side.

The tricky part of asking the right question is discovering the personality type. None of us walks around with a personality tag, nor can most of us even describe our own personality. But by observing a person's behavior it's possible to identify his or her personality type. Behavior can be observed, measured, dealt with objectively, and changed. This means that it is possible to identify a person's primary personality simply by observing his or her behavior.

And that's what we're going to do now. The Five C's are not infallible, but they do help. The following descriptions of the five categories contain behavior clues that should help you recognize the basic personality traits of the people you work with.

The Commanders

The Commander type personality is confident, direct, loves challenge and change, is willing to take charge and go for the action. These people don't wait for things to happen—they make them happen. Commander personalities are often aggressive, self-motivated, goal-oriented, and fast-moving. Surgeons, some entrepreneurs, stockbrokers, and project managers of any kind often have many Commander characteristics. Two renowned examples of the Commander personality were John Wayne and General George C. Patton. In television fiction, Beatrice Arthur's character, Maude, and Jackie Gleason's character, Ralph, are both Commanders.

People with a Commander personality often move up the ladder fast because they get results, but when they carry these qualities to the extreme they can be careless about securing their role within the company. Many consultants I know moved quickly up the corporate ladder because they had such a strong, result-oriented disposition. Eventually, however, they couldn't climb any farther because they had made too many enemies within the corporation. That's when they left and started their own consulting business.

How can you spot a Commander in his or her natural habitat? These merchants of action in the business arena tend to enjoy change in all areas of their lives. At work, Commanders are very conscious of using every minute productively; they like to work on several things at once, and their typical pattern is to arrive at the office early and stay late. Their offices are functional and demonstrate power; for example, visitors chairs are likely to face a window where the sun streams in. Off the job they look for ways to make leisure time or vacations "count." Time off, for its own sake, bores them.

In my seminars I ask Commanders, "How many of you like to solve problems?" They all raise their hands. My reply is "That's good, because you cause most of them."

And they all burst out laughing. Commanders, unlike most other personalities, will laugh at themselves. They also get the most ribbing from other people because they are stress carriers who can take a joke.

Commander personalities tend to be impatient. Their own questions are usually direct. (When they call you on the phone, they're likely to skip the hello. If my husband answers when my friend John calls, John says: "Nonny? John. Dorothy." Or if my secretary answers, he may not identify himself at all: "Is she there?" Some Commanders launch full tilt into the purpose of their call: "When can I get that report from you?") Their favorite question is "What's the bottom line?" Because they are blunt, it's tougher for them to learn how to use open questions to advantage.

Of the five groups, these are the men and women who are least approachable by questions. They don't want to talk, they want to move. One other thing you should know: Because control and power are important to them, Commanders need to have the upper hand. If they see your questions as a subtle attempt to get control, their defensiveness will know no bounds.

Commanders will keep right on pushing until someone stops them. When a Commander is running off the rails, don't hesitate to confront him. Miller, a bank president who hired a Commander to help him implement some new marketing plans, was appalled when the new man told the board of directors that the president didn't know anything about marketing. Later, when Miller went on vacation, the marketing man moved into his office. Miller, himself a Caring personality, was so shocked at this behavior that his only response was to fire the marketing man (although, being a nonconfrontal Caring type person, he gave him a year's severance pay). Direct confrontation would probably have turned the marketing man around: "What the hell are you doing in my office? Out."

Asking Questions of a Commander

When you want something from a Commander, pose a direct question. Keep it brief and to the point. Do not hedge or fool around. Remember that the Commander is interested in results, not details.

If you have a Commander on your staff, avoid boxing him in with specific instructions ("This is the only way to do it"). If you tell the Commander what to do, complain that he or she is falling behind, or throw down a win-lose challenge ("Do it my way or don't do it at all!"), you'll bring out his worst characteristics. If you try to drive or pressure a Commander, you risk a nasty blowup. No one can drive a Commander harder than he drives himself.

The kinds of questions that work best are direct: "What are your goals?"

"How much time will it take?"

"When can I expect to have it?"

"Do you need backup or help with details?"

If *you* work for a Commander, do your homework and act confident. Well-adjusted Commanders can be good to work for, because they are secure and will give you a chance to prove yourself. You can always go far with Commander bosses if you go beyond specifications, beat the competition, and make solid suggestions for improvement. But first make sure you deliver what they ask for. Once you've shown your mettle, they will leave you on your own.

Stay away from "feeling" questions. "How do you feel about this?" is not a smart question for a Commander. Ask questions that stick to the high points, not the little details, questions that get you the information you need to do your job. Smart questions that all Commanders like:

"Where do I need to end up with this assignment?"

"What is the overall purpose?"

"When do you want it?"

"What kind of help will I get?"

"When can we get moving?"

"What's the big picture?"

"How can we beat the other team?"

"What are you seeking to achieve?"

"How can we change that?"

"How can we do it better than everyone else?"

The Convincers

The Convincers are promoters, socializers, persuaders. They're emotional, enthusiastic, and tend to be disorganized. These folks would not be happy working in research, writing for long periods of time, or quietly living alone.

The Convincer's office looks neat when you show up for a meeting, but five minutes earlier he stacked up several piles of papers and put them in a closet. He'll spread them out again when the meeting is over. A sure giveaway: Convincers like to think they know where everything is, but they spend a lot of time looking for it, just the same.

The office will often have one big attention-getting item that is a guaranteed conversation starter (I know one Convincer who has a gravity machine in her office—she never uses it, just likes to explain it to visitors). They also tend to have unusual pets for the same reason.

Convincers are flexible and playful, and they go with the flow. They are open and outgoing, and enjoy working with people. They quickly move on to a first-name basis and are great huggers and touchers. They are seldom in their offices. They are the most stylish of the four types, usually dress well, and keep in shape.

You're likely to find Convincers in positions that require powers of persuasion, such as public speaking, sales, advertising, fund-raising, and public relations. Convincers can make first-rate trial attorneys and impressive evangelists, but they are an asset in any business because they are optimistic and help boost everyone's morale. Joan Rivers ("Can we talk?"), Lucille Ball, and Dom deLuise are classic Convincers.

Convincers are natural persuaders. They excel at motivating other people. When it comes to building better relations with clients or within the company, Convincers are without peers. They love to contact people—the telephone is an extension of their body. The worst torture you could devise for a Convincer would be to put him alone in a room without a telephone.

You can usually hear Convincers' enthusiasm in their voices. Thinking out loud and on their feet is second nature to them. They talk their ideas and then tend to forget them. Others are often disillusioned when the talking doesn't turn into doing, or when they follow through on the idea only to discover the Convincer has already forgotten about it.

In the extreme form, Convincers don't plan enough, and tend to jump to conclusions. They will stick to—and even argue—their opinion long after they are proved wrong. They're easily sidetracked. Too many

Convincers working together, for example, add up to a problem. Convincers tend to hire other Convincers so they'll have somebody to talk to, and as a result productivity may suffer.

A woman I know who headed an important government agency was herself a strong Commander and Convincer personality. Many people have a tendency to hire those with personalities similar to their own. She had a staff full of Commanders and Convincers. Everyone came up with innovations and got along well with people. But there was never anyone in the office doing the work.

Conversely, I once consulted with an old, established accounting firm which was facing some new competition. Everyone in the company was steady and detail oriented. They didn't like change. When they hired marketing consultants they hired people just like themselves. I suggested that they look for someone different—someone with Commander and Convincer characteristics who could shake things up a little.

Convincers often operate best from unconventional platforms. One Convincer executive I know in the beverage industry has a van outfitted with a kitchen and dining table. At noontime he collects whomever he has to do business with and drives them out to á lake for a picnic lunch with beer and wine. Colleagues love the break in routine, clients are enamored of his style, and he is in an environment where his creative juices flow most freely.

Convincers are usually popular, and fear rejection. They also have trouble saying no, because they want to please everyone. The worst thing you can tell a Convincer is that you don't like him. A Convincer will pick out the one person in a group who doesn't approve and will concentrate on getting that person to like him. I've fallen into that trap myself when addressing groups. If someone in the audience seems bored or unreceptive I tend to concentrate on winning that person over. I've trained myself not to react in this situation and to ignore the disapproving individual.

In general, you get the best results from Convincers if you make them feel special and if you are receptive to their ideas and creativity. Encourage their positive traits, and you'll get a positive result.

Asking Questions of Convincers

Convincers respond well to "How do you feel about this?" And "How would you like to do it?" Any question with "you" as the subject is a winner. After themselves, their favorite subject is other people. Don't ask Convincers "what," ask "who." "Whom will you need in this project?" "Who's the best person for this job?" "Who will hear about it?"

If you want to establish better communication with a Convincer, whether you work for him or he works for you, it's important to get him to slow down and organize his thoughts. Your goal is to help the Convincer channel some of his bountiful energy into specific action.

If you have Convincers on your staff, be very clear in your instructions. Get them to agree on what they're going to do and when. And always establish checkpoints for them to report back to you. Asking Convincers the right questions can help them become better focused and more productive. One key to getting their attention is to be persistent in your questions: "That's a very interesting point, John, but how, specifically, can we correct the problem?" The key is to not let them off the hook.

If your boss is a Convincer, you may find his or her personality frustrating. You may want to get to work when he or she wants to shoot the breeze. One executive described her Convincer boss: "He reminds me of my seventh-grade English teacher. We always knew we could deflect him from the subject at hand—grammar—by asking him to tell us about his summer trip to Europe. He would go on for the whole class period, and we'd never have to do any grammar. I loved that in the seventh grade. But now, at the office, I do all the work, and my boss sits around and chats with the client."

You may need a sense of humor to focus a Convincer. Try to pin him down when he's in a hurry: "We've only got five minutes. What are three key issues you want to discuss? I'm counting." Other good Convincer questions:

"What are your main problems?"

"Before we have the meeting can you give me an agenda and timetable?"

"What are the specifics?"

"What are the details?"

Jokingly say, "Can you restate our objectives in ten words or less?"

The next time your sociable boss is headed for a client lunch, write out a list of fact-gathering questions for him to ask.

The Carers

Caring personalities can get the job done and work harmoniously with a wide variety of people. They move slower and are more thoughtful than Convincers. They are good team players, and more and more companies are finding that those who succeed in business, especially in large companies, are Carers.

Carers never pick up and leave a job or a relationship easily. Because they are more loyal and more family oriented they're a great long-term investment for any company. However, if Carers have to choose between job and family, they suffer from the conflict.

How to identify this personality: The Carer works slowly and deliberately. He will be more inclined to leave the office on time, because he wants to be home with his family. They are good listeners and prefer one-on-one conversations. Their offices are comfortable, chairs facing each other. Photos of family and friends, framed letters, or drawings done by their children may decorate the desk and bookshelves.

They are wonderful at socializing and are always willing to come early and help out at parties. As long as they're with friends or family, they can relax and enjoy almost anything.

Carers work best in a relaxed atmosphere built upon sound relationships and harmony. Counseling, human resources, teaching young people, family practice medicine, and nursing are all careers that attract them. They thrive on cooperation and if possible will avoid competition. Group achievement is a Carer hallmark. A Carer would rather refine an existing practice to a high polish than to institute change.

Resistance to change can be a strength or a weakness, depending on the situation. In a balanced work group it is invaluable because the Carer thinks, analyzes, and assesses before committing to change.

Like the other personality categories, when the strengths of Carer personality are exaggerated they often become weaknesses. The Carer can be possessive and somewhat suspicious. Under stress, he or she will withdraw and miss deadlines. Carers tend to be grudge-carriers. They may appear passive, but underneath—because they dislike confrontation—they internalize and build up their resentments. A Carer can suddenly explode and surprise you with an ultimatum. I remember the dismay of one boss when after a routine assignment he found his Carer employee, whom he believed to be happy on the job, clearing out his desk and leaving without notice.

A Carer personality can sometimes be too concerned with the needs of others. More than most people, they have trouble firing someone—like Miller, the Carer bank president who fired his troublesome marketing man but gave him a year's severance pay. They also hesitate to delegate because they worry about overworking other people.

The worst thing you can do to a Carer is to overload or confuse him with sudden, risky changes. When you ask a Carer personality to implement something new, it's important that you explain everything, preferably in writing, so he or she can get a grip on each aspect. List all the advantages, and show how the plan fits into the bigger picture.

The Carer views the Convincer as too artificial, too eager to move without checking details; and he thinks the Commander is intimidating or overpowering. To get along better with a Carer personality, if you yourself are a Convincer or a Commander, be less direct. Show general concern and avoid confrontations. Emphasize cooperation and support.

If a Carer works for you, emphasize the relationship first. Coach and train in a nonthreatening tone, and motivate them by talking about how they can improve relationships.

Asking Questions of Carers

Carers respond best to "how to" or process questions and to "people" questions:

"How is the project being handled?"

"What systems need organizing?"

"Who needs help?"

"How can you make it work for the company and the team?"

"How can you build a better company/work-team environment?"

"How are we going to do it?"

The Calculators

Lily Tomlin once made this comment on her state of mind: "I'm as frustrated as a perfectionist who can't do anything right." That's a perfect description of the Calculator personality. Calculators are competent, conservative, correct, and conscientious. These are the people who follow the rules and regulations. They achieve their goals through planning, education, and persistence. These are the detail people, the perfection-ists.

Engineers and accountants, mathematicians and researchers are usually Calculators. (I recently had a man come up to me in a seminar and tell me that now he understood why he had left accounting. He was a true Convincer, doing a Calculator's job.) In the corporate world, financial people are often Calculators. At their best, Calculators have precise minds and impressive analytical skills. In the days before computers, these people were the computers.

By nature, however, Calculators tend to be suspicious. They naturally question everything and worry a lot. If you have Calculators on your staff, don't make appointments with them in advance without explanation. For example, if you say on Monday, "Let's get together for a talk at the end of the week," they'll worry about it all week long.

If the Calculators in a company are too strong, the company might not be very innovative or competitive, but everything will be done perfectly. The Calculators will be holding things up, analyzing, measuring, counting. They may become overly focused on the quality of the task and fail to see the big picture.

Sometimes Calculators see their role as saving the company from the wild-eyed Commanders who will break the company into pieces with their schemes and changes. For success every company needs both sides of the equation, because the natural tension between the two groups creates its own system of checks and balances.

Calculators are sensitive and intuitive about events and people. Yet it is not in their nature to get personally involved. They leave this to Convincers and Carers.

How to identify Calculators: In his meticulous, formal office, a Calculator may have numerous graphs and charts lined up around the room or placed precisely on the walls. The favorite animal of Calculator person might be a Siamese cat or an owl. His car will be the most efficient and up-to-date, and he will know the precise value and use of every gadget in it. (His favorite publication is likely to be *Consumer Reports*.) Dick Cavett and the Mr. Spock character from *Star Trek* both appear to be Calculators.

I am more of a Convincer, and my husband has many Calculator characteristics. When it's my job to clean up after dinner I quickly and haphazardly load the dishwasher. If I go back into the kitchen later on, I'm likely to catch him carefully and systematically reloading my input.

Calculators are organized and precise. They talk in quality-control terms. Most Calculators (but not all) are silent types, but they will talk to you if they respect you. The better they know you, the more they'll open up.

Asking Questions of Calculators

The main thing to keep in mind about Calculators is that they can't stand criticism of their work. Asking personal questions is also a waste of time. The Calculator seldom volunteers information about herself. ("What did you think of it?" "I liked it." And a direct question will get you a blunt answer: "Is today your birthday?" "No.")

If a Calculator works for you, always give clear and accurate instructions. Give him a new piece of equipment to use, and he needs to know everything about it. He will ask many questions about how to do it, and then go over it with you to be sure. (Commanders and Convincers will take a quick look, say "Oh, I get it," only to go ahead and break it.)

If you work for a Calculator, you'll do well to recognize that they are task oriented. They respond best to specific, analytical questions that pertain to their professional concerns. They listen well to people who are clear and concise. Make a detailed outline of your work and what you plan to accomplish.

"How can we improve the quality of our product [our group, our system]?"

"How does it work?"

"How can it be done better?"

"What cross-checks are needed?"

"Who needs to be cross-trained?"

Calculators will lift their eyebrows if you give them an incomplete or inaccurate report. Prepare well for every encounter—whether it's in person, on the phone, or by letter, and always follow up. Calculators like to be presented with logical, planned options, and realistic trade-offs. I always hope my airplane pilots and the mechanics who work on the planes have a lot of Calculator characteristics. I always worry when the pilot is very talkative and effusive.

The Creators

The Creators are idea and concept oriented. In the business world you may find them working as designers, photographers, as new product developers, inventors, scientists, artists, or writers.

The world would be at a loss without the Creators. When I go through the functional areas of management in my seminars—planning, organization, controlling staff, leadership—one area I focus on is innovation. All managers and staff need to ask themselves, "How can I do it better?" People are valued in organizations not because they maintain the status quo, but because of the new ideas they come up with and the actions they take. Every time an individual discovers a better way to do things his creative part has been at work.

Creators are usually difficult bosses. They leave people alone and expect them to act and respond as they themselves would in every situation. Employees do not receive clear-cut standards to follow. Creators are not specific, nor are they sociable. They are blunt with others, but can be defensive and sensitive about receiving criticism themselves.

They often have a daydreamy quality. They tend not to make eye contact when talking to others, and often appear distracted.

Creators like to work alone. Rather than ask others for help, they prefer to figure things out and solve problems alone. They appear to work in spurts, although even when they seem to be doing nothing the creative process is often percolating inside their minds. When involved in a project they will work for days on end and never notice the time. Because they will keep at a task until it is flawless—which means that they are never completely finished with a job to their satisfaction—they need to be kept to deadlines. However, for them a rigid environment and following rules is high stress, and they do not function well in this kind of company. If you have Creators working or you, you'll get the best results if you leave them alone, but get them to agree to deadlines.

Creators will have an unusual work area that usually reveals their specialty. An architect's office will be laden with blueprints, a designer's with his favorite examples. They can be messy, not because they're disorganized (the driving principle behind the Creators' work is to bring order out of chaos and they are highly organized in their minds), but because outward messiness doesn't bother them. They are more concerned with thinking and creating. They might have papers on all the chairs and if you come to visit there's no place to sit.

Creators can be forgetful. (Their pets might be hungry because they forget to feed them.) There's the story about Albert Einstein who stopped to chat with some students as he was walking along a path at Princeton. After the discussion Einstein asked the students, "Which direction was I coming from?" The student pointed in the direction the famous scientist had been walking. "Good," said Einstein, "then I've already had lunch."

Creators are not strong in dealing with people, although they can be very caring if you can get their attention. Less creative people usually admire the talents of the Creators and their nonconforming style. But insecure people often feel uncomfortable or "inferior" around Creators.

Asking Questions of Creators

Creators do not usually make good listeners. This can be frustrating if your boss is a Creator because it's difficult to pin them down. They often agree with you just to get rid of you so they can go back to their project.

Creators can be unbearable and difficult during the creative process. To get the most from a Creator as a boss or employee you must understand their pattern and find times to deal with them when they are not preoccupied and can concentrate. The best time to talk to any Creator is between creative projects or shortly after the culmination of one, especially if its a success.

When talking to Creators, stay away from feeling-type questions. They don't mind them, but they are more thinkers than feelers. Creators respond best to creative questions, rather than people-oriented questions:

"What are you developing right now?"

"What do you think about it?"

"What are the aspects you are considering?"

"What ideas need developing?"

"What needs to be in place for your creative process?"

"What factors contribute to the whole?"

"What was your most satisfying creative effort?"

"Who can handle the nitty gritty so you can be free to think?"

Personality Combinations

There are some similarities and overlap among the five major behavioral styles. Commanders and Convincers both tend to be active and energetic; they like change and action. The Carers and Calculators are more slow moving and resistant to change; they are more oriented toward the status quo. Commanders, Calculators, and Creators are concerned with tasks, whereas Carers and Convincers are more concerned with people.

We all have all five dimensions in our personalities, but with varying degrees of intensity. One quick trick for learning something about a person's personality type is to ask them a simple question. For example, "Tell me what you enjoy most about your work. What do you like least?"

The Commander is likely to answer bluntly: "I enjoy outwitting the competition." "Bottom-line results." "Getting moving." "The adventure." "The chance for big gains." "That the job changes every day." "Having the whole project under my eyes." "What I like least is being bored."

The Convincer will probably go on at length, especially if you supplied the coffee: "I enjoy the flexibility." "The recognition." "Being where the action is." "Setting my own goals." "The challenge." "What I like least is writing reports."

The Carer might say, "Working with my team and feeling secure." "Developing the process." "Being part of an effective organization." "Helping people develop." "An environment where I can care about what I do and help others." "What I like least is sudden shift in policy."

The Calculator tends to reply: "Planning." "Analyzing situations and projects." "Getting the documentation right." "Having the time to do the job right." "What I like least is incomplete reporting or vague notions."

And the Creator might answer, "Conceptualizing. Freedom from restraints. Working alone. What I like least is being interrupted."

You don't need me to tell you that personality traits are not chiseled in stone. Because a person likes to place his pen precisely parallel to the top of his notepad doesn't automatically identify him as a Calculator. Nor does the fact that she sparkles at parties and can talk a blue streak mean that she's a Convincer in a business setting.

You must watch and listen. Even physical clues can be misleading. I recently planned a management development program with a client who had his office furniture arranged in an open style, with many photographs of his daughter around the room. I concluded that he was a Carer type. During the course of the meeting I asked him a question that I ask most clients: "What do you feel are the key points to include in the program?" I was surprised when he impatiently replied, "You're the expert. That's what I'm paying you for."

His response told me immediately that he was a Commander—someone who doesn't like questions. In this case, the superficial clues around his office were misleading. But when I heard his response to a single question I knew how to proceed. From then on I made all the decisions and just kept him informed of the results.

What Personality Type Are You?

It's important for managers to know their own personality traits and see how they are perceived by others. The following questions can give you a quick reading on your own personality:

Do you like to tell people what to do? (Commander)

Or do you prefer to persuade, cajole, or sell? (Convincer)

Are you a cooperative part of a working group? (Carer)

Are you interested in the task and the thoroughness and perfection in your work? (Calculator)

Do you like to think abstractly and daydream? (Creator)

If you identify yourself as a Commander-type manager, you can probably benefit by taking more time to ask your people questions and listen to their answers. Show that you care. Ask for feedback: "How do you feel about it?"

If you recognize yourself as a Convincer, you can think about how to talk less and listen more to details: "Can you explain to me specifically how we're to deal with this?"

If you're a Carer, you'll be interested in how you can use questions to focus a little more on results and actions: "How can we move things along a little more quickly?"

If you have many Calculator traits, instead of asking "How can it be more perfect?" you might want to ask more about the person you're dealing with: "How can you contribute?"

And if you're a Creator try to recognize that other people are not necessarily like you, and that you also need to depend on others. Spend time looking at and focusing on the people who work for you. They admire your creativity. They usually make exceptions for much of your unusual behavior because of your talents, but don't take advantage. Ask your staff, "How can I help you when I have time?" They will appreciate your concern and understand when you are preoccupied.

By observing a person's major personality traits you can ask questions that minimize hostility and anxiety and capitalize on that person's strengths. Behavioral assessments reveal what's important to different people, thereby suggesting a way of communicating well with them. While there are certain universal, fail-safe questions that work in almost any situation, for the most part when you ask questions—just as in any form of communication—you need to be supremely aware of the individual you're speaking with.

With that in mind, we're going to enter the heart of the Smart Questions System. The value of any system is that it has broad application in a variety of circumstances. When you understand how the Smart Questions System works you can use it across the board—whether you are trying to generate greater productivity from your staff, help people solve problems, or quicken your own pace as you move ahead in your organization.

6

The Smart Questions System

The Smart Questions System involves more than popping questions at random. It recognizes that asking smart questions is a thinking process. Once you learn the system you can gain the advantage in any situation—a job interview, asking for a raise, getting a promotion, handling an assignment, increasing productivity, coaching and leading your staff.

The question itself is only one element of the system. The Smart Questions System begins *before* you ask the question.

Step One: The Windup

Before you can ask a smart question, you need to *know your purpose*. Why are you asking? Ask yourself these smart questions:

1. "Exactly what do I want to gain with this question—cooperation, help, resources, information, commitment, better performance?"

2. "Whom am I asking? My boss? Someone else in upper management? A colleague? A member of the administrative staff? A subordinate?" (Not knowing whom you're talking to is like entering a room blindfolded.)

3. Put yourself in their shoes: "What are their goals?" "What do they want to happen?"

4. The final phase of the Windup is "How can I phrase this question to everyone's advantage?"

Christopher, the vice president of a real estate development firm, told me this story on himself. His firm was trying to get an important group of investors to commit to building a large shopping center. The investors had agreed to the terms of the proposal but were stalling about coming to a final signing. A face-to-face meeting had been postponed several times by the primary investor. Christopher, although certain that the agreement would eventaully go through, needed to get the contract off the ground. As time dragged by, his firm was losing both momentum and income. The company brass decided that the time had come to push harder and told Christopher to call the investor and insist on a meeting.

Christopher tried to develop an opening gambit for his phone call. He needed to convince the investor of the urgency of the situation without alienating him. He wrote out several paragraphs describing his company's objectives, the need to put the plans in action, why they should get started soon, when he would be available for a meeting, what they could hope to accomplish during the meeting, and so on.

When he finished Christopher had five handwritten pages. It occurred to him that he would have a terrible time having a one-on-one conversation with the investor if he had to read this epistle over the phone. Was there a way to get the investor to do some of the talking? He thought about the Smart Questions System and asked himself:

"Who is this investor?" (The head honcho, supposedly with the power to make decisions.)

"What is my purpose?" (To have a meeting during which he will sign the contract and give us a check.)

"What is the investor's problem?" (I don't know.)

Then Christopher threw out all of his notes and devised five smart questions to ask the investor during the phone conversation:

- "Is there something more you need from us to help you move the contract through?"

- "What can I do before we meet to make our time together maximally productive?"

- "Is there anyone else you would like us to talk to?"
- "When do you hope to see this project completed?"
- "When can we get together?"

Christopher then made the call. By asking only five questions, he stayed in control of the conversation, made clear his objectives, and helped the investor clarify his own thinking. As a result, Christopher got a firm appointment for a meeting, set the agenda in advance, and was able to come out of the meeting with a signed agreement and a start date.

Step Two: The Delivery

Once you've identified your purpose and have come up with the most appropriate question, the next step is to *ask the question*. You already know how to open up the question and invite the fullest response. When you ask, make sure you speak clearly, calmly, and directly, and don't rush the other person's thoughts. Maintain a positive attitude; don't let hidden feelings of disapproval or criticism creep into your voice. Because you have thought through the question, you should find it easy to speak without fumbling.

Don't toss the question off or bury it in a stream of other words. Let the person know you expect an answer. Look into his eyes, and let your warmth and intent show in your voice and manner. Let him or her know that you are interested in hearing the answer.

Step Three: The Response

A question is useless if you don't *listen carefully to the response*. At the opening of her seminars on negotiation, Tessa Albert Warschaw often asks participants to talk to as many people as they can within a period of ten minutes. In each encounter, the participants exchange answers to two questions. First, "What assets do you bring to a negotiation?" Second, "What liabilities?" The participants hear over and over again what's helping them and hurting them in their dealings with others.

But it's in their second meeting that the real test occurs. Once again, Warschaw asks the participants to speak to one another. "This time," she says, "tell the person you're talking to one thing you remember about him or her from what he or she told you last night."

Invariably this request is met with nervous laughter. To their intense embarrassment, the participants usually remember almost nothing from their conversations with one another. They realize that they've got to start "attending," as Warschaw calls it.

Much has been made of the virtues of listening. We talk about listening "between the lines," or listening to the "inner message," and a few authors suggest listening overtly—that is, paying attention to precisely what is said and not trying to decode hidden meanings.

Listening well is a skill that requires concentration and effort. For one thing, we think seven times faster than we speak. So while we're listening, our minds are racing ahead. Thus we often project our own ideas, associations, and judgments into what is being said to us. As a result we're not fully tuned in to what the other person is saying. It would be much more constructive to spend this surplus thinking time listening fully and constructing an interesting direction in which to take the interview, based on what you hear.

We also fail to listen when we feel an urgency to express ourselves. We're certain that if we can explain ourselves convincingly, the other person will see us as we wish to be seen. And the best resource we have for explaining ourselves is talking. Right? Wrong. One author lunching with his editor learned this lesson the hard way.

"I had a perfect opportunity," Jake said. "A chance to find out what trends my publisher saw in the book industry, what kinds of books she specifically was looking for, and how I fit into the scheme of this particular publisher's future. But I didn't find out anything."

Jake was so nervous that he spent the entire luncheon talking about himself. "I told her where I thought my career was going, how I wanted to develop as a writer. I learned absolutely nothing about her needs or the needs of the company. If she learned anything about me, it didn't result in any concrete suggestions for my future."

In other words, Jake presented himself as a person with a set of problems that needed to be solved and asked the editor to be his doctor. "*I* should have been the doctor," he said with sharp hindsight. "I should have found out her needs—symptoms—and looked to see what I could do to help her. I wasted an ideal opportunity."

Another typical reason for not paying attention is that we're not really interested in what the other person is talking about. But one way to make sure that you are interested is to ask questions.

When you're hopelessly bored while listening to someone else talk, consider this: Listening covers your weaknesses (you can never look or sound foolish, even if you're in way over your head). Listening gives you time to think and to consider all the information relevant to the particular situation. When you do speak your words have greater impact. Even though most of us feel compelled to talk, listening—when you learn to enjoy it—is actually less stressful than speaking.

But before you pat yourself on the back for being a good listener, remember that you can fall into your own trap. If you are listening in order to be thought captivating, don't let your eyes wander around the room as you nod your head agreeably. Rather than bask in your own charms, concentrate on what is being said. Some people are so enchanted with the impression they create as a good listener that they fail to hear what the other person is telling them.

Are You a Good Listener?

According to a recent report from Sperry Rand, 45 percent of a manager's time is spent listening. Listening absorbs your time in one-to-one conversations, in meetings, and on the telephone. There is no communication unless someone is listening.

You can judge your listening skills by asking yourself these questions:

Are you willing to learn about other people, places, and things?

Would you welcome your staff's opinion about your listening ability?

Do you listen for the main ideas being expressed?

Do you take care not to interrupt?

Do you curb the impulse to complete the other person's sentences?

Do you tune in to the speaker's feelings as well as his words?

Do you try to get beyond your own judgmental attitudes?

In other words, do you practice listening skills? If you have six or fewer yes answers, your listening could stand improvement. To quote Epictetus, one of the more observant Greek philosophers, "God has given us two ears and one mouth so we may hear twice as much as we speak."

Step Four: The Evaluation

As you listen, you need to *evaluate the answer.* This is the processing stage of the system. You may need to ask another question, or questions, before you get what you're looking for. You may want to ask a clarifying question to make sure you have the details straight. Or a probing question to get deeper into the heart of the issue or to discover where hidden resistance might be.

Good salespeople have learned that they can pin down a sale by asking questions that dig progressively deeper into the issues. The curtain rises on this conversation between a probing, calm, and concerned salesperson and the head of purchasing in a clothing manufacturing firm:

"Research has shown that our threads outlast our nearest competitor's by 17 percent, and other competitors' by much more than that. Yet our price is the same. Therefore our threads will save you money in the long run. How do you feel about saving money?"

"Well, who wouldn't like to save money? But convenience counts too. Our people are used to the present threads and salespeople. We're generally satisfied with what we've got now. With your product we'll have to change our threading process."

"When you say you're satisfied, does this mean that there are no problems?"

"We have a little trouble occasionally, but nothing we can't handle."

"I know nothing is perfect. What kind of trouble are you having?"

"Nothing serious, but I've noticed that we don't get as long a last from our present threads. We've been getting more garments returned because of split seams, and I've seen some reports about problems with the thread in the machines. It seems to break and put the machine out of commission for about ten or fifteen minutes until it's cleaned out.

"What percentage of returns are you getting?"

"I'd estimate about 8 percent."

"That's at least twice the number you should be getting. Our research shows that with our threads you should get returns down to 2 percent or even less. Can you judge how much total time you're losing?"

"Overall, we're averaging about fifteen to sixteen hours a week in lost time."

"You should only be losing about eight hours. With our easier threading and stronger thread, most of our customers lose only five or less. I'm comparing your company to companies with similar garments and number of employees. Wouldn't it be to your advantage to save problems with your machines and reduce the returned merchandise?"

"Yes, of course, but there's more to it than product viability. Threading is only a minor item in our production line. Replacing it with a new product could upset the procedure. Frankly, it isn't worth it. It means a new set of operating instructions and a period of confusion during the changeover, which usually means a lot of errors."

"I know what you mean—change is always upsetting. I can understand your wanting to avoid confusion and errors, but I wonder if this is likely to happen? How long have you been using your present product?"

"About three years."

"Then about three years ago you shifted from one thread to the brand you're now using. Is that right?"

"Yes, that's right. But what are you getting at?"

"I'm just looking to discover how difficult the transition period was. How much trouble do you recall having during that changeover?"

"Well, let's see. . . . Once or twice when things went wrong somebody blamed it on the new thread, but we straightened it out pretty easily."

"Then aren't you paying a lot more to avoid some trouble that isn't even likely to happen, from your own experience?"

"You know how people love to complain when you institute a change, and I don't always have the time or the energy to deal with it. On the other hand, I've been a little annoyed about the problems we've been having with the product. Maybe it wouldn't be that hard to switch, especially if the new stuff makes it easier to thread the machines. Suppose you send me a trial order of your thread and we'll see how it works out."

Through pointed questioning, this salesperson held the initiative all the way. The initial questions stirred the buyer's mind to activity rather than leaving him in a state of inertia. Subsequent questions moved his thinking until he himself reached out for a trial order.

Asking the first question, however, was only the first step. The critical factor was that the salesman *listened* to each answer—and responded to the answer with another question.

I once called on a personnel director in a large advertising firm. When I asked what concerns she had, she answered, "I really don't have any concerns. We have several outside consultants and they all say we're doing a good job."

As I listened to her I recognized that her defenses were up, but I stuck with the questioning approach. "That must make you feel good. But there must have been one or two small things bothering you or you wouldn't have called me. Are there any areas in which you've never done training?"

As I probed around with nonthreatening questions, she agreed that there were a few minor things, and then went on to list many problem areas that were bothering her.

So stick with it. If you give up after asking one question, the conversation is probably over. Listen, evaluate the answer, and be ready to ask another question.

Step Five: The Payoff

You've asked a smart question, listened to the answer—and then what? To make smart questions pay off, a good manager must act on what he or she learns. You gain the respect of other people only if you capitalize on the information. If you ask for suggestions but fail to use them, people will stop volunteering.

The same thing is true of your colleagues and staff. When you ask for participation, when you ask people to delve into their minds and emotions to answer your questions and then ignore what they've told you, you've undermined all your good work. If you have a company suggestion box and never use it, people stop contributing. Likewise, if you ask for advice and disregard it, people stop providing it. What, after all, was the point?

Not every question and answer needs a direct action. Sometimes it's enough to listen and respond, letting the person know that you appreciate their thoughts and input.

Often action means simply following up. If an employee's work improves as a result of a questioning session, acknowledge it. Action can also mean mentally or physically filing away the information you gathered for future use. But, for example, if you discover in a questioning session that the reason deadlines have been missed in your department is because a supplier is consistently late, act on that information and solve the problem.

Taking action for the sake of doing something is not a good move. Just as smart questions, not just any questions, are the first step, smart actions are your goal. Knowing that your eventual aim is to take an appropriate action can help you to formulate your questions in the first place. The purpose of asking smart questions is to improve things, and that only happens when you act. Unless you go beyond what you have already mastered you'll never grow.

Five Steps for Best Results with the Smart Questions System

1. The Windup—know your purpose and your person
2. The Delivery—formulate your question
3. The Response—listen to the answer
4. The Evaluation—probe further if necessary
5. The Payoff—take action

Getting into the habit of asking smart questions takes some effort. It involves breaking an old habit (making statements) and creating a new one (asking questions). It's a matter of retraining your responses. However, when you try the Smart Questions System you see the benefits so quickly that it's easy to continue doing it. It's much easier to change when you see the rewards.

Asking smart questions is a technique that can become automatic, just like brushing your teeth, driving a car, or hitting a tennis ball. Studies show that it takes between seven and twenty-one conscious efforts to create a new habit. Pay attention to your communicating style for a week. Notice how you initiate conversations, how you talk to employees, how you respond when someone asks you a question. The next time you're ready to lecture someone or make a statement, stop yourself. Count to five and take a deep breath. And ask a question instead.

The Smart Questions System offers a wonderful and immediate reward. You will notice the difference the first time you use it, and those benefits will encourage you to keep experimenting. For the remainder of this book we're going to describe specific applications of the Smart Questions System. Part Two concentrates on your role as manager—how you can use smart questions to help everyone on your staff bring out his or her greatest potential.

PART TWO

Getting the Most from Your Staff

"Hard questions must have hard answers."

—Plutarch

7

The Quiz: Part Two

I once observed Sally, a customer-service manager, give instructions to her staff. "This is the way I want you to deal with complaints," she said, and she went on to describe the technique she wanted the representatives to use. Sally spoke quickly and to the point. At the end of her talk, she asked if there were any questions, but made it clear that she expected efficient action and not a lot of conversation. No one had any questions. Her staff, feeling not a little apprehensive, started to work. Over the next week, few of them were able to deal properly with customers. Sally was annoyed. She had been clear enough, hadn't she? Why hadn't anyone listened to her? A few weeks later she gave the lecture again, with the same poor results.

When it comes to getting the most from their staff, one common sin managers commit is telling people what to do but failing to discover if they've understood the instructions. Most managers like to lecture and feel uneasy with two-way conversations. A conversation means that you must ask questions and must establish an atmosphere that encourages people to ask questions of you as well. It takes more time, and it means that you leave yourself open to challenge. But a questioning approach is the way mistakes are corrected, comprehension is expanded, and co-operation becomes a byword of the department.

I ran into a similar problem with my own answering service. I recently called the service and gave the manager instructions on how I wanted my phones answered; I assumed that the information would be passed down to all the operators and it would work out. But they continued to make the same mistakes.

I called the manager again and asked, "How do you get the information to all the other operators?"

"We write it on your card," she said.

"How do you know that people read it?"

"We don't."

This was puzzling, but complaining didn't seem to solve the problem. So I asked a question: "What can you do to be sure that everyone who answers the phone gets this information and understands what has to be done?"

The manager thought about it, and came up with the idea of briefing all the operators at least once a day and asking for feedback to make sure everyone understood the new instructions. The same technique was used with the night shift. Only by verbal questions and answers would the information get through.

Part Two of *Smart Questions* deals with using questions to get the most from your staff and to establish better understanding so that people know what you need. The main reasons people fail at work are because they don't have the ability, they have a poor attitude, or they don't know what's expected of them. One way to be a superior boss is to clearly express your expectations. And smart questions will help you do that.

It will also help you develop your staff to their maximum potential. Many managers have talented people on tap, yet wind up doing much of the work themselves. Or they continue to use the same individuals for the same jobs, assuming that they know the abilities and goals of each person. But in fact we usually know very little about the people who work with us. By taking time to ask questions, managers can expand their knowledge of each individual on their staff and devise the most productive ways to make use of their talents and ambitions.

Again, it's important to answer these quiz questions with your first response. Before change can take place, it's necessary to become aware of the present reality. Only if you answer the questions honestly—not the way you think they should be answered—can you become a better questioner.

Are You Getting the Most from Your Staff?

1. When organizing a project team you usually:

    a. Select people you like.

    b. Ask "Who are the best people?"

    c. Ask yourself "What is the goal of the project and who are the best people for it?"

    d. Choose people you can control.

2. Recently your staff people have been making a lot of mistakes in written reports. You:

    a. Accept the situation as a normal part of doing business.

    b. Ask yourself how you might improve your instructions.

    c. Criticize them for not following directions.

    d. Ask them for solutions.

3. You can't decide between two qualified candidates for a position in your department. You:

    a. Ask a colleague to sit in on their interviews.

    b. Develop more probing questions to find out more about them.

    c. Look for a way to hire them both.

    d. Kick the decision upstairs and ask your boss to decide.

4. Your assistant tells you he can't meet an important deadline. Your immediate response is to:

    a. Ask "What am I going to tell the senior vice president?"

    b. Tell him he has no choice.

    c. Ask "What's the problem?"

    d. Tell him to get whatever help he needs to finish the job.

5. After giving an employee complex instructions for an assignment, you:

    a. Ask "Do you have any questions?"

    b.   Leave and give him time to work out the assignment for himself.

    c.   Ask him to repeat the instructions.

    d.   Ask him to describe in his own words how he interprets the assignment.

6.   You can't finish a project on time. You:

    a.   Think about which of your employees you can approach for help.

    b.   Stay up all night to finish because you assume your staff is overworked.

    c.   Ask your closest peer associate for help.

    d.   Ask yourself who else would most benefit from working on this project.

7.   Two of your best staff people are involved in a personal conflict. Your normal response is to:

    a.   Call them both into your office together for a problem-solving session.

    b.   Talk to each of them individually.

    c.   Tell them to work it out between them.

    d.   Transfer one person to another department to alleviate tension.

8.   When you plan a job interview for a prospective employee, you:

    a.   Write out a series of questions to ask.

    b.   Bring along the job description and use it as a guide.

    c.   Structure the interview around the applicant's resume.

    d.   Wing it, under the premise that spontaneity allows more freedom to explore the person's potential.

9.   One of your employees has a long-standing personal problem. You:

    a.   Get involved and try to solve it.

    b.   Send your employee to personnel.

    c.   Ignore it.

    d.   Strongly advise getting professional help.

10.   You have a new supervisor reporting to you who doesn't delegate enough. In a coaching session, you:

    a.   Laud the advantages of delegating.

    b.   Tell her that she must delegate more.

    c.   Ask her why delegating should be important to a manager.

    d.   Send her for training in delegation.

11.   You schedule exit interviews with several employees who have resigned. You:

    a.   Go through the formalities and wish them luck.

    b.   Ask your remaining staff how they see the situation.

    c.   Try to discover the real reasons for their leaving.

    d.   Emphasize that they are making a big mistake by leaving.

12.   Morale is sagging in your department. To solve the problem, you begin by:

    a.   Thinking it through objectively on your own.

    b.   Calling a full staff meeting and ask for each person's contribution.

    c.   Asking your key people to investigate.

    d.   Asking the people who are most discontented how they perceive the difficulty.

13.   When you interview a new clerical employee, you say:

    a.   "Tell me about yourself."

    b.   "I guess personnel has told you all our policies."

    c.   "What has personnel told you?"

    d.   "What do you know about our company?"

14.   At a technical training session for your staff, you:

    a.   Lecture and answer questions as they come up.

    b.   Start off with a joke, then keep talking.

    c.   Ask open-ended questions 75 percent of the time.

    d.   Ask for frequent summaries throughout the session.

15. Your staff people have been late and ill a lot in recent months. You:

   a. Figure it must be the weather.

   b. Tell them to come in on time.

   c. Suggest they have physical checkups.

   d. Ask them, "What can we do to add more job satisfaction for you?"

16. You have a strong potential job candidate who was late for his first interview. You:

   a. Ignore it.

   b. Ask for his references and call them.

   c. Ask him why he was late.

   d. Ask him to come in for two or three interviews and see what happens.

17. You are always the last to know the bad news in your office. You:

   a. Ask yourself why you don't get this information earlier.

   b. Ask your group why they don't share with you.

   c. Complain that no one seems to care.

   d. Ask your boss for help.

18. You've hired two losers and are apprehensive about hiring the present job candidate. You:

   a. Ask "Can you describe in detail your previous job and the standards you were expected to fulfill?"

   b. Ask "What were your job duties?"

   c. Describe the job you have and ask, "Do you feel you can handle it?"

   d. Ask the personnel director for his or her opinion.

19. You feel uncomfortable in your new job because you are much younger than the people you've been hired to manage. You:

   a. Ask them "What do you feel makes a good manager?"

   b. Hope you'll prove your worth by actions.

   c. Try to cultivate your best personality so they'll get to like you.

    d.   Ask them for help in those areas where experience is important.

20. You feel your staff does not operate as a team. You:

    a.   Give them a pep talk.

    b.   Talk to them individually.

    c.   Ask your corporate trainer about a team-building program.

    d.   Ask them, as a group, to bring to the next staff meeting suggestions for improvement.

21. The third excellent employee you've hired has been lured away into another division of your firm. You:

    a.   Decide not to hire such good people.

    b.   Ask them why they go.

    c.   Register a complaint with your divisional vice president or the vice president of human resources.

    d.   Feel good that you have such a great network within the company and ask for a raise.

22. Several of your staff people regularly come late to meetings. You:

    a.   Wait for the latecomers.

    b.   Ask your boss to come in for your next meeting.

    c.   Ask the staff to decide on a penalty for latecomers.

    d.   Start all meetings on time with important information for each person.

23. During your summer vacation things fall apart in the office. You:

    a.   Wait for fall.

    b.   Plan a cross-training project.

    c.   Ask your employees for their suggestions.

    d.   Ask yourself if you've been delegating properly.

24. Three of your top people have just returned from an expensive seminar. You:

    a.   Request a report from each.

  b. Ask each one what he learned.

  c. Ask each what he is going to do differently.

  d. Watch to see the improvements.

25. Managers succeed with their people because they:

  a. Clearly express their expectations and ask their people to clarify their own expectations.

  b. Have high goals.

  c. Ask for frequent feedback.

  d. Keep an open-door policy.

Answers

1. a = 2 b = 3 c = 5 d = 1

We all prefer to have people we like on our project teams (*a*), but they aren't always the best choices. Nor are the all-round "best people" (*b*) always the right choice for a given project. The best answer is to match the people with the project (*c*), which should give you the best people for the particular job. You're in managerial trouble if you automatically choose people you can control (*d*).

2. a = 0 b = 3 c = 0 d = 5

Your staff people recently have begun to make mistakes. The operative word in this question is "recently." If they had not been making mistakes before, something has gone wrong. The best answer is to ask them for solutions (*d*): your staff knows what is creating these problems. The answer would be totally different if you had a new staff and they were making a lot of mistakes. In that case, the best answer is to ask yourself how to improve your instructions (*b*).

3. a = 1 b = 5 c = 2 d = 1

It's tough to decide between two qualified candidates. There's nothing wrong with asking a colleague for some help (*a*), but you must make your own decision. If you've got an unlimited budget, look for a way to hire them both (*c*), because you never can have enough good people.

And you might also ask your boss for advice; however, if you're looking to get ahead, don't ask your boss to decide for you (*d*). The best answer is to develop more probing questions to find out more about each candidate (*b*). It takes time and effort, but in the long run it's worth the trouble.

4.   a = 0   b = 1   c = 5   d = 3

Your assistant tells you he can't meet an important deadline. You lose if you condemn, immediately generate guilt, or worry about your own skin (*a* and *b*). Telling the person to get help (*d*) is not a bad answer because the realities of the workplace don't always allow time for individuals to complete their personal projects. But even when time is pressing, the best answer is (*c*): "What's the problem?" There may be a specific obstacle that can be worked out to allow your assistant to complete the project successfully.

5.   a = 2   b = 0   c = 4   d = 5

One reason people make so many mistakes is that managers don't ask for feedback. If you have a good working relationship with an employee, asking "Are there any questions?" is helpful (*a*). Letting the person work out the assignment for himself (*b*) is a waste of time unless the person is a mind reader. Both (*c*) and (*d*) are good answers, although just asking someone to repeat the instructions (*c*) can make the person feel like a child. Asking him to describe the assignment in his own words (*d*) is the most tactful and effective approach.

6.   a = 3   b = 0   c = 2   d = 5

Many new managers feel that when they're behind on a project it's up to them to stay up all night (*b*) or do whatever it takes to complete it alone. You may get the job done this way, but it's not a good solution. In an organization we all have to help each other. Asking your peers for help (*c*) does not take advantage of your managerial powers. Asking your employees for help (*a*) is a good idea, but you can maximize the situation by asking yourself "Who can benefit most from working on this project?" (*d*), thereby turning it into a growth experience for a staff person.

7.   a = 5   b = 1   c = 2   d = 1

When there are personal conflicts within your department, in most circumstances the best solution is to talk to the people together (*a*). Speaking to them individually (*b*) takes away their power to solve their problems jointly; and telling them to work it out between themselves (*c*) doesn't show enough concern on your part. Transferring one person (*d*) without getting to the bottom of the problem brands you as a manager who fails to deal with problems.

8.   a = 5   b = 4   c = 1   d = 0

The best way to interview prospective employees is to have a series of questions planned (*a*). The job description (*b*) is important, as long as you have read it before. Personally, I don't think resumes (*c*) are useful, from either the interviewer's or the candidate's point of view. Questions should be built around the job, not the resume. And while spontaneity sounds nice, a job interview isn't a party—far from it. If you wing it (*d*), you'll wind up with nothing.

9.   a = 0   b = 2   c = 0   d = 5

It's always difficult when employees have personal problems, but there's only one good answer here. As manager you can listen, but if an employee has a long-standing serious problem your goal is for the person to get professional help (*d*). Good managers often have a list of professionals or organizations to refer their people to. Sending someone to personnel (*b*) is passing the buck, although in some cases personnel might be able to help find the appropriate help.

10.   a = 2   b = 1   c = 5   d = 4

When a supervisor doesn't delegate enough, talking up the advantages of delegating (*a*) may help because at least it's positive; simply telling your employee to delegate more (*b*) is unlikely to have any effect. The two best answers are (*c*) and (*d*). Your goal is to get your employee to recognize for herself the benefits of delegating, which makes (*c*)—"Ask her why delegating should be important to a manager"—the best answer. It's also possible that an outside trainer (*d*) might help the person develop her delegating skills.

11. a = 1   b = 3   c = 5   d = 0

Smart managers make exit interviews work for them. If you merely go through the formality of shaking hands (*a*) or pontificate that the person leaving is making a big mistake (*d*), you fail to maximize the opportunity. Since in this situation several people have resigned, asking your remaining staff how they see the situation (*b*) is a good choice. But the best solution is to ask questions of the people leaving, to discover the real reasons they are resigning (*c*). Such insight can help you correct situations in your department; you may also gain important feedback about your management style and how it affects your employees.

12. a = 5   b = 3   c = 2   d = 4

Sagging morale rarely corrects itself. The best response is (*a*): before you take action, think through the problem objectively on your own; ask yourself some introspective smart questions about what's going on in your department. Then ask your problem people how they perceive the morale situation (*d*), since they are the ones having the problem. Asking your key people to investigate (*c*) is the least helpful of all the responses because your top people are not usually the ones having the problem. Calling a full staff meeting and asking for each person's contribution (*b*) can work, but it's taking the long way around. It's better to focus on those having the morale problem and try to correct it with them.

13. a = 0   b = 1   c = 5   d = 1

"Tell me you about yourself" (*a*) is the worst question you can ask anyone during a job interview. It makes people feel defensive and confused, and seldom gets you any worthwhile or specific information. This question merely shows that you don't know what you're after. "I guess personnel has told you all our policies" (*b*) doesn't do you much good, either. Asking "What do you know about the company?" (*d*) has little value if you're hiring a clerical person but can be useful if you're interviewing someone for a management position. Overall, "What has personnel told you?" (*c*) is the best answer. It opens the conversation, it lets you find out what the person has already learned, it saves time, and it starts the interview off in a questioning mode.

14.   a = 5   b = 1   c = 1   d = 4

The key word in this question is "technical" training (as opposed to "human resources" training). To provide technical training for your staff you need to give input, but as with any training, you should also answer questions as they come up (*a*). Many technical trainers start off with a joke and then plunge into their talk (*b*), but this lecturing mode doesn't help people learn. Nor are open-ended questions (*c*) helpful when it comes to training someone in a specific skill (they're great for interpersonal or human resources training). In any training session, asking for frequent summaries (*d*) is good; summaries help reinforce the training and allow misinformation to surface and be corrected.

15.   a = 0   b = 2   c = 2   d = 5

When people come late or start calling in sick it's always a sign of deeper problems. Never ignore it (*a*). Telling them to come in on time (*b*) may work for a few days, but it won't solve the problem. They may have some physical problems (*c*), but don't count on it. Always investigate (*d*)—try to find out what's behind the lateness and sick days. If people are bored with their jobs you may not be able to do anything about it, but there's often the possibility of cross-training or other changes that might motivate your staff.

16.   a = 1   b = 4   c = 3   d = 5

What do you do when someone comes late for a first job interview: Do you assume they are always late? If punctuality is important in your office you don't want to ignore it (*a*), nor do you want to jump to conclusions. You can ask for an explanation (*c*), but that tends to get the interview off to a bad start (anyone can be late once). One good solution is to call the person's references and ask about past history (*b*); the best thing is to schedule two or three more interviews and see what happens (*d*).

17.   a = 5   b = 4   c = 1   d = 2

If you're the last to hear bad news in your office it means that people are afraid to tell you things. This happens to many managers, and it's dangerous. The best solution is to ask yourself why you don't get this information earlier (*a*), when you still have time to do something about it. Asking your group why they don't come to you when things go wrong (b) is not a bad approach, but if people are already afraid to talk to you they probably won't speak up. Complaining (c) and asking your boss for help (d) are not worth talking about.

18.   a = 5   b = 4   c = 2   d = 1

There's no foolproof way to select good job candidates, but your best chance comes if you can find out what the applicant did in his previous jobs and what standards he met (a). It's important to know what the person's job duties were (b), but without knowing the standards it isn't enough information. If you describe the job and ask the person "Can you handle it?" (c), you're doing the talking and the applicant naturally is likely to answer in the affirmative, which doesn't tell you much. And finally, asking personnel for an opinion (d) won't help you much because they can't know the job requirements as well as you do.

19.   a = 4   b = 3   c = 2   d = 5

When you're younger than the people you manage, it can help to ask them what they feel makes a good manager (a). They know as well as you that age has nothing to do with managing, and having to think about it will put them on the right track. But an even better strategy is to make the more mature people feel important (d). It's all right to prove your worth by actions (b), but it takes longer; try the other two strategies immediately. And putting on your most pleasing personality (c) may smooth the way temporarily, but you will still have to come to grips with the situation.

20.   a = 2   b = 3   c = 4   d = 5

If you want your people to operate as a team, giving them a pep talk (a) or talking to them individually (b) isn't going to do the job. Training (c) might help, but the best solution is to get them together as a group (d). A great way to start is to ask them to bring suggestions for improvement, and take it from there.

21.   a = 0   b = 4   c = 1   d = 5

Whenever you hire good people you run the risk that other departments will want them. Deciding not to hire such good people (a) is hurting yourself. Asking them why they accept the new offers (*b*) is a smart idea, because it may turn out that if all the top people are moving out of your division you might want to move out, too: you might work to change your management style if you discover that is the problem. Complaining to your boss (*c*) is silly. Overall, my philosophy is to enjoy the fact that you have such a good network in the company (*d*).

22. a = 1 b = 3 c = 4 d = 5

The worst thing you can do with latecomers is wait for them (*a*), because then you're rewarding bad behavior. Asking your boss to attend the next meeting (*b*) is not a bad idea; and deciding on a penalty (*c*) has worked in many companies. But the more subtle, effective thing to do is to start the meetings on time, and start off with important information for each person, information that they cannot easily get elsewhere. It should cure the problem almost immediately.

23. a = 1 b = 4 c = 3 d = 5

If things fall apart in your office when you're away, you must ask yourself if you're delegating properly (*d*). The next best thing is to plan a cross-training program (*b*) so that people can help each other when you're away. Asking employees for their suggestions (*c*) is not as specific, but it is helpful. The only thing that will happen if you wait until fall (*a*) is that the leaves will change color.

24. a = 5 b = 3 c = 4 d = 2

When you've invested a lot of money sending people to a seminar you want to maximize its value. Asking for an extensive written report (*a*) helps reinforce the information and gives the seminar extra impact. It's also good to sit down and talk to each person who attended (*b*), but it's more important to find out what they're going to do differently in the future (*c*). (You might want to wait a while for the new information to sink in before asking this question.) If you passively watch to see the improvements (*d*), you are indicating that you don't really care if they learned anything and that sending them to a seminar was just going through the motions.

25.   a = 5   b = 3   c = 4   d = 1

The main cause of employee failure is unclear or unverbalized expectations. If you clearly express your expectations (*a*), you should be well on your way to being a successful manager. And the way to know if people understand your expectations is to ask for frequent feedback (*c*). High goals are important (*b*), but unless you express those goals clearly they remain your personal secret. I don't believe that managers should keep an open-door policy (*d*), because if they're available all the time people don't learn to make decisions on their own.

Scoring

100–125 Points

Your profile is the ideal for today's manager: you are concerned with both people and results. You ask questions throughout the workday, and you evaluate and act on the answers you receive. You are confident, calm, well organized, and able to delegate. Your people work hard for you and give you their best. You hire people at least as talented as yourself and don't feel threatened when they are promoted. Productivity in your department is high. You are respected by your staff as well as by upper management.

85–100 Points

Deep down, you really don't accept the fact that if your staff looks good, you look good. But you are ambitious. By asking more questions, listening more, and increasing your staff's involvement you could improve the overall performance of your department, as well as your own.

65–85 Points

Although you know that today's standards require you to be more of a people manager, you still hold on to an autocratic management style. Because you make all the decisions and insist that everything be done your way, your people do not produce as much as they could, and several of your employees feel frustrated. Because you take over so much, they don't feel fully involved in the job and consequently do not give it their maximum effort. You can improve if you give fewer orders, ask more questions, and listen more to your people.

Less than 65 Points

Managers who prefer to work alone are usually in this category. They are often detached and tend to avoid problems and confrontations.

Here also is the manager who can't say no. He is often overworked and disorganized, a person who relinquishes all control and decision making to other people, with little or no direction. This manager would like to put all his responsibility on others. As a result, staff people often feel he is both weak and unfair.

These two management styles are inadequate for today's business. Any manager who fits these profiles could improve his or her management skills and overall performance by developing a questioning approach.

The issues raised in Part Two of the Quiz are important because they show how your own management technique affects the morale and overall performance of your team. While managers can do much to enhance the enthusiasm and dedication of their people, success depends largely on choosing the right people to begin with. Selecting people with talent and ambition is your most demanding task. Your influence and success as a manager depend on your ability to make the right choice. The next chapter reveals how smart questions can help you find the best people for the job.

8

Quality Staffing: The Right Stuff

Volumes have been written about motivating employees and helping people bring out their best. But those managerial tasks are a thousand percent more profitable if the employee you're working with has "the right stuff" to begin with. Perhaps your most important function as manager is bringing on board the right personnel. And in this capacity smart questions serve as your shrewdest skill.

Set your standards high, and hire the best people to meet them. Sounds easy? It's not.

Jack was the production chief of a national magazine, and like production chiefs throughout the journalism industry he was overworked and understaffed. With a double issue going to press and a special year-end edition in preparation, Jack once again pleaded with upper management to add staff. The managing editor finally agreed and gave the necessary permission for Jack to look for someone new.

Jack was so anxious to relieve the pressure that he urged personnel to fill the job as soon as possible: "Get me a body, and get it fast."

And fast it was: he hired the first experienced person who passed the computer typesetting test. The result: four months later, his group of eighteen typesetters and proofreaders were squabbling among themselves, fighting over overtime, refusing to cooperate with each other—

in effect destroying the coordinated team effort essential to producing any regular publication on schedule. Why?

The new employee, it turned out, was fast on the computer but disaster on the team. Jack had completely missed the boat on the hiring decision. He thought he needed an extra pair of hands, but what he really needed was someone who would fit smoothly into the tightly knit group, remain cheerful under pressure, and be empathetic to a myriad of sensitive, volatile personalities—in other words, someone who could help the team function at peak performance. Competent hands were only a part of the task.

Jack hadn't taken time to ask himself the right questions: questions that, first, would help him *define the real job;* and second, that would help him know exactly *what kind of person* would best fill it.

Nowhere do you have more at stake than in hiring a new employee. Not only do you look bad if you choose the wrong person, but like Jack's, your company may be stuck paying thousands of dollars in unemployment compensation because of your mistake.

Many managers are like movie producers. Just as producers try to sign up big-name talent with proven box office draw, managers look to hire people with the right credentials, references, and experience. The reasoning in both cases is the same: self-protection in case something goes wrong. If the movie fails at the box office, the producer can look the investment banker in the eye and say, "I hired top names who had been successful in the past. It wasn't my fault if it didn't work." If an employee flops, the manager can say, "He went to Harvard and his references were impeccable. How could I know?"

This need for self-protection causes managers, like movie producers, to flop. Quality staffing is based on much more than credentials and references. Selecting the best person for the job requires that a manager be more than an executive—he or she must be something of a soothsayer.

Every day of the week, able people successfully step up into jobs they've never performed before. Sometimes it's brilliant strategy to take a chance on an individual of above-average ability, charisma, or ingenuity, especially when you're hiring for a growth job. An officer of a direct-mail marketing organization, interviewing senior account executives, discovered a candidate who had no experience in the field. But she did have all the vital attributes—ability to contact, establish a relationship, get information, sell creative concepts, close the deal. The firm took a risk, and the new employee helped multiply their business by 40 percent in the first six months.

What if you could accurately predict the future performance of any candidate who applied for a job? If you could pick winners and avoid personnel disasters? Obviously, if you hope to avoid the bad bets and spot the winners you've got to come up with the smartest possible questions to ask during the interview. And that means doing your homework. The reason that 90 percent of managers cannot pick a winner is that they're focused on the wrong aspect of the hiring process. They're willing to ask questions of the candidate, but they fail to ask questions about the job itself.

Before you can find the best person for the job you must, above all else, have a crystal clear understanding of the job itself. If you really know what the job is—not just the particular skill involved, but the kind of temperament needed to carry it out and the required level of performance—then finding the right person is relatively easy. You can never be 100 percent certain that the person you choose can do the job for you, but when you have a thorough understanding of the job's requirements, you can more easily take a chance and bet that he or she has what it takes.

Creating the Essential Job Profile

Reaching this thorough understanding is the key to hiring the right person. Most managers set out to hire "the best person for the job" without determining what is "best" for that particular position. It's the Rocky Graziano approach to hiring: "I pondered the situation—and it hit me!"

What you're after is a way to distinguish vital skills from irrelevant skills and to pinpoint the subtle qualities that will put the candidate over the top. By asking yourself some smart questions, you can put together the Essential Job Profile; from there you can go on to develop smart questions to ask during the actual interview.

The Essential Job Profile is a comprehensive outline which considers all aspects of the position—skills, personal traits, team fit, and special talents—the crucial as well as less important requirements.

To arrive at this profile you must answer four important questions:

- What type of person does your team need?
- What is the hidden job description?

- What are the success factors?
- How well do you want the job done?

Write each question on a separate sheet of paper. You can also ask people on your staff to help you with your homework by writing up their version of a particular Essential Job Profile. This can be an interesting project, and you and your group may learn a great deal from each other in the process.

What Type of Person Does Your Team Need?

Each time you hire a new person, the impact reverberates throughout your team. Everything shifts as the new employee finds his way to fit into the group and the group finds a way to adapt to him. This is true even if you run a two-person "group" and you are the only person the newcomer directly affects.

Understanding personality types is invaluable for smooth team transition. You also need to know something about your group's style. Take a good look at your team; think about how a new person might liven things up a little. If your people thrive on action and deadlines, then a slow-moving member might retard their momentum. On the other hand, such an addition might help moderate the team if it tends to foul up because of too high a speed.

Consider the descriptions in Chapter 4 of the 5 major categories of personality types. Commanders are the fast moving leaders, the merchants of change. Convincers will also come up with ideas, and will promote them. Carers will keep the peace, cooperate, and get the work done. Calculators will be sure it's done right. Creators will come up with new ideas and concepts. Most teams do best with all 5 types represented.

As a manager you also want your new employee to complement your own style. For example, if you're a Commander looking for a secretary or assistant, you should look for a Carer or Calculator to complement your weakness. *Hire your weakness*—someone who is strong in the areas where you are weak.

Ask yourself and your team these questions:

"How can I improve the group when I hire a new person?"

"What kind of person will fit into our team best?

"What talents or personality types would help to balance the team for maximum productivity?"

"Have I complemented my own weaknesses?"

"Can this person make up for my shortcomings?"

"Are we lacking a Carer or a Calculator type who would complement our group of Commanders and Convincers?"

"Do we need an idea person, or a peacemaker?"

"Do we need a person who loves detail, or someone who loves to talk to people?"

"Are there any parts of this job that someone else on the team would like to do?" (Hiring is a good time to reassess the team and see if other jobs should change.)

"Is there a way that this new circumstance will let me improve the present situation for my team?" (More space? Increased budget or more team training? This is a perfect question if you're hiring people to work with newly installed technology.)

Write down all your answers. They will form the basis of interview questions.

What Is the Hidden Job Description?

Many jobs already have a formal job description. A good one usually includes things like educational requirements, experience necessary, major responsibilities, lines of communication, and special considerations.

But every job also has a hidden job description—those things you wouldn't or couldn't or shouldn't write in the formal job description. A formal job description gives the facts: what the person is expected to do. The hidden job description covers the intangible requirements. You expect a salesperson to have confidence and to cope well with frequent rejection. And you want a copywriter to be sensitive to trends and change. And a personnel administrator who is a good listener.

Sometimes even the "best" skills are useless if the person isn't happy with the work. A simple question to ask yourself is "What should this person enjoy doing?" Or "What unusual circumstance should he or she be able to tolerate?"

David, who was hired as an administrative assistant in the training department, wanted to be a trainer although he had no experience. Even though he was a whiz on the word processor he resented it and peppered every passerby with comments like "Elaine is out there enjoying herself while I'm stuck at this miserable computer."

It's important to find people who really like their work. Hiring a manager who doesn't like people would be like hiring a chef who doesn't like food. Likewise, an administrator should love organized systems, and a secretary should enjoy being efficient. While these traits seem obvious, you can't take it for granted that because someone applies for a given job they automatically have the appropriate predilections.

Probing around these intangibles gives you the fodder to create a lot of smart interview questions. For example, if you note that frequent policy changes are a fact of life in your company, you should devise questions about the candidate's reaction to change. If several people have left recently for other companies, some interview questions may concern loyalty.

The hidden job description helps you focus on qualities, such as loyalty and energy, that can make a big difference when it comes to choosing the right person. To pin down these elusive factors, ask yourself—and your team—these ten smart questions:

"What personal qualities are necessary for this job?" (Enthusiasm, steadiness, flexibility, love of detail?)

"What type of behavior will suit this job?" (Energetic, placid, talkative, silent?)

"Who has failed in this job and why?"

"Who has succeeded in this job and why?"

"Who are the difficult people this individual will have to communicate with?"

"Are there any unusual circumstances in the organization that the person will have to cope with?" (Change? Moving? Working alone?)

"What are the toughest conditions of the job?"

"What kind of work should a person thrive on in order to be happy doing this particular job?"

"What kind of atmosphere should this person most enjoy?"

"If I had to describe the person who could best fill this job, what would I say?"

What Are the Success Factors?

There are almost always one or two outstanding characteristics that a person needs to excel in a job. I call these special talents or skills "success factors."

When you have defined the job and have determined the kind of personality that would best carry it out, you need to know something more: "What is the most important quality or ability the candidate must have to succeed in this particular job?" This could be both a quality or a skill or a combination.

Some people might say "An MBA," or "Writing reports." But those answers are wide of the mark. The success factor addresses itself to the essence of the job. For example, it's essential for the CEO of a controversial corporation (a power company, for example) to be a dynamic public speaker and a good media personality. And a telemarketing person must have a warm, confident telephone voice and the ability to close sales. A court stenographer must be able to record 150 words per minute. If the essence of a certain job involves complicated dealings with high-level authority, a candidate needs special talents for both politicking and negotiating. Desire and enthusiasm for the job are not enough. An opera singer, no matter how hard she works, cannot succeed without a great voice. These are the special abilities needed for these jobs—the keys that allow the person to excel.

If a job applicant is missing the success factor or factors, no other assets, no matter how exemplary, can make up for it. Too often we hire ducks for running and rabbits for swimming.

In my own office, for example, I hope that an administrative assistant will deal pleasantly on the telephone with clients, be an excellent typist, write good letters, and generally have good ideas for the company. But none of those assets is the success factor. The primary quality an administrative assistant must have is an unfailing ability to follow up and handle details.

Identifying the success factor can save a lot of time. If a Broadway producer or a real estate developer can raise funds, any other talents they have—or don't have—are irrelevant. Likewise, if a job requires 75 percent research, a highly gregarious Convincer, even if he or she is eager to tackle the research job, is the wrong choice.

You can sometimes arrive at the success factor if you think in terms of your company rather than an individual's capabilities. A prospective account executive may have a great track record landing new accounts, but perhaps his success has depended on a lavish expense account. Limited by the low budget your firm can afford, his hands will be tied. Another candidate may be able to land one king-size account in six months, but in fact you might need someone who can pull in several smaller accounts right away.

Janet Tweed, executive recruiter for Gilbert Tweed Associates, recently described one of their worst hiring decisions: "We wanted a president to oversee five companies, each with its own problems. The person chosen had unbelievable credentials with a Fortune 500 company. However, we learned he could manage different plants making the *same* product but lacked the flexibility to handle five *different* situations."

Some jobs have more than one success factor. There is the top success factor, and then others of lesser import. For example, many consultants whose business is conducted outside the office have trouble finding and keeping good secretaries because the person is alone so much. Although functioning well when alone is not the top success factor, it is vital and should be included. A good list of success factors should contain at least one—but not more than three—elements without which the job cannot be performed with excellence.

Five questions will help you determine the success factors for a particular job. Ask yourself, and write down your answers:

"What is the one talent and/or skill this person must have to do this job well?"

"Are there any other secondary qualities and/or skills necessary for good performance?"

"Are these factors crucial, or only important?"

"If a previous employee failed in this job, was there one quality lacking that made the difference?"

"How does that quality alter the list of success factors?"

Here's an example. Let's say that you have a position open for a technical researcher.

The first question is "What is the one talent and/or skill this person must have?" You answer: The person must be a persistent, dedicated researcher.

"Are there any other secondary qualities and/or skills necessary for good performance?" You answer:

1. Telephone interviewing.
2. Organizing a tight outline from many different sources.
3. Ability to write reports in clear, nontechnical prose.
4. Ability to type a clean, attractive presentation.

"Are these factors crucial, or only important?" You answer: Numbers 2 and 3 are crucial. Telephone interviewing and typing could be done by someone else.

"If a previous employee failed in this job, was there one quality lacking that made the difference?" You answer: The person who held the job before could amass information but had trouble picking out what was important.

"How does that quality alter the list of success factors?" You answer: I would change Number 2 to read: Ability to ferret out important information, *conceptualize*, and develop a tight outline from many different research sources.

After answering these self questions your list of success factors would read like this:

1. Dedicated, persistent researcher.
2. Able to select important information, conceptualize, and develop a tight outline from many different sources.
3. Able to translate outline into clear, nontechnical prose.

How Well Do You Want the Job Done?

The level of performance you would like to see in the work of an employee is the fourth vital element to add to your Essential Job Profile. During job interviews few things look more promising than an enthusiastic new employee; unfortunately, few things can be as misleading. Too often you find that your new employee's level of energy doesn't match his level of skills.

Managers often miss out on the right people because they fail to set standards of performance. Interviewers typically ask themselves "What is the job I have open?" A smarter question—the question that will get the best person—is "How well do I want the job done?"

A public-relations executive recently had to fire a newly hired account man; she realized that although he could write a press release in three days, she needed someone who could turn one out in half a day. Most of us have only a vague notion of the performance level we require in a job—someone who types "well," or someone who can handle a "variety" of projects.

When I ask in seminars "How fast do you want your secretary to type?" most executives answer "Around 50 words per minute." In my office I hire only people with 70 wpm or better. For most managers productivity will increase substantially if the secretary types 70 to 75 words per minute, and many people out there fill the bill.

Your interview questions aren't designed merely to learn what the applicant did in his last job; you want to find out how well he did it (and how well he would do it for you). Only when you establish the performance standard you require can you discover whether an applicant can perform at that level. If you want to excel, don't lower your standards—keep raising them.

Questions concerning standards will vary according to the job and the job requirements. Each major job requirement should have a matching performance standard. For example, if typing is one job requirement, you will have to set a minimum speed. You will have a separate performance standard for telemarketing, and so on. For each job requirement, ask yourself:

"What specific achievements do I expect from the new employee?"

"What do I want never to happen?" (No complaints from customers.)

"When do I expect the person to master the job?"

The questions should be aimed at the specific job at hand. For example, if a product manager will have to develop "several" new product lines over a twelve-month period, how many do you actually expect? How close to market-ready should suggested products be when presented to upper management? How successful do you expect them to be in their first year on the market?

Or if you're hiring a new account person: Do you expect him or her to eventually handle one or two product lines alone? Three or four? And how soon is "eventually"?

Or if you're hiring a new receptionist: Do you want the person simply to be pleasant and efficient? Or do you expect him or her to field tricky phone calls with tact and intelligence? Will you expect the receptionist to recognize all your clients after being with you a month? Two months?

Final Preparation of the Essential Job Profile

When you have answered these questions on your four sheets of paper, you have everything you need to arrive at the Essential Job Profile.

By developing the Essential Job Profile you are forced to think clearly about the forthcoming interview. Even if you do nothing further, you are already way out front in the hiring process.

However, it's best to take it one step further: to spell out a series of smart questions that will help you discover if the job applicant has the qualities revealed in the Essential Job Profile. Every hiring situation is different. As much as possible, each question you ask should be tailored to the particular situation and person involved. As you develop the Essential Job Profile for your job opening, put your notes in writing; outline important issues and start thinking of smart questions that relate to each issue.

A much-traveled-never-in-the-office colleague of mine asked me to help him hire an administrator to run his office. We used this system to create the Essential Job Profile. Here is what we wrote:

TEAM FIT:

Even-tempered; must complement me. Someone who enjoys being a self-starter and can work alone. Definitely need a Calculator personality.

HIDDEN JOB DESCRIPTION:

Someone to take over the administration and financial aspects of the business. Someone who will work overtime when necessary and not be a clock watcher. Want someone interested in doing the job right. Take-charge attitude, able to cope with high-pressure office. Clearly detail oriented.

SUCCESS FACTORS

1. Highly organized and detail oriented.

2. Must like to take over and operate without direction.

3. Must be able to hire good people.

PERFORMANCE STANDARDS

Record keeping: All books must be balanced each week with no errors.

Level of complaints: Complaints from clients are unacceptable.

Must be able to direct staff so that everyone is in office on time—without fail.

Here is the list of smart questions my colleague came up with to discover how job applicants matched his Essential Job Profile.

"What are your restrictions about overtime?"

"What in my ad attracted you?"

"In what specific ways do you consider yourself precise and detail oriented?"

"How would you define a self-starter?"

"Can you describe in detail the complexity of the projects in your last job?"

"How many projects did you have going on simultaneously?"

"What were your follow-up procedures? Your quality-control checks?"

"Describe how you interview a job candidate."

"May I talk with one of your former employers?"

The list of questions you devise will create a structure to carry you through the interview and keep you relaxed and on track, no more than that. Trying to follow a script is counterproductive. Overplanning and programmed questioning can be nervewracking to the interviewee and may lead to rigid and insipid answers.

Your goal is to have enough smart questions prepared so that in the interviews you will not be talking more than 30 percent of the time. (If you talk more than that, you're not finding out enough.)

Hiring Gives You a Competitive Edge

Hiring a new employee gives you the perfect opportunity to go beyond the ordinary and make a run for excellence. Aside from creating a first-class staff, nabbing the right person for a job is also a great way to make positive changes in your department and to shine up your image with upper management.

Each time you have such an opportunity, ask yourself these smart questions before you take any action:

"What goals do I want to achieve by hiring a new person?"

"Is there anyone else who should be involved in this hiring process?" (A peer whom the person may occasionally report to? A subordinate who will work closely with the person? Your own boss?)

"If so, what are their expectations?"

"What are the advantages (or disadvantages) of discussing the hiring decision with my boss?" (If you're perceived as weak in the decision-making department, you can prove otherwise by making an excellent choice by yourself. On the other hand, if you've been told you should be more of a team player, now is an ideal time to show that you do indeed value input from other people.)

"Where have I fouled up in the past in terms of hiring?" (Perhaps you weren't willing to spend money. Or you didn't really know what you were looking for. Or you chose someone because you liked him. Or you were afraid to hire someone who might outshine you.)

It is not uncommon for people to avoid hiring applicants who are "too good." One executive found a way to overcome her anxiety about hiring people who outperformed her: "I learned that coming up with good people made me look good. As a result one or two may have moved past me. But I'll tell you this: I've got the best network in the company." She has also earned herself a reputation for picking winners.

Managers who succeed understand that the best leaders follow this wisdom: Hire and promote people who are better than you are, because when they shine they make you look good. The eventual result is that when you reach a senior position, the entire organization is seeded with your talented charges.

The abiding philosophy of David Ogilvy, of the renowned Ogilvy & Mather advertising agency, is this: "If each of us hires people who are smaller than we are we shall become a company of dwarfs. But if each of us hires people who are bigger than we are, we shall become a company of giants."

People who get ahead in corporations see every hiring situation as an opportunity to thrust their careers forward. They ask themselves, consciously or unconsciously, this one smart question: "What can I do to maximize this experience—for myself, my team, and my organization?"

In the following chapter we're going to take quality staffing out of the theoretical and into the actual interview—one place where asking smart questions offers an immediate payoff.

9

The Smart Questions Way to Hire

You look across the desk. The job candidate smiles back at you. You notice that with his well-tailored blue suit and white shirt he's wearing gleaming black Italian loafers, an elegant tie, and a matching handkerchief peeking out from his breast pocket. "Why did you choose our company to apply to?" you ask.

Enthusiasm spills out of every pore: "I think what you're doing here is innovative. This organization is known to have its finger on what's happening around the country."

As you take in his appearance and his attitude, one question runs through your mind: "Is this person the right one? Is he the best possible addition to my team?"

There's only one way to find out. Resumes, credentials, and references can tell only part of the story. Impressions and "vibrations" add a little more. But your total picture of the applicant can be filled in only by asking right questions and evaluating each response.

When you interview a job candidate your immediate goal is to reduce tension and encourage forthright communication. Aim for a relaxed and unpressured pace.

The interview situation is likely to distort your sense of time, so don't rush things. Studies show that when interviewers estimate the length of a period of silence they typically magnify it by a factor of 10 to 100. As a result, whenever there is a pause in the conversation most interviewers rush to fill what they perceive as an awkward gap. Don't let anxiety make you answer your own questions because you can't bear the silence. Take your time and let the candidate fill the pauses with his own thoughts and answers.

Interviews should be one-on-one. If a colleague or your boss is also going to interview the candidate, their interviews should be in separate meetings. If the applicant must meet several people at once, for example a board of governors, let him know in advance and give him some advice on what to expect.

Always tell the applicant your purpose and objectives: "We're together to discuss the position that's open, and whether it's the right one for you. So this is a discovery process for us both." Suggest a give-and-take discussion.

One school of interview techniques is gaining popularity among managers desperately looking for easy answers to the hiring dilemma. This theory holds that the only purpose of the job interview is for you, the manager, to gather information. As the interviewer you give out as little information as possible and conduct the interview strictly as a question-and-answer session for yourself. I don't believe this method has value. High-quality candidates will not appreciate being treated like specimens to be examined at the discretion of the interviewer.

Many interviewers divide the interview into two parts—in the first part the interviewer asks questions, then during the second part the candidate can ask questions. This is better than the first technique, but it still creates unnecessary tension. In my opinion, conforming to such a rigid pattern is the sign of an insecure interviewer.

First-class interviewers encourage job candidates to ask questions throughout the interview. The idea is to establish a genuine rapport from the moment the session begins. Tell the person that you welcome questions, and then make it easy for him or her to ask: "I'll ask some questions, and feel free to ask any you might have as we go along."

Study the candidate's resume *before* the interview. You've got a real live person there, so don't relate to the paper when you can relate to the human being.

Some managers use the interview to sell applicants on the merits of the job—and later wonder why they hired the wrong person. Your success depends on your accurate assessment of *the candidate*, not vice versa.

Another fatal flaw: managers tend to hire people they like, or who are like them. Some managers are misled by the so-called halo effect. That is, they judge an individual in terms of the impression he or she makes. Managers often let the personal appeal of the candidate overshadow their judgment.

Interviewers must concentrate on past behavior as an indication of the person's potential. The fact that someone is charming, for example, doesn't guarantee that he or she can bargain with vendors for lowest prices. But the fact that the person had successfully run a dinner theater does strongly suggest that he can negotiate with a variety of suppliers for the best deal.

Begin with Open Questions

With the preliminaries over, just how does a manager go about asking the right questions? In a research project that concentrated on interviewing techniques, Samuel G. Trully, who teaches management courses for the School of Business Administration at the University of California, analyzed the recordings of one hundred job interviews. Trully discovered that successful interviewers always began with broad, open-ended questions and worked their way into sharper, more direct questions toward the end of the meeting.

If you ask closed questions right from the beginning, the interview becomes awkward: "Have you spoken to personnel?" "What are your salary requirements?" "What was your previous title?" "Did you get along with your last supervisor?" These questions are guaranteed to bring the conversation to a screeching halt.

In contrast, broad, open questions give the candidate plenty of room to reveal himself. He can talk about what he feels is important and can expand into areas that he thinks are vital. That means that you, the interviewer, have an opportunity to listen and learn.

Open questions stimulate discussion:

"What are some of the reasons you're interested in this position?"

"Why would you like to work for this company?" (Shows if the candidate has done some homework and found out anything about your company before the interview.)

"What has personnel told you?" (You find out what they know and don't know.)

If you succeed in establishing an easy flow with open questions, people will answer questions honestly. And because they encourage the person to talk freely, such open questions also let you learn about strengths, secrets, or problems that wouldn't be mentioned on a resume or in a more formal interview.

Later in the interview the conversational tone you've established will let you pose unusually intimate questions. For example, you might try the favorite interview questions of Robert Half, America's preeminent hiring pro:

"What did you do the day before yesterday—in detail?"

"Why do you think we should hire you?"

"Where does the power come from in your organization?"

Overall, however, you're searching to discover if the candidate has the strengths highlighted in the Essential Job Profile. Some interviewers probe for a person's weaknesses, but in fact, if the candidate fills the role described in the Essential Job Profile, his or her weaknesses are irrelevant. Everyone has weaknesses.

Matching the Essential Job Profile

The meat of the interview should involve questions that grow out of your Essential Job Profile. Here's where you find out whether the candidate's personality fits in with your team and matches the basics of the hidden job description; whether the applicant boasts the success factor or factors; whether in your judgment this person will perform up to your standards.

Looking for Team Fit

If the person you're looking for will have to deal with authority figures, you might ask:

"What kind of people did you have to deal with in your last job?"

"Can you describe the person or people with whom you got along best?"

"What were your least successful relationships? Why?"

"Tell me about two serious interpersonal relationship problems you've had on the job."

Even though I advocate a give-and-take exchange of information, it's important not to pose leading questions which have the answer built in: "You don't mind working alone, do you?" A better question is "What do you like best—working in a group or working solo?"

If they answer "both," press for a decision: "Give me examples." Or, "If you could choose between working on a team and doing research, which would you select?"

Probing for the Hidden Job Description

When considering the hidden job description, you should ask questions that reveal behavior tendencies and work style.

Past behavior is the best indicator of what someone can do for you. It's unrealistic to assume that a Convincer with loads of energy and a need for interaction is going to grow into a research job. If you know a person had a chronic problem meeting deadlines on their last job, it doesn't matter why. The only thing that matters is that the person isn't good at making deadlines.

The hidden job description often involves an individual's temperament and behavior patterns. Michael, the director of a pharmaceutical firm, hired a new vice president of direct marketing. Because the company was in the midst of growth and reorganizing, all of the new executive's time was devoted to budget and long-range planning instead of producing direct mail. He did such a good job that Michael offered him a promotion to do more of the same. But by this time the executive was ill from all the stress the job had caused him.

If you want to test temperament and behavior, try:

"Describe an interpersonal problem you had and how you resolved it."

"In what areas do you feel you would like to develop further?" (Look for concrete answers. A person might answer vaguely: "I'm looking for a job to sink my teeth into." Keep probing for specifics.)

"How do you plan to achieve these goals?"

"Can you tell me in more detail what you mean?"

"How do you see this job fitting in with your plans?"

This is also an appropriate time to find out whether the person is a Commander, Convincer, Carer, Calculator, or Creator. Ask questions that deal with working style, such as:

"Would you describe yourself as people oriented or task oriented?" Or, "Do you like to produce a product yourself, or do you like to delegate and supervise?"

"Can you explain why?"

"Do you solve problems by examining all the available data, or by creative trial and error?"

"What process do you follow in solving problems?"

"In groups do you often emerge as a dominant figure? What do you feel causes this?"

"Are you a competitor or a cooperator? Can you give an example?"

"When you have a problem with a co-worker, do you prefer direct confrontation or tact and delicacy?"

"What methods do you use to make decisions?"

An imaginative question can also reveal a person's behavioral tendencies: "Suppose you have to leave right away to sell a strange and totally unfamiliar product door to door. If you can ask only three things about the product before you go, what would they be?"

There is no right or wrong answer. If the candidate's unhesitating answer is "Price, product lifetime, primary use," you've got a quick thinker with an innate ability to pinpoint the bottom line—a Commander behavioral tendency.

On the other hand, an immediate response along the lines of "How will it make me feel or look better? What benefits does it have?" may indicate great marketing ability. This is more of a Convincer response.

Perhaps the candidate analyzes the question and comes up with "Who can fill me in on this product? How can I get the rest of the team involved in a sales campaign?" You probably have a Carer who presents a balanced view and likes to work with the full resources of a team behind him.

If the person asks "What are the facts about the product?" "Where is my sales manual?" you've got a Calculator. If he asks "What does this product do?" "How does it fit into the overall product line?" or "Why did you select me?—I'm not a good salesperson—I want to create a new product," you've got a Creator.

Don't stop after learning one dimension of the person. Probe further. For example, you might want to know how a candidate handles the issue of honoring company policy: "Were there ever times you had to get around, ignore, or change company policy in order to get a project done on schedule?"

If the applicant answers "Yes," don't jump to conclusions. Ask him or her to describe the details. Then follow it up with another question: "Was there ever a time that you followed company policy, even though you found it difficult?"

Since you've asked both questions, the applicant can't intuit the answer you're looking for. You're after a multi-dimensional picture of whether the person supports the organization he works for, and how he responds to rules and regulations.

When you're probing for the hidden job description, it's important to listen to *how* the person answers as well as what he says. Does the candidate have a pleasant voice or a grating one? Is he or she especially articulate, blunt, commanding, intimidating, tactful? Poised, outgoing and somewhat theatrical, full of irrepressible energy—or more like the Rock of Gibraltar and just as dignified? Careful observation can also give you keys to a candidate's personal strengths and perhaps to untapped potential.

Probing for Success Factors

Questions that probe for a given success factor will depend entirely on what kind of talent you're looking for. Seth, a clothing manufacturer, was looking for a designer who would develop four new lines each year and supervise a difficult, conflict-prone staff of twelve. The previous designer had ignored the people totally to meet the deadlines. When it came time to interview a new designer, Seth asked these smart questions:

"What were the pressures on your last job?"

"Most executives are jugglers. How do you handle the need to juggle many different elements?"

"In detail, what did you have to produce in your last job?"

"What kind of problems did your people have?"

"What results did you accomplish?"

"How did you develop your key people?"

"What do you consider your three greatest career achievements?"

"Why did these give you such satisfaction?"

"What are the most difficult aspects of your job? Not that you can't do them, but the ones that cost you the most time and effort?"

"If you had two people in serious conflict during a major deadline, what would you do?"

"If a key person wanted to quit during a deadline crisis, what would you do?"

"What do you consider the three essentials of success in developing four new lines and supervising a contentious staff?"

"If I were to interview a person on your staff, how might they describe you?"

"What is your interpretation of success?"

Smart Job Performance Questions

It's easy to ask a typist "How fast do you type?" It's more tricky to get subjective information about previous performance levels. Job applicants often know what success factor you're looking for and will give the expected answer. For example, I once made a poor hiring decision when I was looking for someone who was detail oriented. During the job interview I asked the applicant, "Are you good at details?" and she answered "Yes." I took her word for it, and went on to something else. I was impressed by her nice personality and by the ideas she had for running the office.

After the new person had been in the job for two weeks it became clear that while she had all the other necessary qualities, she was not interested in the follow-up work which was the heart of her job. When it came to the success factor, I should have probed beyond her immediate response and asked a series of questions designed to uncover this one important element. If I had been hiring an opera singer, I could have asked her to sing. But how do you audition an administrative assistant to discover if she's good at details? The only possibility is to ask smart questions:

"Are you good at details?"

"Describe how you handled the details of your last project."

"What have you done to ensure the quality of your employees' work?"

"Can you give me an example of how you would set up a cross-training program?"

Suppose you ask someone who was a project leader, "How well did your projects turn out?" You can bet they'll answer "Fine." Instead, try these smart questions:

"What kind of projects did you handle?"

"How did you select people for your projects?"

"To what extent did you delegate responsibility?"

"Tell me about a problem you had on a project."

"How did you handle it?"

Ask people for specifics:

"Describe a specific assignment and the specific results you achieved."

"What tools, resources, and people did you have to work with?"

"What were your accomplishments?"

"Over what period of time?"

"What was your budget?"

"If you had to do that project over again, what would you do differently?"

Listening and Evaluating

Since you've gone to so much trouble to devise smart questions, make sure you listen carefully to the answers. Throughout the interview, your questions should shift as you listen and evaluate the candidate's responses. Allen E. Murray, Chairman of the Mobil Corporation, says, "My first priority [when interviewing someone] is to make sure I hear and register all the answers, including the implications. After all, that's what prompts my next question."

What an Applicant's Questions Reveal

A good interviewer also listens carefully to the applicant's questions. If you've encouraged a mutual exchange throughout the interview, the candidate's questions will give you insight into the way his or her mind works. For example: "Where can I go in the company?" If an applicant asks this question in the first three or four minutes of the interview, you know this person is eager for a job with promotion potential.

Other questions asked early in the interview may suggest past problems or frustrations:

"Will I be responsible for coming up with ideas?"

"Will I have to present it in person?"

"How much red tape will I have to deal with?"

These questions require you to probe further. Ask "Is that a problem for you?" or "Why are you asking?" Make a genuine nonthreatening inquiry, so that you actually understand why the person is asking the question.

Before you answer any question, consider that you may learn more by first countering with a qualifying question:

Candidate:	Is there any overtime?
Interviewer:	Why do you ask? [It sounds as if she wants to make extra money, but that may not be the reason.]
Candidate:	Will I have to work late?
Interviewer:	Is that a problem for you?
Candidate:	Will there be much travel in this job?
Interviewer:	It's possible. How do you feel about traveling?
Candidate:	Some travel is all right, as long as it isn't too frequent.
Interviewer:	What do you mean by too frequent?
Candidate:	I don't want to be away all the time.
Interviewer:	Tell me what your specific travel concerns are.

If the job applicant doesn't ask any questions, you've learned something about her anyway. Supposing you're looking for a conscientious researcher, a newspaper reporter, or an aggressive salesperson? If the applicant doesn't probe they can't fit the bill.

Gaining the Winning Edge

You gain maximum advantage in the interview when you keep turning your question around until you get the most from the candidate's answer. When you ask a question, the first answer you get is often a programmed reply. Keep rolling the question over, keep probing, keep asking applicants to explain their answers: "Why did you say that?" "Under what circumstances did that happen?" "What would do if you were doing it again?" "Tell me more about that."

Ed Weihenmayer, Vice President of Human Resources at Kidder, Peabody & Co., says that during an interview he looks for a person's work ethic and their technical expertise. "I'll ask several questions to probe into these areas. The rule is, never let people off the hook. Be a detective. Move in on them. It makes for an incessantly tough but interesting and rewarding interview."

Ending the Interview

Significant bits of information are often revealed towards the end of the interview when participants have loosened up a bit. If you end too abruptly, you're likely to lose a valuable player. As you are getting to the last third of your questions, set up the ending: "Before we finish there are a few more things I'd like to go over with you." This gives the candidate a clue that the session is drawing to a close.

A brief summary also helps because it gives both participants something to think about afterwards. But get the *applicant* to summarize the interview. Here is the smartest interview question you can ask: "From our discussion so far, how do you see this job?"

When you bring the interview to a close, you don't want to commit yourself either way. But you do want to be cordial and to leave the person feeling good about himself: "Is there anything we haven't covered that you'd like to know?"

Part of the conclusion should consist of a plan of action, something to be done by either or both parties: "I'm interviewing several people for the job, but I will get back to you within two weeks. I thank you for coming in; I've enjoyed talking with you." Stand up and walk the person to the door and back to the reception area.

Post-Interview Analysis

During an interview, jot down notes of your impressions and the applicant's significant answers. These notes will help you reconstruct the interview at a later date. They also provide a framework for planning the next interview. Having something on paper lets you review the interview accurately. In the process, you may see flaws in your technique that may show you how to improve your approach. Without benefit of such hindsight, you tend to repeat your mistakes. Writing out overviews of the candidates can also help you compare applicants fairly so you can make the best choice.

Smart Questions for Reference Checking

Reference checking is often difficult these days because many people hesitate to give out any information about former employees. This means that it is even more important than ever to ask good questions when you check a job candidate's references.

I recently interviewed applicants for an office manager position. When I tried to call references I got the reply "Henry Rowan worked here" and that's all they would say. At first I accepted that, but by asking some nonthreatening questions I was able to get more information. For example, to one reference I said, "These new rules and regulations are really tough! What do *you* do when you need information about job applicants?" Soon we were talking and I got all the information I needed.

Here are some basic rules to remember when calling references:

1. Always let the candidate know beforehand that you will check their references.

2. When you call up for a reference, keep the conversation short, and concentrate on asking about those areas that most concern you, especially those that involve the success factors:

    "What kind of presentations did Elizabeth make?"

    "How much help and guidance did George need from you?"

    (This is a helpful question if the person must work on his own.)

3. Don't give away the answer you're looking for ("Was Elizabeth good about following company policy?" Better: "How did Elizabeth handle the issue of sticking to company policy?").

4. The smartest question: "If you could work with Elizabeth again, would you?" "Why?" "Why not?" If there is a significant pause, you can assume there were reservations. If possible, probe further. Usually if someone was a superior employee, questions are always welcome.

Great All-Purpose Interview Questions

Some interview questions apply in just about any situation. Put these on your list:

"How have your past job experiences prepared you directly or indirectly for this position?"

"Describe a normal day at your present job . . . a busy day . . . a great day."

"What did you like most about your last job? What did you like least?"

"How did the company's philosophy or attitudes affect you and your work?"

"How would you describe your previous boss's management style?"

"How did you work together?"

"In what ways were you alike—and different?"

"Who were your best employers and your worst?"

"What do you require from your boss?"

"Where did you fit on your last company's organizational chart?"

"What were your responsibilities?"

"What authority did you have?"

"What was your staff like?"

"What was your budget and how did you manage it?"

"What specifically were you accountable for?"

"What improvements did you make?"

"What or whom did you really go to bat for?"

"What were your three most impressive tangible contributions to your company?"

"What are your pet peeves—in a boss, in an organization?"

"Give some examples of situations in which you have been criticized."

"How did you react and why?"

Robert Half has said: "There is something that is much more scarce, something rarer than ability. It is the ability to recognize ability." When you ask smart questions, hiring becomes an art. Nothing can make a manager look better and perform more productively than a great team. Every time you are in a position to hire, you can enhance your opportunity for upward mobility. A good staff makes you less indispensable in your present position and more promotable.

I recently worked with a young woman who beat out three male engineers for an important promotion because she had gone into a failing department, hired some new people, and turned the department into a cohesive and productive work group. Because the department could then run on its own, upper management was convinced that she was the only person to handle the new and more challenging job.

Even when you have put together a superior team, however, your work as a people manager is just beginning. After you have them on board, you must look for ways to manage and motivate your staff on a day-to-day basis, to help them achieve their fullest potential. There are a number of vehicles with which to accomplish this, from encouraging them when things stall out, to offering direct advice on how to achieve their goals, to coaching and counseling. All of these techniques come under the umbrella of motivating your people to achieve maximum potential.

10

Ask the Most from Your People—And Get It

Millions of managers in thousands of different industries want the answer to the same question: "How can I motivate my people?"

Despite all the new management trends and alleged cure-alls, motivation remains a critical problem in today's business. Each of numerous theories has had its day in the sun, but no single idea can be applied universally. Theory X and Theory Y, job enlargement and job enrichment, increased responsibility, cross-training, job switching, situational leadership—all are good ideas that work in some instances and fail in others.

The fact is, managers cannot motivate other people. The best they can do is choose the right people for the right jobs, establish the right atmosphere, and ask for excellent performance.

Inspirational speaker and sales trainer Alan Cimberg often begins his seminars by asking a female member of the audience to come up and give him a kiss. Someone always fulfills his request.

"Why do I get the kiss?" he asks. "Because I ask for it. But when I ask the same woman, 'Will you take off all your clothes and give me another kiss?' she never does."

Cimberg's example graphically illustrates the difference between asking someone for something they can do or that they feel comfortable doing and asking for something they can't do or feel terrible doing. Understanding that difference is the essence of motivation.

As many experts on management emphasize, true motivation only comes from within. You cannot "start up" a human being the way you would switch on the ignition of a car. What a manager *can* do is help employees motivate themselves and get their own engines revved up to top speed.

The overriding question every manager should ask himself is "How can I encourage employees to perform with excellence because they want to?"

Smart Questions

You can motivate people only on their own terms. People respond for their own reasons, not yours. You may want someone to increase productivity to meet department quotas, or to enhance efficiency to reduce overtime. But the person actually carries out your program because he or she wants to go home on time, hopes to be paid well for satisfactory performance, or has some other personal motive. Sometimes the reason is that they want to please you. But motivation is most enduring when someone has his own inner goal, and when you recognize the nature of that goal. The reason most motivational techniques fail is that they do not focus on the individual.

The most universally successful way to motivate is based on discovering what the other person needs. And smart questions give you the tool for discovery. Smart questions are not limited to one company, or to a certain kind of person, or to a particular motivational technique. The right questions can help you discover the needs of individual staff members as they develop, and as jobs grow and change.

Self Questions to Get Started

To learn how to use questions as a motivating technique, begin by asking yourself:

"What do I want to happen as a result of my efforts to motivate?" (The answer is usually that you want people to *want* to do their best.)

"Why should this person want to do his best?" "What's in it for him if he does do his best?" (Promotion? Less strain? More challenging work in the future? More money? More freedom?)

"If I were this person, what would I need to get me moving?"

"What can I do to enhance his job so he will want to aim for peak performance?" (Make it more interesting? Give him more responsibility? Take away some of the pressure? Recognize his efforts?)

When you ask these questions, be specific, for this will bring you more in touch with the person's particular goals. For example, if you answered "Give him more responsibility," specify what kind of responsibility. More client contact? Seeing projects through?

Leadership Style

Even when we accept the idea that motivation must come from within, a manager still has to set the scene and develop the atmosphere that permits self-motivation to take over. You can't create the proper atmosphere simply by handing over the reins to your staff. The way to be democratic and at the same time maintain authority is by no means clear-cut. As one middle manager put it, "In my company, being a manager is still a choice between being a babysitter and being a son of a bitch."

Neither extreme will bring you much in the way of respect from your staff. Research shows that the most successful managers are flexible. They are able to adapt their styles to fit the situation and the people they're working with. True, a manager may need to be an autocrat in a crisis. But when things are running smoothly again, and you have talented people in your group, you should loosen your hold. Different situations call for different tactics. Brainstorming sessions, for example, require a free-wheeling, nonjudgmental atmosphere.

The successful leader is one who can respond appropriately in a variety of situations. If direction is in order, she is able to direct; if considerable participative freedom is called for, she's ready to grant such freedom. Thus in today's business world the successful manager is one who can accurately gauge the situation, determine the most suitable behavior, and act accordingly. Flexibility is the key.

Unfortunately, too many managers carry the same set of responses into every situation, especially if a certain method has served them well in the past. Jerry was hired by a large record company to pull the organization through a major crisis. He had built up a reputation of "saving" companies in tough times. This particular firm was faltering because it had failed to keep up with new technology in the industry. Just as he had in similar predicaments, Jerry clamored and pushed—and pulled the company through. Everyone rallied to his battle cry. But after the problems subsided, what did Jerry do?

He kept right on pushing. He treated every situation as though it were an emergency. He kept his people at such a stressful pace that everyone suffered from the daily strain. "It got so that ordering a taxi was a crisis," his secretary recalled. "Instead of walking to the elevator, he ran. Instead of making a request, he barked an order. It seemed we were forever throwing water on a fire that never got put out." The result was a big turnover in employees, as people grew tired of catering to his self-created tantrums.

Self Questions to Enhance Your Flexibility

We are all accustomed to reacting spontaneously in our usual way, whatever that "way" may be. It's difficult to let go of old habits and develop a more flexible managerial style. Leadership is tough. That's why corporate leadership is such a challenge.

Questions can help you become more flexible and establish an atmosphere where people can express the best in themselves. Here's one way to do it. When you encounter a problem, pose these quick questions to yourself:

"How is this situation unique?"

"What is my usual mode of dealing with people problems?"

"What works?"

"What doesn't?"

"What's the best way to handle this particular situation [or this particular person]?"

"When was the last time I handled something in a new way?"

"How might I change my approach to get the most out of each person on my team?"

"Where would applying pressure help?"

"Where would it hinder?"

"In terms of my bottom-line objective, how would I like this situation to turn out?"

"How can I get out of my own way and make that happen?"

Golden Rules of Motivation

Through hundreds of research reports one message rings out loud and clear: To increase motivation, create an atmosphere where people motivate themselves. When people feel personally involved in a plan, they work to make it happen. How do you do it? Show respect for the worker's opinion and experience; listen to ideas as well as problems; remove the obstacles that mar the employee's motivation.

There are seven questions that managers can ask themselves to help create a self-motivating atmosphere. Each one involves improving communication with your team.

1. Do Your People Know Your Plans?

Make it a point to share information vital to your business or organization—annual reports, quarterly updates, monthly operating results, comparative performance among divisions or units—with everyone on your team, including those at the entry level. Do all hands know, on a regular basis, how their group is performing according to the ten or fifteen most important criteria? How their group stacks up against other groups? Do they know how the standards were arrived at, and why?

It pays to be direct. Discard what Bob Collings, CEO of Data Terminal Systems in Massachusetts, calls the "Mushroom Theory of Management—the one that says keep your employees in the dark and throw a lot of manure on them." The best way to motivate people is to let them know the plan so they can participate in it. Tell them your goals and the goals of the organization. Let them see the picture as a whole and get a sense of their part in it.

Sharing builds motivation. As Collings says, "When people are highly motivated, it's easy to accomplish the impossible. And when they're not, it's impossible to accomplish the easy."

2. Do You Give Feedback?

People need feedback the way they need air. Even well-motivated employees "die" without it. They want to be encouraged if they're doing well, and if they're not doing well they want to know why. The more they know about how they're doing, the more effort they'll put into their work.

Give feedback immediately. When you see a good or a bad performance, tell the performer about it right then. Don't wait a year to correct a problem or to give recognition for a job well done. Pounce on it. Let the person know—now.

Feedback is a two-way process based on asking smart questions ("This looks good. Did you have any problems with it?"). When you give feedback you help keep communication channels open. If your people know you're willing to discuss performance with them, they'll be more likely to bring you their problems and questions and to keep you better informed. Feedback helps you avoid the NETMA (Nobody Ever Tells Me Anything) Syndrome. Create an atmosphere where people are not afraid to tell you when something is wrong, and you will have fewer surprises.

3. Do You Build on Strengths?

In their book, *Leaders,* Warren Bennis and Bert Nanus isolate several factors that mark superb leaders. At the top of the list: Instead of focusing on weaknesses, they build on strengths—their own as well as the strengths of their employees. When I train public speakers I ask people in the class to identify their strengths and their weaknesses. Invariably they say, "I don't know what my strengths are, but my weaknesses are. . . ." We've been so programmed to focus on weaknesses—as though any imperfection would negate or detract from any strength. But this is not so. All success comes from strengths. A person who is bright but shy succeeds because of his brightness and in spite of his shyness. If he merely dwelled on his shyness, he might not have allowed his intelligence to surface.

Once you get people operating from a position of strength, it is easier to motivate them. They will enjoy what they're doing and they will do it better. Positive—not negative—behavior should be looked at first.

For example, after a meeting, ask yourself: "What went right? How can I apply that in other situations?" Know the strengths of your people so you can help build on them. Know your own strengths so you also can continue to grow.

4. Do You Give Constructive Praise?

Successful managers sandwich criticism between layers of praise. Criticism and praise are both valuable parts of feedback, but some managers are reluctant to give either.

W. Timothy Gallwey, writing in *The Inner Game of Tennis*, observes that people wait for praise, and when they don't get it their performance falters. However, as Gallwey says, you cannot praise every move they make from start to finish. To help people learn, praise must be specific and precise. "You did a great job" is better than nothing, but if you want to help someone grow, try: "You did a great job. This is what made it great. . . ."

I have always admired the technique of a piano teacher who was known for launching superb pianists. After a student played a new passage during a lesson she would say, "That's very good. Try it with a little more action in the fingers." Or, "Try to draw out the legato in the fourth measure." Or any number of other improvements. She frequently made it seem as if she was correcting herself: "Let me see if I can give you a better fingering for this passage."

In other words, she *never* criticized, even when it was apparent that the student hadn't practiced or was giving a lackluster performance. As students followed her advice they saw and heard the improvement, and drove themselves until she would say, "Ah, that's much better. Keep doing that."

Her philosophy was that criticism kills pride, shatters self-esteem, and destroys desire. Constructive praise, on the other hand, builds new skills, stimulates self-confidence, and enriches performance.

For those times when criticism is necessary, engrave this message on your mind: *Give praise publicly; keep criticism private.* I will always remember one successful company president who made this offhand comment: "If you want to give a person credit, put it in writing and circulate it around the company. If you want to give him hell, do it on the phone."

Perhaps the most golden rule of people management is "Never be too tough on a person when he's down." When an individual is upset over failure, harping on the negative can hurt him and quench any incentive to improve. Even when giving criticism, you can create a positive framework: "I don't think this is up to your usual standard. What can we learn from it?"

5. Do You Give Rewards?

If people meet their agreed-upon objectives, they should be rewarded with more than kind words. Money and a promotion are among the tangible ways a company can proclaim a "Most Valuable Player." Adam Osborne, the one-time computer whiz who is now the head of Paperback Software International, Inc., in Berkeley, California, says, "Nothing is more important than developing a team that is willing to work with every bit of enthusiasm they have. The way you do that is by being fair—and a little bit more than fair—in the distribution of wealth that comes from your success."

But giving everyone the rewards isn't sound. When it comes to cost-of-living increases, for example, give the top performers the most, the satisfactory people a modest increase, and the poor performers nothing. Otherwise you are rewarding nonperformance.

The best-motivated organization that I've observed is a large graphics company where all raises and bonuses are based on merit and quality. If there are no errors or rejects, each month everyone gets a bonus. Individual merit is rewarded at the time of performance appraisal. The standards are clearly defined and everyone knows the rules. This company has very low absenteeism and is at the top of the industry in quality and creativity.

One of the best rewards you can give a high achiever is your time. Most managers spend the bulk of their time with the poor performers and let the best ones fend for themselves. When someone does a good job for you, recognize their efforts and set aside time to develop projects that will help them get ahead.

When you do give a person a raise, that's the time to increase his responsibilities. Reward him for what he's done and at the same time motivate him to do even more.

One good way *not* to motivate: If you always give someone else's work to a person who finishes a job quickly, then you're punishing, not rewarding. (You've rewarded the poor performer who was inefficient.) Or you might have someone on staff who helps out by doing a dirty job and doing it well. After a while, that person ends up with all the dirty jobs. A willing, effective worker should not be punished for being helpful; he or she should be given a raise, a promotion, or a new title or award. Or assign him a job he's eager to do.

6. Do You Listen and Learn?

It's reported that after finding himself at a dead end, out of money and out of prospects, Thomas Edison once asked his janitor this question: "I'd like to ask your advice, Pop. What do you think I should do in this situation?"

The janitor was stunned. "Nobody ever asked for my advice before," he replied.

"Well," said Edison, "then you should have a lot of good ideas stored up."

No matter what other techniques you employ in your quest to motivate your staff, you have to be prepared to ask questions and to listen at least as much as you talk. Managers who listen—to both ideas and problems—make the difference between a mediocre company and a great one.

It's essential that managers encourage all of their people to contribute and come up with ideas for improvements. Let's say you're in the manufacturing business. By asking questions and listening to your people in the field, you're able to develop products that are the direct result of demands from customers.

No one's ideas should be missed. Acknowledge all correspondence sent to you. You needn't seize on every suggestion, but if you don't at least get back to the person and say "That was a terrific idea" and thank him, he'll never give you another one. A thoughtful response lets people know they count with you. Always give proper recognition for every valid suggestion.

7. Do You Set an Example?

The best manager is a good role model. If you want your staff to perform in a stable, balanced manner, for instance, you cannot be an emotional yo-yo yourself.

A good manager accepts responsibility for the group, as opposed to expecting the group to be responsible for him. This means that he or she does not routinely delegate unpleasant matters. Anyone can muddle through ordinary events; it's the difficult tasks that show leadership. If you have to fire someone, for example, it's up to you to do it. If you don't handle unpleasant jobs personally, you forfeit clout and respect. Public relations expert Henry C. Rogers, author of the popular *Rogers' Rules for Success*, advises managers to "always take the blame, because doing so puts you in a leadership position and enhances your image." A good manager also knows how to say no, to be tough but fair.

Art Williams, founder and president of A. L. Williams, one of the fastest-growing life insurance and securities marketing organizations in the country, concurs: "I see so many of our leaders who talk about winning but who sit back and let others do the tough things. When one individual leads by example, he can become a very powerful force."

In other words, if you don't handle the responsibilities of your own leadership position, you can't expect your staff people to live up to their job responsibilities either.

Recognition of Performance

When you motivate effectively and your people consequently improve and succeed, what do you do next? You push them forward as fast as is practical. Such a policy is tonic to the ambitious, and it serves as a catalyst for the entire staff.

Business has come a long way in this regard over the past few years. Many big corporations used to have unwritten rules about cutoff points for certain employees (women, blacks, non–college grads)—points beyond which they could not move, regardless of their dedication or ability. Also, higher-ups often typecast individuals in their current roles and did not give them a chance to prove they could do more. For the promotion system to have a positive effect within a corporation, advancement must be based on merit. When an employee feels that movement is blocked regardless of performance, motivation falls off.

If the fact is that specific employees will not be promoted, for whatever reason, you, as a manager, have two choices. You can motivate them so they get the most enjoyment from what they're doing—switch job tasks, cross-train, look for ways to liven up the existing job. If they reach a point where they're no longer turned on and you cannot seem to spark any interest, you can move them somewhere else in the company. (Or, if there seems no alternative, suggest that they go elsewhere.)

Self Questions to Rate Your Motivational Skills ˜

"Are my staff people in the right jobs?" (Every manager should strive to match the job with the person—and keep them matched. This is one important key to motivation.)

"Do my employees know specifically—not just vaguely—what I expect of them?" (Would each of them agree with your answer?)

"Can each person describe his job in terms of the Essential Job Profile?"

"Do I know what each person lacks to make him a good performer?"

"Do I show my concern about each person's performance in a helpful, nonthreatening way?"

"Are there any company policies or procedures which might be blocking them?"

"Do I consistently act in a supportive manner?"

"Do I frequently remark on their improvements?"

"Do I provide sufficient help and training for my staff?"

"When I delegate a task, do I also delegate authority?"

"Do I practice what I preach?"

"Am I careful not to punish good performance, and do I reward poor performance?"

"Do my employees have confidence in me?" (If you're the last one to know when there's a problem, your answer should be no. Remember the NETMA Syndrome.)

"Do I keep my people informed about company matters that are important to our department and to them?"

Any manager who can answer yes to twelve or more of these self questions can give himself a high rating in the motivational skills department.

Using Motivational Techniques

Managers generally think of motivating when employees aren't performing at peak levels. But in fact, successful managers are motivators all the time. They instinctively vary their approach to meet the needs of this person at this time, or that group at that time.

In his most vital role, a manager may motivate by *delegating, coaching, counseling,* or *confronting*. Each role is slightly different, but each has the same goal—to help people learn and grow, and to encourage creative ideas from all hands, all of which further your organization's overall purpose. When used skillfully, each method can stimulate motivation. When used inappropriately, however, the same methods can demotivate and crush morale. In the following chapters you will see how the Smart Questions System can make the most of each of these opportunities to motivate.

In all of these roles the manager is striving for maximum people potential—to get the best from the individuals who comprise his staff. And in all of these roles the Smart Questions System provides the key. The objective in every case is to ask questions that let the other person determine the means to growth, and to let that person take the responsibility for his or her own personal development.

11

Questions That Help You Delegate

Are you typical of many managers? Do you come in early and leave late while your employees are out having a good time and sleeping in? I once ran a three-day training program for the American Management Association during which one highly placed executive was always being called out to answer panicky telephone calls from his office; he missed one entire afternoon of the program because he had to attend to a staff emergency. By coincidence I was later called in to consult with his company. I learned that he was considered a poor manager because when he wasn't around everything fell apart.

Bear this in mind: If you've rendered your staff helpless without you, your boss won't be able to promote you—he'll know that chaos will result. You may have preserved your sense of control, but you've forfeited your chance for advancement. Further, refusing to delegate is the surest way to keep yourself bound to your desk twenty-four hours a day.

Delegating demands a sense of security. You have to trust others to come through without your constant coaching, and you have to be willing to give someone else a chance to succeed.

"The hard thing for me when I moved up to sales management," said a stockbroker promoted to branch manager, "was to admit that someone on my staff could sell as well as I used to, and in some cases even better. Even harder, though, was to learn to be patient with someone who

139

wasn't as good as I was. To give them time to learn, instead of jumping in and doing it myself, was my managerial trial by fire."

Delegating is something you're expected to do for your own good. Yet even with all of the outstanding benefits—more time, less stress, greater productivity, more opportunities for growth—many managers still insist on being a one-person band. If you're inclined to do everything yourself because you think it's the only way it will get done right, then you are doing something wrong.

For you to get ahead, you have to learn how to delegate—to give other people important tasks and move aside so they can accomplish them. If your group doesn't stand out as a group, you will reach a managerial impasse.

Smart questions can help you delegate work imaginatively, in a way that gets the work done successfully and at the same time helps your people grow and develop.

Why Delegate?

Delegating is a superb tool for motivating your staff and getting the most from your team. The objective is the long-term development of each person, which in turn contributes to the performance of the team and ultimately the organization.

Frederick Herzberg, Professor and Chairman of the Psychology Department at Case Western Reserve University, has discovered that the only way to motivate an employee is to give him challenging work that is meaningful to him, for which he can assume responsibility. The message is that responsibility improves morale and encourages people to work harder and with more enthusiasm.

Finding the Right Approach

The most delicate part of using delegating as a motivational tool is making sure you don't demotivate the person in the process. A manager must tread the fine line between guiding the person and letting go so he can succeed on his own. If you give a person a task and then tell him not to come back until it's done, he may feel abandoned and in over his head. On the other hand, if you keep too tight a grip on the reins, you risk suffocating him. The latter error is more common—most managers tend toward too much control rather than too little. But both can cause you trouble.

It's essential that you learn to overcome that impulse to dominate the situation and yet never let the individual feel that you've lost interest in him. Good managing is personally guided autonomy, and you're the chief guide. You can turn things over to people gradually, with ever-widening intervals of reporting back to you, until they are ready to fly solo.

And if handling a task has given an employee a degree of expertise, let him follow through, especially in decision making. If you ask someone to research a new computer system for possible purchase, for example, let him or her be in on the final decision.

Delegating Authority

Nothing is more destructive—and self-defeating—than for a manager to delegate a job, then make it impossible for the employee to successfully carry it out. The easy part of leadership is telling people what to do; the hard part is giving them the authority to do it.

For example, Janice delegated a major time-study job which required a great deal of interaction with other departments. But instead of letting those involved speak directly to the person delegated to handle the job, all return calls had to go through Janice. Aside from being a waste of time, this was demoralizing to the staff person. Janice gave him responsibility, then essentially took it away.

In another instance, a manager in a word processing unit delegated the responsibility for hiring a team of skilled, quality-conscious workers. Although he told his subordinate to find the people, the manager made the hiring decisions. By reserving the final authority for himself he defeated the purpose of delegating.

Alex, a senior manager in a communications conglomerate (who should have known better), told Pat, a middle manager, to integrate three groups into one. Pat considered the assignment carefully, then offered her ideas for carrying out the process smoothly. Alex rejected the suggestions. "This is the way I see it," he said. "Do it my way."

Pat was forced to carry out a plan with which she did not agree and to defend the plan to the three diverse groups, who didn't want to be combined in the first place. There was no way for her to reach the goal on her own terms.

The result was unhappiness among the three groups, frustration for Pat, and a rough and disorganized transition period—all because Alex had insisted on doing it his way. It turned out that his middle manager knew the situation best because she had firsthand knowledge. Ultimately, because of employee dissatisfaction and union involvement, most of her original ideas were incorporated after all. But the overall result of the mishandled situation was distrust and disharmony between staff and management.

Thus, when you delegate a job, the two most important questions to ask yourself are:

"Am I also delegating the appropriate amount of authority?"

"Will this be a growth experience for the person, or merely more work?"

Good managing is making sure that others do their jobs smoothly, harmoniously, and productively. That means not only delegating tasks, but conceding the authority and status necessary to accomplish them.

Delegating Opportunities

When you delegate you should think of how you can polish and fine-tune the overall performance of your group. Look for opportunities for each person. If a new public-relations project comes in, you might give someone who normally implements and oversees projects a chance to become a promoter and improve his public speaking. When somebody leaves a team, see if another staff member might want to learn a new skill or take on some of the responsibilities the previous person held. Being given the chance to explore their potential is a tonic for boredom. When your people realize that you're looking to develop their potential and promote their careers, their interest level will continue to be high.

You can find opportunities to delegate in even the most static situations. At least part of what every manager considers routine would offer an interesting challenge for staff members. These routine tasks shouldn't be mere drudgery, however, but responsibilities that captured your own interest before you mastered them. In my office, making sales calls is routine for me but a great challenge to my assistant. Although it takes time and coaching to train her, it's worth it because of her great satisfaction when she makes a successful call.

There are other delegating possibilities: any project that has been sitting, stone cold, on the back burner. That one project you keep meaning to get around to someday—but somehow never do—is perfect for assigning to a staff member.

Another idea involves task swaps among staff members. There is bound to be interest and excitement for one person in what used to be a challenge for another. Your people may have their own notions of advantageous job swaps and promising projects. It's up to you to ask them.

The purpose of delegation is not to delegate chores you don't like. Nor should you keep all the boring or tough tasks for yourself. Self-sacrifice is not a virtue. Strive for a good mix for everyone on your staff. That doesn't mean you have to pass along a task you thoroughly enjoy. I know the managing editor of a publishing company that produces art books. She assigns a working editor to each book but always retains at least one book each season for which she does the hands-on editing because, as she explains, "I love it. I would be miserable in my job if I couldn't spend at least some time actually working on a book of my own."

When you delegate in this manner, what can you expect to happen? A number of staff members will respond wholeheartedly. Doing a tougher job will give them confidence; they will discover ambition. You won't get maximum results from everyone, but you can count on a heightened interest which will motivate staff members to build on their strengths.

Self Questions to Discover Opportunities

To be a good delegator you have to look for opportunities. Ask yourself these questions:

"Am I alert for situations where I can help people learn other jobs and take on new responsibilities?"

"Do I feel unthreatened by an individual's exceptional skill or ability?"

"Do I honestly want my people to succeed?"

"If not, why not?"

How Not to Delegate

Of course, there are some tasks that you should not delegate; never fall into the trap of thinking delegating is synonymous with passing the buck.

Employee conflicts, performance appraisals, any situation in which you risk losing face—these you've got to handle. Dumping on others all those things you hate to do is not the way to delegate.

Further, if you've agreed to personally take care of something for someone, you can't turn around and delegate it, regardless of how busy you are. One way to prevent this situation is to say, "My team will handle it for you. I trust that's all right?" or "We'll take care of it." Also, you shouldn't delegate anything you don't fully understand yourself. The idea, remember, is to assign tasks and improve the effectiveness of the team. You can't toss someone a problem and hope that somehow it will be resolved.

Cross-training can be valuable in many situations, but rotating people through various departments of a company with the idea that the movement will encourage them and keep them from getting bored presumes that all skills are interchangeable. They're not, and the people are more likely to get dizzy than inspired. It's as if a hospital administrator said about an obstetrician, "He's great on deliveries; next week let's have him do open-heart surgery." Having some experience in one area doesn't necessarily translate into skill in another.

If you force a switch on people, you risk losing their respect. Anna, the new owner of a large printing company, was looking for ways to reduce costly errors as well as eliminate some jobs. She observed that one group was responsible for setting type on the computers and another for proofreading galleys and checking for accuracy. Anna's idea was that she could increase efficiency and reduce errors if these two groups were combined. Also, with one person doing a job previously done by two, at least a few people could be dropped from the payroll. Anna quickly instituted a program to carry out cross-training: the typesetters would learn to proofread and copyedit, and the copyeditors would learn to set type.

This plan antagonized everyone involved. The typesetters felt that their job was impossible without excellent computer skills, good manual dexterity, and an ability to produce in a hectic, pressure-filled atmosphere. The copyeditors felt their job required thoughtfulness, a high degree of linguistic expertise, and a broad knowledge of many subjects. Both groups took pride in their own accomplishments. They all felt that the new owner had little understanding of what their jobs entailed and were furious when suddenly ordered to switch jobs and cross-train. Within the first two weeks, 80 percent of the staff left.

And yet Anna's idea could have worked. If she had understood their jobs, polled the people in both groups and asked who wanted to expand their skills, and matched up pairs in a positive manner, she might have pulled off a productive transition.

When to Delegate

The time to delegate is when you know your staff people are ready to take on more responsibility and make special contributions. Your staff then gets greater experience and a showcase for their talents.

Consider your team. If you have people who fit these descriptions you should be looking for opportunities to delegate:

Is there someone on the team whose performance is consistently high or exceptional?

Is there someone ready for promotion or increased responsibility?

Would it help to broaden someone's experience by exposing him or her to other areas of the department or the company?

Is there a promising performer who should be brought to the attention of colleagues or upper management?

What to Delegate

Many people don't delegate because they feel they must have one person to delegate an entire task to. But with analysis of the task and of the people on your staff, you can break a project into parts and have several people work on it. Take a good look at all the duties assigned to you personally, as well as to your group. Ask yourself these smart questions:

"What are my responsibilities?"

"What are the responsibilities of my department?"

"What can be delegated?"

"What would be gained?"

"Who is ready to do it?"

"Can it be broken into parts?"

"Who can carry out parts of the assignment?"

"Who could do it with training?"

Matching Assignments to People

Consider each individual in your group. Ask yourself:

"Who is a possible candidate for my job?"

"What particular skills does each of my people possess?"

"When does each person sparkle the most?"

"With whom does each one work the best?"

"What work does each one find most rewarding?"

"What are each person's long-range goals?"

You should have a delegating plan for each person on your team. Sit down with each individual and discuss what he or she wants to achieve. Before you assign a particular job to someone, ask yourself:

"What can he or she learn from this job?"

"What authority does he or she need to carry it out?"

Questions to Prepare the Person

Once you've decided what to delegate and to whom, smart questions can help the chosen employee get the most out of the opportunity. Before the work begins, ask the person:

"How do you see this project, overall?"

"Specifically, what is your objective?"

"What steps will you take to carry it out?"

"What kind of feedback do you plan to give me, to keep me abreast of your progress?"

"How often should I expect to hear from you?"

"In what form should I expect your final results?"

"When do you think you'll be finished?"

"How much authority do you need?"

"Do you need anything from me?"

Post-Delegation Questions

In terms of motivating your people, the most valuable questions are the ones you ask after the job is completed. The delegation process should always be a learning and growing experience for you and your employee. At the end of the project, ask the person:

"What's the most important thing you learned from this assignment?"

"How would you do it differently the next time?"

"What kinds of problems did you have?"

"How could you have anticipated problems sooner?"

"Should you have asked for more help?"

"Could you have done the job with less assistance?"

"Did you use all the resources available to you?"

"Did you enjoy and profit from your increased responsibilities?"

"How could I have been of more help?"

Overall, delegating is a superb motivational tool. It offers your people a way to develop their skills, show off their competency, and get ahead. It also offers you the chance to train your replacement, which means that you become more promotable.

Delegation is the essence of management. It works best when you have willing, problem-free employees. But managers also may need to use some special, often misunderstood, motivational techniques to help staff people develop. The most consistently valuable of these is training and coaching.

12

Questions That Train and Coach

When your Rolex watch goes on the blink, why don't you throw it out and get a new one? Because it's more practical and less expensive to have it repaired. The same philosophy applies to people management. When a person goes on the blink—when he or she loses motivation, or needs to develop new skills or sharpen old ones—it's much more productive to retrain than it is to hire someone else.

But a preconceived attitude works against many of us. We'd rather tell someone to go away than tell him how he's fouling up. We don't want the aggravation that comes with confronting a person with criticism. And yet managers who want to achieve a motivated, excited working group must tune in to the idea of helping people change. Asking smart questions offers a easy, rewarding way for managers to overcome their own resistance to training and coaching.

Training, coaching, and counseling are closely related motivational techniques, and many managers use the terms interchangeably. However, training is defined as a technique to teach new employees, or to train employees to use new equipment; coaching is used when an employee is failing in a specific task; and counseling is applied when an employee's overall performance is dropping. (Counseling often involves an employee's personal problems; for this reason, although the counseling technique is similar to coaching, it is treated as a separate subject in the following chapter.) All three techniques can be used spontaneously or in planned, formal sessions.

The hallmark of all three techniques is the Smart Questions system. The axiom is: People remember best those things they discover, learn, and experience themselves. If you want someone to digest and remember something, he has to think of it himself. The only way you help someone accept an idea as his own is to ask him a question and let him give the answer back to you.

I once observed the president of a sportswear chain put this principle into practice. Her vice president of marketing had to develop a sales promotion campaign for a new line of running shoes. The president had her own ideas about what would work, but rather than pushing them asked the vice president, who seemed stymied, this question: "If you were buying these shoes, what would get you excited?" That question got him started and he wound up with a great and successful campaign. I subsequently asked the president if their ideas had matched. She said she was pleased with the vice president's campaign, but never told me whether her ideas had been better.

The manager's role as a trainer or coach is to encourage and to educate. What you're looking for is better performance from your staff, but you also want to increase their self-confidence. To achieve both goals you must do three things: ask questions that encourage feedback, listen closely to the answers, and show appreciation for growth. Ask . . . listen . . . appreciate.

Feedback: The Principal Tool

Training and coaching the Smart Questions way is primarily a feedback technique that meets a genuine need from your staff. As a motivator you should continuously give feedback to let your people know how they're doing and to encourage them to strive to do even better. As a trainer and coach the second channel for feedback is open to you: you ask questions, and the person you're training or coaching feeds back information to you. This is the single most important element of successful coaching.

Feedback is the only way to confirm that your message has gotten across. Getting feedback on what may seem like simple instructions can save days, and even weeks, of work. More than that, by feeding back answers to your questions the individual discovers a way to solve the problem—whatever it is—for himself. Such independent discovery builds confidence and ensures that the information being learned is fully absorbed.

Showing Recognition

Questions are the main device for successful training and coaching. But there is one other valuable tool the manager must employ if he hopes to succeed: Always notice and reward progress in some way, even if it's just a thank you or an appreciative nod. And do it even when it's something you feel a person should have been doing all along, such as arriving at work on time. Many people disagree about this notion of reward when the person does what he's expected to do. But when you compliment a notoriously tardy person for arriving on time you're rewarding the change in behavior, not the person specifically. Change, even when it is relatively minor, is hard for everyone. Remember that if you want the change to become a permanent behavior, you must reinforce it with recognition.

By the same token, if you don't speak up when things go wrong, you're sending a signal that it doesn't matter. Even the most creative and spontaneous workers want guidelines.

Smart Questions That Train

Training is necessary when new systems or changes are instituted, or when an employee first joins the staff. The emphasis is on learning specific new material.

And yet in many companies new employees are simply brought in, shown to a desk, and within six weeks to three months evaluated on their performance. Often they aren't even told the difference between good performance and excellent performance.

Dr. Evans, physician-director of a surgical center in Kansas City, spent two hours telling four administrative assistants how to field phone inquiries. Evans's instructions included details about insurance forms and scheduling for surgery, as well as medical information about his specialty. At the end of the session, he asked, "Got that?" The four assistants nodded.

Dr. Evans went about his business. A few weeks later he tested the efficiency of his staff by asking a friend to call his office and pretend to be a prospective patient. The friend tape-recorded the disastrous results.

All four administrative assistants gave out wrong information about virtually everything. They did not know how to elicit information from a patient, nor were they able to answer the caller's questions. After hearing the tapes, Evans stormed into the office and fired everyone. He instructed the office manager to start hiring a new team, "and make sure you get people with brains this time."

This waste—of time, money, and human potential—could have been avoided had the doctor taken the time to ask a series of smart questions after his initial lecture. For example:

"How would you describe in two or three brief sentences what services we offer?"

"How would you advise a caller who has no medical insurance?"

"What information must you always elicit from the caller?"

"What will you say if the caller asks you a question you can't answer?"

Important Training Questions to Ask Yourself

Before you initiate any training program, ask yourself the Big Four Questions:

"What do I want this person to know, or do, as a result of the training?"

"What is the best way to impart this training?" (The more active and involved the method, the better. For example, questions and answers and hands-on training are better than lectures.)

"Who is the best person to carry out this training?"

"How can I reinforce this training?" (Ask for feedback and follow-up at scheduled intervals.)

Smart Questions That Coach

Coaching can take place all the time, under many different circumstances. It can be as informal as an enthusiastic cheer from the sidelines or as formal as a structured learning session. Whether it is informal or structured, coaching has a goal: to help a person improve performance in a specific area.

Coaching can be used to make simple, brief corrections, to improve poor performance in a specific task, and to provide encouragement before or after a "first" (first client presentation, first board meeting).

Many situations can be turned into informal coaching sessions. For example, a debriefing following a presentation illustrates the classic Smart Questions coaching formula. Immediately after the presentation (or meeting or production failure or submission of a written report), ask the person to think for a moment and then answer three questions:

1. *"What did you like about what you did?"*

Everyone has a gut feeling about what was right and what was wrong about their work. As time passes, however, they lose much of their objectivity. If they did a less than adequate job, for example, their memory clouds over as protective rationalization rushes to the defense. (An actress failing an audition may say, "I didn't get the job because the director wants his girlfriend in the part." An account man losing an account may say, "The client wasn't interested in doing something really different.")

On the other side, some people go too far the other way and berate themselves for the slightest flaws, losing sight of what they did well.

An evaluation is most accurate when it is done immediately after the event. Close to the reality, the individual usually comes out with a pretty fair assessment of what he or she did right.

2. *"If you could do it over again, what would you do differently? What would you change, and how?"*

Anyone performing a complex task should have the opportunity to look at what has been done, evaluate it, and consider what might have enhanced or enriched it, much like a writer revising a manuscript or an illustrator retouching a drawing.

Co-workers at an elite package-design firm make it a policy after each client presentation to evaluate the meeting. "We started doing it because our president does it on her own performance. After every presentation, she informally relives the meeting. She describes what was good about it, and then talks about how she might have made it better, how she could have answered a question better, or how she wished she had asked something or other. She doesn't berate herself, but she makes mental notes of how she would do it differently the next time. We all caught on to her style, and it's become a habit."

When you ask the first two questions most people readily uncover their major problems, especially when they are given support and feel they can express their thoughts without fear of negative criticism. During the evaluation the person may come upon a problem that he can't solve, which leads to the third and final smart question from you:

3. *"What help do you need from me?"*

These three smart coaching questions let the person clearly evaluate what was right and what was wrong about the job at hand, and provide an avenue for change. You may have your own ideas about the person's performance and how you would do it differently. But the goal is for the person to discover for himself what he can do to improve. People can change only when they see the need for change.

When to Coach

Coaching can be used productively across the board to solve a variety of managerial problems. Athletic coaches, for example, do more than just train; they offer support, provide frequent advice, and keep people going. Ask yourself these smart questions:

"Does someone on my staff need specific information to enable them to contribute more fully?"

"Are people performing poorly?"

"Is someone showing signs of discontent—coming late, long lunches, many personal phone calls?"

"Are performance expectations unclear?"

"Does someone need to expand a specific skill?"

"Do I need stronger teamwork?"

"Are there some moderate performers in my group who need to push themselves?"

"Do I need an active way to show support for my group?"

"Do I need to show more enthusiasm?" (If you're feeling low and acting low, think about how tough it must be for your staff.)

If you answer yes to *any* of these questions, you have a situation that could benefit from coaching.

Whom to Coach

Before undertaking a formal coaching session with anyone on your team, you should ask yourself a series of questions. If you answer no to *any* of the following, coaching is in order.

"Could this person do the job if he or she wanted to?" (If the answer is yes, you might have an emotional issue on your hands. If the person isn't performing well because he or she is annoyed or demotivated, the situation may require counseling.)

"Does this person really know how to do the job?" (Always question the person directly about the training they received for the job. Then if your answer is "No, he doesn't really know how to do the job," coaching is appropriate.)

"Have the organization's goals been clearly communicated?"

"Did the person receive effective guidance?"

"Did I point out how to approach various people in the organization, and how to deal with them?"

"Have I spent enough time with the person?"

Rate Your Coaching Skills

To examine whether or not you as a manager are using coaching for maximum effectiveness, ask yourself:

"Do I show substantial support for my team?"

"Do I think team members would give me a high rating on understanding their problems?"

"When I apply pressure do I also offer support?"

"Do my people hear from me when they perform well?"

"Do I take time to encourage my team before an important event?"

"Do I repeat the encouragement afterwards?"

If you can answer yes to all of the above, you are using coaching skills consistently and productively.

The Coaching Session

The whole idea behind productive coaching is to help people to solve their own problems. You cannot and should not solve the problem, or tell them how to solve it. You can, however, contribute, and you can make suggestions.

The usual dialogue at a coaching session runs like this one between Linda, the manager of the electronic data processing department of a large toy manufacturing company, and Tom, one of her supervisors.

Linda: Tom, the monthly progress reports are late again.

Tom: I've been busy—half the people are out of the office with the flu.

Linda: I need to get the reports on time. It's making us look bad to the front office.

Tom: I'll do my best.

Linda: Thanks.

What's wrong with this approach? Everything. And the inevitable result is that the reports go out late again next month.

The interesting part about coaching is that given a chance to talk, most people have the solution to their own problems. However, people don't always come up with a neat answer the first time you ask; if it were that clear to them they'd be doing it right the first time. It's worth your while to do some imaginative probing and find out how to get the person headed in the right direction.

The first—and most difficult—step to productive coaching is getting the person to agree that a problem exists. Establishing an opening gambit is the toughest part of a coaching session, and this requires some creative questioning. Let's give Linda and her supervisor another chance, this time using the Smart Questions coaching system:

Linda: We need to talk about scheduling your reports. I'm not sure you see it in terms of its effect on the overall department. What do you think happens when reports are late? [Linda already knows the ramifications, but by asking the question she's transferring the thought to Tom's mind. She must wait and listen for Tom's answer.]

Tom: I guess the departmental report goes in late.

Linda: Anything else?

Tom: It makes you look inefficient.

Linda: What are some of the ways that might affect the position of our group with upper management?

Tom: We might not get the new computers we asked for. They might go back and use the outside consultants and cut down our staff.

Linda: Any other ideas?

Tom: We might not get much budget for raises or any bonuses at year end.

Linda: That's what I'm thinking, too. Do you agree that we have a problem? [Until Tom agrees that there's a problem, the manager can't move on to a solution. If Tom answers, "That's true, but. . . ." he hasn't agreed. "But" signals that he's unconvinced.]

Tom: Yes.

Linda: Let's talk about a solution. What are the main reasons for the delays?

Tom: We're short-staffed, and don't have the budget for overtime.

Linda: Any other reasons?

Tom: I don't like the details and checking the data. I tend to leave it for last.

Linda: What are your ideas for a solution?

Tom: I'll have to get to it earlier and spend more time on it. [Tom's response is not sufficient. He needs to tell the manager what specific actions he's going to take. If Tom continues to do the same thing, he'll continue to miss deadlines.]

Linda: How will you do that?

Tom: I could start collecting the information earlier in the month. I could also have a department meeting and set up a plan.

Linda: How would that work?

Tom: It would get everyone thinking about the problem and setting a schedule to meet the deadline.

Linda: You said you don't like checking the data. Any ideas about that?

Tom: I have one person in my group who's a stickler for accuracy. I could get him to check everything before I sign off on it. [The idea is for Tom to give his manager numerous solutions. Some of these might involve changes in the way other people do things—or even in the way the manager does things.]

Linda: Those sound like good possibilities. In terms of overall effectiveness, which solution do you think will work best?

Tom: Perhaps a combination, starting with a departmental meeting. We can set up a flowchart, and get people to check with me twice a week so I can gain better control.

Linda: Is there something I can do to help you put the plan into action?

Tom: What I would like is extra staff. Barring that, I think it would help if you came to the meeting yourself and reinforced the importance of the reports.

Linda: There's a company-wide hiring freeze on, so for the time being hiring outside people is not an option. If you still feel you need more staff after you implement the new plan, there may be an opportunity later to transfer someone in from another division. For now, I'll back you up in the meeting. So, what have we agreed on? What's the goal?

Tom: I'm going to implement a new plan for the monthly reports.

Linda: What's your first step?

Tom: I'll call a meeting for next week.

Linda: When can we expect to see some results?

Showing Support

Coaching means expressing approval or admiration, applauding, and commending small and large victories. But warm words are not enough. Coaching is the act of helping. While Tom's boss didn't solve the problem for him, she did ask what kind of help he needed. And she helped Tom solve the problem for himself. Like Tom, we all usually have the answer to a problem tucked away somewhere in our minds. A good manager looks for ways to build small successes into a solid track record. Support is shown by the personal commitment of the coach, proven through his or her consistent imaginative interest in helping each person progress.

The manager who has listened to an employee's problems and helped solve them is rewarded when he sees that person come into his own as a result. Training and coaching the Smart Questions way are fine motivational techniques that let managers accomplish this goal. But sometimes the root of the problem is emotional, and when this is the case the manager needs some very special motivational tools if he or she hopes to help. Emotional issues require sensitive, careful counseling from managers, and in extreme cases, a more dramatic confrontation. Both methods are difficult business techniques made simple by asking smart questions.

13

Problem Solving with Problem People

When the manager's job is to help an employee improve a specific performance problem, the best technique is coaching. But when a manager must deal with an employee who has personal or professional problems—problems that are damaging his overall effectiveness—a different technique is needed.

In some of my middle management training programs I use a problem called the Joe Bailey maze. Bailey is a fictional employee who is absent on too many Mondays. The problem is to decide how Joe's manager should deal with him. Seventy-five percent of the thousands of managers who have taken this program keep going around in the maze and never get out until they fire Joe or he quits, without ever getting to the root of the problem.

Smart questions offer managers a way through the maze. The manager's role as counselor is to ask a few opening questions, listen, and give support. The emphasis is on problem solving, with long-range change as the goal. The manager hopes to steer the individual towards renewed commitment, towards taking responsibility for his own problem. Throughout the counseling process the manager must be encouraging and positive.

The best way to begin is to ask one or two questions, and then be quiet and listen for a response. The worry is that a question the manager asks may be too intrusive. A thin line separates interest and concern from an invasion of privacy, and managers should guard against interfering in personal problems when their attention is unwelcome.

I once had a long-time employee who had always been reliable and whose work had always been excellent. Over a period of several weeks she had been arriving late and wasn't getting her work done on time. At staff meetings she was silent and contributed little. I knew I had to talk to her, but she seemed so withdrawn and defensive that I didn't know what to say. One day when she was in my office explaining why a report was late, I offered her a cup of tea and took the opportunity to bring up her unexplained drop in performance.

The company had come to rely on her excellent work, I started, "but lately you seem worried and distracted."

She didn't answer. I drank my tea and thought about what to say next. My first thought was, this counseling business isn't easy, but maybe I can get through it if I ask her a question.

"Is something wrong at home?" I asked. She nodded, but still didn't speak.

"Is there anything I could do to help?"

That one question unleashed the whole story. She was separated from her husband of twelve years and they were in the midst of divorce proceedings. She hadn't wanted to tell anyone about it and didn't want to offer her personal problems as an excuse for her diminished performance.

We talked for a long time, although not about her work performance. Afterwards, I inquired from time to time how things were going, but never asked her directly about her husband. Her work improved immensely. While I didn't solve her problem, it was enough that the two of us were able to talk about it.

It's up to the manager to decide the extent to which he or she should discuss an employee's personal life. But when personal problems become work problems, it may be more appropriate to step in than to pretend the problem doesn't exist.

Being a good counselor means going beyond the obvious, and this demands time and sensitivity. Some work problems can be smoothed over by correcting a misunderstanding or moving somebody into a different work station. But others will take patience and continued effort. Regardless of where the problem comes from—home or work—the counselor's role is to help the person understand the problem and then surmount it.

When to Counsel

Before you take on the counseling role in any situation, ask yourself one question: "Does the situation really call for it?"

A person should be given a reasonable chance to turn things around under his or her own power, with your wholehearted support but without your interference. Counseling is not another name for meddling—getting involved without the right or the invitation. Too soon can be as disastrous as too late. You should counsel only when asked, or when a performance problem seriously threatens an individual's job or the productivity of the team.

In most instances, you should counsel only if you have tried to coach first. There are one or two instances when counseling is applied immediately—for example, when someone suffers a sudden setback a little counseling can help him over the rough spots. But for the most part, counseling is preceded by coaching attempts.

A manager shouldn't try to be a psychologist. Some situations require help from professionals. If serious help is needed, be prepared to send the person on to someone else for professional assistance. It's a good idea to have some names that you can refer people to.

To discover if managerial counseling is appropriate, ask yourself these questions:

"Does the person who's not performing well have a solid track record?"

"Has training or coaching failed to make a difference?"

"Has the individual asked for my help during a personal crisis?"

"Does he or she seem to be at a loss, unsure of how to proceed?"

"Is someone having trouble coping because the organization is growing fast or is undergoing drastic changes?"

"Is an individual accustomed to success unable to bounce back after a failure or disappointment?" (This might occur unexpectedly when someone's role has been broadened by promotion.)

If you answered yes to any one of these questions, you have an individual and a situation in which counseling can help.

Pre-Counseling Self Questions

If you decide that counseling is warranted, it's time to extend a purposeful hand. Before setting up a counseling session, ask yourself these smart questions:

"What is my goal?" (Your overall goal is to make headway with the employee in order to get him or her back on track.)

"In what way do I expect the person to change his behavior?"

"What results can I expect?" (This is crucial; if you are vague or unclear in your own mind about what you want to accomplish, how can you hope to address someone else's confusion?)

"What is reasonable?" (If someone has been very depressed and looking terrible, you can't expect him to turn around and be Mr. Clean overnight.)

"What is my basic approach?" (Remember the 5 C's. Commanders will accept a direct approach. Carers will internalize all their grudges. Convincers will be easier to talk to. Calculators will be defensive, but will respond to a reasoning approach. Creators will be vague and withdrawn especially during the creative process.)

When you are prepared for the session, choose a time for the meeting. Counseling is a promise you must keep. Don't squeeze it in, and once you set the time, don't cancel. Pick a time when you both can give it your full attention, but do it during working hours. Sitting over a drink in the local cocktail lounge doesn't work.

Once you've chosen the time, ask the individual early in the day if he or she can meet with you at some later hour. Do not suggest an overnight—or even worse, a whole weekend—waiting period. If counseling is warranted people usually know something is wrong, and you instill needless anxiety by putting it off. Occasionally an opportunity will spontaneously present itself, but in most cases the best idea is to establish a time for the meeting and keep the appointment.

Counseling Questions

Here are some guidelines and questions that will help you through the Joe Bailey maze.

Open the session with a brief, straightforward statement of why you suggested the meeting: "I want you to be effective, and I know that you want to be effective. Let's see how we can work together to achieve that."

Let the person know that you are genuinely concerned about them. Try not to be intimidating or accusatory; that's the quickest way to seal the problem. Also, assure the person that whatever they say will be kept private. Once you open the discussion, lead the session with a few questions, and be prepared to listen.

"What do you think is at the root of the problem?"

"How do you think the problem could be solved?"

"Who or what has contributed to the problem?"

"How have I contributed to the situation?" (This is a tough question to ask, but be prepared to accept your own involvement as a possibility.)

Once you know where you're headed, establish the means to get there. Put together a plan of action.

"What needs to happen?"

"When?"

"What kind of assistance do you feel you will need?"

"What do you need from me?"

"Is there anyone else who should be told or involved?"

"Do you feel getting professional counseling would help?"

"What are you going to do to take action?"

"When would you like to talk again?"

Before the meeting ends, set up another one to check on how things are going and to see how you can help and support progress.

The key to a good session is understanding your role. You're not there as a psychologist—you're there as a manager. Your goal is always to get good people who have become problem people to solve their own problems. And by being supportive and asking the right questions you can create an environment that helps them do just that.

Elaine, an administrative assistant in a large law firm, was experiencing a problem with adapting to change. Not only did her boss install a new computer but he expected her to learn two software programs in two weeks. Elaine panicked, started arriving late or calling in sick, made careless mistakes in her work, and generally made her co-workers miserable. Her boss was furious.

Finally her boss calmed down and asked this question: "Since it's important for you to learn these systems within two weeks, what do you suggest?" He asked the question seriously, with the genuine intent of finding out how she would solve the problem.

Elaine came up with a perfect solution: the secretary could learn one while she learned the other. During the next month they would cross-train each other. For the same amount of money, the boss then had two people trained on the computer and was in good shape for future absences and vacations. This also reduced the stress that Elaine was feeling—the panic over sudden and extreme change—and allowed her to operate with much less daily tension.

Many problems are deeply personal. Dennis, ordinarily a fine team player, became withdrawn and uncooperative. When co-workers asked him what was wrong, Dennis answered, "Nothing." His manager was concerned and spent some time drawing him out:

Manager: "I'm concerned about you and want to help. How do you see this problem affecting your work?"

Dennis: "I can't help it. My wife's children have moved in with us and one of them is using drugs."

Manager: "That's a tough one. How are you dealing with it?"

Dennis: "I'm not, at least not very well. I don't know what to do."

Manager: "I can suggest some help. A friend of mine had a similar problem, and got some help from one of the youth organizations. Would you like me to ask who he saw?"

If you run into resistance in an attempt to counsel, you can always ask:

"How long will it take to clear up the problem?"

"How can I help?"

And if the problem doesn't improve, you can try a follow-up counseling session. Although you have to set time limits, everyone goes through difficult periods sometimes. When I had cancer I was devastated by the experience. It took me several months to mentally recuperate. Fortunately, because I worked for myself I had a sympathetic employer, but I'm sure most employers would have been supportive if I had shared this problem with them.

Confrontation: When Counseling Isn't Enough

When performance problems persist despite repeated efforts to counsel—when an individual is undeniably failing in his or her current role—then it's time to bring things to a boil. It may be an employee who yesses you to death but never changes. Or a willing, amiable employee who for some reason cannot seem to do the job the way it needs to be done. Or it may be a conflict between two people or among a whole team. Occasionally, depending on the person you're dealing with, confrontation happens sooner rather than later. In a simple instance, when someone flatly refuses to come in on time, or fails to deal with customers pleasantly, you may cut directly to confrontation, bypassing coaching and counseling. The basic principles of confrontation are the same, whatever the situation.

Confrontation means that change is imperative. It means making a decision and setting a deadline to carry it out: job reassignment, restructuring of the current job, curtailing current job responsibilities, or dismissal.

Done by the best, confrontation is a forceful form of counseling in which the alternatives and consequences are clear and close at hand. Provided you previously did everything you could—coaching and counseling—to foster improvement, confronting can be a constructive, caring response to an individual's chronic low performance. Confrontation is always a face-to-face meeting where you bring a person's attention to the consequences of unacceptable performance. Confrontation is one of a manager's toughest responsibilities.

Even when viewed in its most positive light, confronting someone is an anxiety-producing situation. Frustrated managers often lose perspective and unload a personal attack or an ultimatum. There is a tendency to lecture and rehash previous discussions and harp on minor details. The greatest danger is that confrontation can flare into an all-out blaming session, in which you fire the person out of fury or the person quits in a huff.

The key to positive confrontation is to stay cool and to discuss sensitive issues without overdramatizing them. Both manager and employee have to be willing to get past the old obstacles and look ahead for solutions. A questioning approach allows you to confront different types of problem employees without letting things get out of hand. Asking smart questions gives you a way to get into the situation, minimize anxiety, and avoid becoming hostile: maximum results with minimum stress.

As a confronter, a manager must be positive, supportive, firm, and calm. The manager's job is to set limits, establish clear expectations, and stay centered on the subject.

Don't allow the employee to manipulate you ("You never told me that we had an inflexible deadline"). The normal reaction is to defend yourself ("I told you at least four times, and you're supposed to know it anyway"). The Smart Question reaction is never defensive ("I could have told you more *often*—but what do you think happens when you miss a deadline?").

Questions also get problem people to commit to change themselves. As in counseling, the key is to ask sensible questions and be willing to listen.

How to Confront

There are small confrontations and large ones. Letting a person know that he is abusing the lunch hour is a small confrontation. But a manager who deals with small problems immediately will have fewer large ones

Confronting poor performance should never come as a surprise to the person. A true confrontation situation is always the last step, never the first. By the time you decide that the situation requires confrontation you both should be familiar with the issues.

All overtly nonconforming behavior is intended to get attention. You can help someone solve the problem if you build on their self-esteem. The better they feel about themselves, the more receptive they will be to your criticism.

One of my clients had a supervisor in the communications department who was always complaining, griping, and generally bad-mouthing everything and everyone. In addition, she was power-hungry and tried to pit people against each other. The director of the company, who valued this supervisor's creative contributions, repeatedly told her to improve her lousy attitude or she would never get ahead. But no change ever ensued.

After thinking over the director's problem, I suggested that he ask the supervisor a smart question: "How would you improve the low morale in the department?" Almost immediately she focused her attention on finding a creative solution. She got so much attention from her positive action program that she abandoned her gripes and complaints. It was a miraculous turnabout.

Decide that you will ask questions and provide assurance. Remember that people will resist what you tell them, even though deep down they might agree.

When Howard, a vice president of marketing, kept extending the lunch hour, his boss, Trevor, the executive vice president, was at his wit's end. Howard was great in the mornings but useless all afternoon. His unlimited expense account wasn't helping the situation. Previous suggestions to improve had not helped because Trevor, himself a likable and friendly Convincer, hated forcing the issue. Looking for a way to solve the problem without making an enemy of Howard, Trevor devised a strategic question. At their next meeting, he asked Howard, "What do you think will happen to your expense account if you continue like this?"

Now, Howard really loved the five-star restaurants and first-class travel arrangements. When he realized that Trevor was serious, he answered, "I'll probably lose it." That thought was so sobering that Howard made some serious changes in his work habits.

Think of ways you can use questions to get at the heart of the issue. Instead of offering a solution, ask for the solution: "What do you think would solve this problem?" The best way for a manager to improve poor performance is to get problem people to answer questions and arrive at their own decisions to change.

The biggest obstacle, as in counseling, is getting people to confess to having a problem. Sidney, the senior partner of a large law firm, was forced to confront a close friend and associate who had a long-term drinking problem. The lawyer in question for years had handled his alcoholism so that it didn't interfere with business. But in the last year his work began to slide markedly, and clients complained that the lawyer failed to file court documents on time, confused various legal papers, and was late with tax returns and other important financial matters.

Sidney confronted the lawyer and said, "Larry, you've got to straighten things out or we're in trouble." For a few months Larry improved. But then he rapidly deteriorated again, and soon became worse than before. A showdown was imminent. But Sidney couldn't get to first base:

Sidney: What's troubling you, Larry?

Larry: Nothing. Just been busier than usual.

Sidney: Are you drinking?

Larry: No, I've been on the wagon a long time. You know that.

Sidney: Because if you are, perhaps we could arrange a leave of absence for you at a sanitarium.

Larry: I said I wasn't drinking. I'm fine.

Sidney: Then what's happening to your work?

Larry: I don't know what you mean.

Sidney: The Vox Foundation taxes are long past due. Should I give that account to someone else until things ease up for you?

Larry: Certainly not. I've handled that account for eighteen years. I have a court extension, so there's nothing to worry about.

Sidney: But they don't want to be on extension.

Larry: I'll take care of it by next week.

If Sidney cannot get Larry to admit he has a problem in an agreeable way, he has only one recourse left: "If you can't solve this problem and improve performance, what might happen?" (There's only one answer: "I guess you might let me go.")

It's only when they actually believe that their behavior may have dire consequences that many problem people shape up. But if you keep barking threats at them without actually doing anything, no one is going to change. People will improve when they see that you stand behind the consequences.

It's too late for a "let's try this and see what happens" approach. By the end of the discussion you will have reached a definite plan of action. There is going to be a change in the structure of the present job, a shift to another job, or steps will be taken that lead to termination.

When to Confront

If you are considering confrontation, first ask yourself these smart questions:

"Have I given the person every reasonable opportunity to succeed?"

"Have I coached, trained, and removed any obstacles for achievement?"

"Am I sure this person understands what is expected of him?"

"Have I done enough counseling?"

"Have I really worked hard enough?"

If you answered yes to all of those questions, confrontation is in order. Now, ask yourself one more question: "Is this person worth the time and effort it will take to save him?"

If your answer is no, then try to find the gentlest and most expeditious way to fire the person.

If your answer is yes, then do not delay a confrontation. And be prepared to put in the effort and time necessary to deal with it.

Before the Confrontation

The people you have to confront are the people who've been giving you a hard time already. So you have to be extra strong and keep your objectives firmly in mind during the confrontation. Make sure you ask yourself this one question in advance: "What results can my team and my company live with?"

Smart Confrontation Questions

Before the session, think of the questions you're going to ask. When an employee displays apathy, for example, you might try:

"What are some of the things that you think make for a productive work atmosphere?"

"What do you think of the correlation between your behavior and productivity?"

"Six months ago you agreed there was a problem, but nothing has changed. What do you suggest we do about it?"

"What do you think is behind your lack of support and involvement?"

"Do you look forward to coming to work in the morning?" (If answer is yes, follow up with: "What can you do to show it more? I want to feel that you like to come to work." If the answer is no, then ask: "What do you want to do about it?")

"If you're not happy with the job, is there something specific we can do to change things?"

With a confident or more abrasive person, you can afford to be more blunt: "You're driving everyone around here nuts—what are you going to do about it?"

When the problem is poor performance, ask:

"How do you perceive this job?"

"What do you think I'm looking for in terms of results?"

"What do you think is getting in the way of your job performance?"

"How can it be solved?"

"What are you willing to do to solve it?"

"If you don't think it can be solved, what options do we have?"

"Do you see a way the job could be restructured that would help you?"

"Is there some other way that you feel you can contribute to the company?"

"If you don't think there are any solutions, then what is the alternative?"

Letting Someone Go

When you use smart questions during a confrontation the options become clear, and usually the individual will tell you what he thinks is the best solution. If he informs you that after examining all the possibilities he sees no way to improve his performance, then termination is the only option left.

Firing should never be a surprise. According to Robert Half, author of *Robert Half on Hiring*, "80 percent of us have been fired, and only 22 percent of the time was it a complete surprise."

When you decide to give up on someone you should act at once. Get him in your office, close the door, and tell him why, without mincing words. You owe it to him to let him know the full story. It's no favor to anyone to drag out a bad situation; the company is being shortchanged and so are the others in your group who must take up the slack. Certainly the person being fired is better off the quicker it's over with. For employees who simply cannot cope, it will be a distinct relief—the struggle is over and they can move on to something new. I'm sure that everybody who has ever lost a job because he or she was in the wrong business wishes in retrospect that somebody had recognized it earlier so they could have had a head start in some other career.

Act swiftly and with consideration. Do everything you can within company policy and Equal Employment Opportunity regulations to make it easy for the person. If possible, leave him the choice as to whether he would like to use the office for some period of notice or receive pay in lieu of notice. Find out what he would like others in the group to be told. In sum, treat him as well as you can. Or as you'd like to be treated in the same situation. Being thoughtful toward those who don't make the grade cannot fail to encourage those who do.

Exit Interviews

If done without bitterness, exit interviews can give you some good information for the future. Don't be afraid to ask the person who's leaving a few smart questions:

> "How could I change?"
>
> "How could the department change?"
>
> "Why did you fail?"

You've motivated, trained, coached, and counseled, and even confronted. All of these techniques are important. But without the formal document described in the final chapter of this section you have no permanent record of what has transpired over the course of a year. The performance appraisal is a permanent record—not only of how the employee has progressed but also of how well you've been doing your job as manager/coach. Performance appraisal is a way to officially applaud progress and yet another opportunity to motivate employees to a higher standard of excellence.

14
Performance Appraisals That Work

Carrie, an engineer in a highly structured naval architecture firm, comes into her supervisor's office for her yearly appraisal. The boss smiles nervously and says, "Take a chair. Well, how are you?"

"Fine."

"I'm just going over the past year. You've done a fine job for us. But I can only give you a token raise because you don't get to work on time, and this really works against you here. We all have to punch the time clock. I've spoken to you about this before and you haven't done anything about it. If you make an effort to improve perhaps I can do something for you next time."

"OK."

"Is there anything you want to discuss?"

"Not really."

"Well, OK. Thanks for coming in."

The supervisor scratches a few notes on his rating sheet for this employee, including "excellent performance" and "lateness a problem." And yet he seems baffled when, three months later, Carrie informs him that she's leaving the company.

The performance appraisal is one of the manager's best tools for motivating people, yet it is seldom, if ever, exploited to its full potential. As typically handled, performance appraisals are virtually meaningless. When 200 managers in a large New York company were asked about their own last performance appraisal, only 10 of them said they had received a thorough give-and-take appraisal interview. Some had received no more than a token pat on the shoulder and a charge to keep up the good work. Others had been subjected to a harangue and a long list of gripes.

Yet almost all companies demand a review of each employee at least once a year. Such reviews may range from formal rating sheets where managers are asked to grade individuals on different skills to informal bull sessions.

Value of Performance Appraisals

What is the purpose of performance appraisals? Performance appraisal is usually a systemized, company-wide process by which a company rates people objectively, grants promotions and raises when due, and sets new objectives for the future. Such a review gives upper management a sense of what's happening with employees at all levels. The appraiser's task is to learn how a person has performed in his job during the year. Then the appraiser is supposed to match his perception of the individual's performance with the employee's own perception. Together, appraiser and employee are supposed to reach a consensus and plan for the coming year.

During a job appraisal a manager helps his people see how their objectives fit in with those of the department and the rest of the organization. The result is usually a written document that is passed on to personnel and upper management.

Everyone in the company is appraised, so the person doing the appraising will in turn be appraised by his or her boss. What we're going to discuss here is how you, as manager, can use performance appraisals of your staff as a tool for increased motivation.

Performance appraisal lets you develop each person on your team to full potential. The overall goal is to get each person to a higher level each year—or every six months—until ultimately they're working at their peak.

Regular appraisals, especially in a big company, keep good people from getting buried in the system. Equally important, nonproductive people don't have anywhere to hide.

Perhaps most important, a regular review system forces a dialogue between manager and staff. In an ideal world, no special structure would be necessary to ensure that kind of interaction. But even if a manager doesn't work closely with someone (he might, for example, have supervisory responsibility for someone in a different location), or if he doesn't get along well with a member of his staff, they still have to sit down and decide what they're going to accomplish together in the months ahead. Because there's no way to avoid this meeting, their working relationship is likely to improve as they gradually come to know each other better.

The performance appraisal gives managers an overview—as though on a panoramic screen—of how each person is coming along. Managers get to know their staff better and to establish themselves as thoughtful and interested leaders. Performance appraisals also let people sort out problems and prevent a buildup of aggravations and disappointments.

These are only a few of the benefits of a good performance appraisal. And yet these goals are seldom even touched upon in a typical appraisal.

Theoretically, appraisals should provide a nonthreatening structure for discussing sensitive topics with employees. The main reason they are shunned, however, is that the appraisal invariably involves giving criticism, and no one enjoys the anxiety inherent in such an emotionally laden situation.

It's difficult to be in a position where your judgment can affect a person's life. Further, managers hesitate to commit themselves to a statement that might cause trouble later. In companies that use a five-point appraisal scale, most managers sidestep the whole issue and rank everyone a three.

To be worthwhile, a performance appraisal takes both time and responsibility. Sure, it has the potential to be emotionally upsetting. And you can never predict how individuals will react. While a job appraisal can be couched in all-positive terms, no good appraisal will be 100 percent positive. A simple pat on the back or a smug "Keep up the good work" is by no means sufficient. Even if someone is doing a good job, you need to guide them as to where they can go from there.

Knowing how to ask smart questions helps you make any appraisal review fair and on target, and also softens the foreboding edge. Using questions as a guide gives both parties the opportunity to approach the situation objectively. Managers who ask smart questions get the most from performance appraisals and also eliminate tension by getting the person to be his own appraiser.

Timing of Appraisals

Most managers don't do appraisals frequently enough. Scheduling an appraisal only once a year turns it into an ominous day on the calendar. It also creates the temptation to let grievances and complaints pile up. "Hold it for the performance appraisal," you may think. Twelve months is too long between appraisals—and yet every week would be far too frequent. The optimal interval is every six months or every three, even if your company only officially requires they be done annually.

Whatever interval you establish, prepare yourself in advance for the appraisal interview. There's nothing worse than telling someone, "I don't think you're doing very well," and when they ask for examples your mind goes blank. Just as bad is giving a yearly rating based on the last thirty days.

It's better to evaluate as you go along: keep each person's file open and make regular notes on performance, including both achievements and trouble spots. Keep a daily or weekly list of pluses and problems. Write comments in terms of the person's observable behavior: "Fred's meeting with client went well today—he had done his homework and presented the ideas succinctly. When client asked questions Fred answered directly and to the point."

Or an entry might be something as simple as "Cy's department failed to meet production quality this month," "Cy hired a winner in Debbie," "Ben's performance appraisals for his group were incomplete." All notes should be specific and dated. A performance appraisal should never be general. During the appraisal you should always be able to refer to specific events and specific dates.

How Smart Questions Make Appraisals Productive

Smart questions turn performance appraisals into a prime motivational tool. Asking questions forces you to plan in advance. Questions help to clarify your thinking and also serve to clarify your employee's thinking. When people know they will be asked questions, they usually come to the meeting prepared to illustrate their past performance.

Consider these other benefits:

- By asking questions, you talk less and therefore obtain more information.

- You can lead the discussion without appearing to do so (because the other person will be doing most of the talking).

- Questions put responsibility on the other person. (If an employee protests "You give me too many things to do at once," you can say, "Can you give me specific examples?")

- Using questions keeps you both from becoming defensive. If the individual puts you on the spot with a question, you can always ask for clarification before jumping to conclusions. ("Before I can answer that, can you tell me more about why you're asking?" Or, "That's a good question. What's the reason behind it?")

- Questions encourage you both to be more objective, as opposed to getting caught up in personal value judgments. Instead of "You have a lousy attitude" or "You don't seem to care," ask, "How do you think your team feels when you leave early when we're in the middle of a crisis?"

    "You're so uncooperative" can be turned into: "Why didn't you help Steve when he needed it?" Or, "The last five times I've asked you to stay late you refused. Can you tell me why?"

    Accusations are a dead end: "You're doing the same thing all over again. You're all bogged down and nothing is getting done." Questions lead somewhere: "How do things get bogged down?" "What can we do to correct it?" "Let's look at your work flowchart and see where it's going." "Can we set a goal for improvement in that area?"

- Questions let you deal with a person's behavior—what they've done and what they're going to do—not with the person himself.

Let's go back to Carrie's performance appraisal and see what might have happened if her manager had asked a few smart questions:

Manager:	Good morning—come on in and have a chair. It's that time of year again. How's it going?
Carrie:	OK.
Manager:	Do you want to plunge right in, or is there something you want to talk about first?
Carrie:	Let's get to it.

Manager: OK, why don't you tell me what you think went especially well this year?

Carrie: I think we were running smoothly; the work got out quickly and efficiently. We were almost without mistakes. Adding Jim as a backup was a good idea because it freed me to concentrate on quality control. Overall, I think we were operating at top performance.

Manager: I agree with you. Are you having any kinds of problems?

Carrie: Well, the physical layout of the office is still a problem. I don't like being cooped up in that small inside office with Jim working at a table behind me. There's no privacy, and it's just too much togetherness, if you know what I mean.

Manager: Well, nobody else even has a backup. I had to move heaven and earth just to add him to staff. How can I also request another office?

Carrie: I don't know. You asked me, and I'm trying to tell you.

Manager: OK. Let's put that on hold for a moment—we'll come back to it. Tell me, are you having any other problems?

Carrie: Do you mean about being late in the mornings?

Manager: Yes. There's got to be a reason—you're doing such a good job, and you know what a stickler the company is for punctuality. That time clock is a real pain for all of us. What's behind the coming in late in the mornings?

Carrie: It's just hard getting up and getting downtown so early. I'm not a morning person.

Manager: We all have to do it.

Carrie: I'm not sure why. I'm often here until 7 or even 8 o'clock. No one needs me in the morning—I'm supposed to be here at 8:45 because that's what the company says, not because there's any particular reason for it.

Manager: Well, just to take up your argument for a moment, how do you think everyone else in the group feels when they're at their desks at 8:45 and you come at 9:30 or 10 o'clock?

Carrie: I see your point. It's just so restricting—the whole company is like being in the army.

Manager: Is that really what's bothering you? I mean, we all live
              with rules and regulations. It seems to me that something
              else is behind this. Can you get at it? Can you say what's
              really troubling you?

Carrie: I think I'm just bored, that there's nowhere for me to go.
              I think you'll have me sitting behind that same desk for
              the next twenty years. Nothing ever changes, and I can't
              help but feel that I'm smarter than a lot of other people
              upstairs.

You can see what's happening with Carrie's performance appraisal
now. By continuing to ask questions, her manager has let Carrie fill out
her own appraisal about her performance. He's also done a lot more.
He has taken the opportunity of the performance appraisal and used it
very much like a counseling session. Rather than merely scolding Carrie
for not coming in on time, he's helped her uncover a fundamental
dissatisfaction with her job.

Carrie has revealed herself to be a high achiever who's at the point
where she needs a change. Lateness was not the real problem—the real
problem was job dissatisfaction. If her manager doesn't find a way to
move her up or add some interest to her job, he's going to lose her, in
either body or spirit.

Many companies are satisfied with adequate performance and don't
look for ways to challenge their people. For the last ten years I've met
a scientist from a major computer company at an annual Christmas party.
He's exceptionally bright, and his job bores him to death. He stays on
board because of the financial security. Yet I know he can't possibly be
giving his best to the company.

Job dissatisfaction shows itself in many ways. A sure sign of demo-
tivation is when people become deeply involved in outside activities.
When you have someone running for political office, or spending nights
and weekends singing in a choral group or auditioning for plays, or
accepting time-consuming positions in various outside organizations, you
have people who are not deriving enough satisfaction from their work.

In Carrie's situation, chronic lateness was a clue that she was losing
motivation, and it alerted her manager that he was in danger of losing
a valuable member of his team. His next step is to see how he can help
Carrie set goals that keep her productive and yet still tie in with the
department's goals.

The Smart Questions Performance Appraisal

The biggest trap many appraisers fall into is the "lecture mode," where they monopolize the entire conversation. It's tempting to lecture, because you feel you have to defend any criticism as well as justify any praise. But if you ask four or five good questions you'll accomplish much more than if you lecture for a full hour. Before the session, keep this message in mind: "I'm not going to talk too much. I *am* going to ask questions."

When you handle job appraisals the Smart Questions way, your managerial role will begin to shift. Gradually you become less of an intimidating authority figure and more of a consultant.

The question to ask yourself throughout the whole process is "What are the strengths of this person, and how can I use them most effectively?" The only time to mention someone's shortcomings is when you bring them up in relation to their strengths. ("You're excellent on the telephone. I was surprised to see you had difficulties with that telemarketing project you assisted with last summer. What do you think happened?").

This is where you can build upon the golden rules of motivation. Concentrate on strengths, and ask people for feedback about their own performance: "Were you satisfied with the way the project turned out?" Usually, if you've established a trusting atmosphere, people are tougher on themselves than you would be.

If the person seems unresponsive or vague, be persistent. Keep asking. Rephrase the question and ask it again until the person gets the gist of what you're looking for and does give a response. Remember, you don't have to accept the first answer you receive. Keep turning the questions around and keep probing.

Don't be too predictable with your questions. Instead of setting up a tedious pattern, look upon the appraisal as a real opportunity to develop your questioning skills as well as to improve the person's attitude and productivity.

Openers

The normal procedure during an appraisal is to start with all the good things, then zap them with all the negative data you've been filing away.

Years of observing such interviews reveal that it's preferable to integrate the good with the bad throughout the interview.

Careful selection of opening questions is important because it establishes the tone of the meeting. Here are some smart openers:

"Is there any special place you would like to start this discussion?" (You're giving them the option to bring up something that's been weighing on their mind and get it out in the open.)

"How would you like this appraisal to work for you?"

"How would you like to feel at the end of our session?"

"What information would you like to have?"

"Of the objectives we agreed to last time, which is the one you'd like to start with?"

Exploring Questions

"How well is this current project being done?"

"How could it be better?"

"Tell me how you feel about what you've accomplished and what still needs to be done."

"One of your objectives was to improve communication with data processing—how did that go?"

As long as a person feels that he is not under fire and doesn't have to defend himself, he will undoubtedly be critical and objective and give you an accurate assessment of his performance.

You've eased the way by letting people evaluate themselves; that's why questions work so well. If they say they've done a good job, it's good for them to say so, and you can confirm it. If they criticize themselves, you can be supportive while they examine how they could have done better.

Expanding the Appraisal

The stage is now set to carry forward the performance appraisal so that it becomes a unique opportunity to build motivation. Consider these smart questions:

"What do you consider your main accomplishments this year?" (This is a smart question to discover whether the person's priorities coincide with your own.)

"What obstacles were most serious for you?"

"Which are permanent? Which are temporary?"

"What did you do to deal with them?"

"What could you do in the future to deal with them more effectively?"

"Where do you think you could improve?"

"How could I help you more?"

"If you could redo the year, given the same circumstances, what would you do differently?"

If your assessment of the job is radically different from the person's, ask: "Why do you think our ratings are so different?"

Setting Goals

The one final move that lets you exploit the performance appraisal to its fullest potential is asking the person what he hopes to accomplish during the next interval. First, this allows an individual to act as his own boss and to set his own goals. Second, it encourages self-motivation. Third, new ideas bubble up to the top because you're talking about more than one task or issue. Appraisals also force managers to consider what they expect their people to accomplish next and to learn how they intend to go about it.

This is the time to help the employee ask himself "What can I do this coming year that will make a noticeable difference—not only for my department but for the company?"

William Oncken, Jr., and Donald L. Wass, writing for the *Harvard Business Review*, have described the five degrees of initiative that managers can help their staff people pass through: (1) the lowest level is having the employee wait until instructed; (2) next, the employee should ask what to do; (3) then make recommendations and take actions; (4) act independently but feed results back to you immediately; and (5) at the highest level, act independently, then routinely report back at intervals.

Ideally, by setting higher goals with each appraisal you will be able to help each of your people to move through these levels of initiative until they can all function at the highest level in their key responsibilities.

When an employee states his goals, it's your responsibility to evaluate each one. For example, as someone describes what he hopes to do in the coming months, you can guide ("Is that a little ambitious?"), suggest ("It sounds good, but how will it affect your priorities?"), or approve ("That sounds good. Is there anything I can do to help you?").

People can set goals for themselves in various categories: personal development goals, key result goals, routine and procedural goals, and unusual contribution goals. Sometimes a member of your staff will set a goal for himself and fail to live up to it, because the goal was unrealistic, because of a mistake, or because the individual didn't follow through. Regular performance review gives you both enough time to salvage the situation. Because the employee set his own goal, he realizes that this is his problem.

When goals are not reviewed in this productive way, the person may hammer away at the wrong job for years, continually setting the wrong goals and continually failing to achieve them. Ultimately he falls into such a failure mode that he can't regain a positive footing.

Sometimes an employee reaches a level where no further promotion is possible. In these kinds of situations, however, the manager can be the most helpful if he's frank. In Carrie's case, for example, if there is clearly no promotional prospect for her—if there is simply nowhere to go or no more to learn within her department—her manager can be pretty sure that her enthusiasm for the job is going to deteriorate, as is already evidenced by her tardiness. Sometimes shifting job responsibilities or cross-training can help. If that isn't possible, the best thing the manager can do for Carrie is tell her the facts. Knowing where she stands and what her prospects are, Carrie is free to make her own decision.

As Harry Truman loved to say, "The buck stops here." When an individual's performance appraisal stops on your desk, that document should clearly reflect whether or not the employee has been doing his job and also whether you, as manager, have been living up to your obligations.

Regular performance appraisals bond people together in a constructive way, headed toward appropriate and agreed-upon objectives. They are, consequently, prime motivational tools. The Smart Questions performance appraisal can become a mutually satisfying experience—the mirror that shows how well you've been using your managerial skills to get the most from your staff.

In Part Two we've explored the primary tools at your disposal to help your people grow and develop, and have discussed how asking smart questions can maximize each of those techniques. In the final section of *Smart Questions* we're going to talk about you and your future—how asking smart questions can help you stand out in the crowd, gain visibility within your organization, and get ahead.

PART THREE

Getting Ahead

"Where do you want to go from here?"

—Cheshire Cat to Alice

15

The Quiz: Part Three

The final section of the quiz is designed to test your visibility quotient and your getting-ahead mentality.

Everyone wants to get ahead, but not everyone is willing to pay the price—which involves making yourself visible to upper management, striving for creativity, and working overtime to develop a smart-questioning approach. It's clear at this point that it's never enough to ask questions. You have to ask the *right* questions. That's what Part Three of the book is all about.

Those who get ahead regularly ask themselves one question: "What can I do to make myself stand out?" The top executives we interviewed for this section of *Smart Questions* pointed out certain essential areas: (1) figure out what needs to be done (fill the vacuum); (2) solve problems creatively; and (3) try to gain visibility in every area, from seeking job interviews to running meetings.

People who get ahead don't back into success. They know where they want to go, and they go after it. However, having ambition doesn't mean that you can rush into things. Introspection is the smart manager's most valuable asset. As a manager moves higher up, his or her actions become more visible, and each decision requires more time and thought. Smart managers stop, think, and ask the right questions of the right people.

With a questioning approach you stand a much better chance of gaining lasting success.

If you want to stand out, advance quickly, succeed where others fail, consider how you would cope with these situations.

Do You Use Questions to Get Ahead?

1. At a job interview you're told that the department you will head is functioning in very limited space. You:

   a. Accept the fact.

   b. Ask "What effect is the small space having on the staff?"

   c. Ask "Can I have a commitment for more space before I start the job?"

   d. Ask "Are there any other major problems?"

2. An opportunity to make a difficult, time-consuming presentation is given to you. Your response is:

   a. "When can I get started?"

   b. "Who will be there?"

   c. "What is the purpose of the presentation?"

   d. "How can I avoid this presentation, since I'd as soon jump off a bridge as make it?"

3. You are making a presentation when a key decision maker asks a question that you do not understand, and may not know the answer to. You:

   a. Ask the person to rephrase the question.

   b. Ask if they can see you after the presentation.

   c. Say "I don't know, but when do you need an answer?"

   d. Ask yourself, "How can I double-talk and blur the issue?"

4. You have an opportunity to work on a long project with a person whom you dislike intensely, but you know his expertise could save you at least a year of research. You:

   a. Ask yourself, "How can I set aside my emotions and make the best of this situation?"

b. Ask your boss for advice.

c. Ask "Why should I give myself all this stress?"

d. Accept immediately.

5. You are chairing a meeting and two of the three key people bow out. You:

a. Ask the two who canceled when they can commit to a definite time.

b. Ask your assistant to run the meeting.

c. Have a brief meeting with all three and ask if the third person can carry the ball.

d. Ask your boss to talk to the two key people.

6. You've been asked to relocate in a company where moving is necessary for upward mobility. Your spouse has a great job and doesn't want to move. You:

a. Refuse the offer.

b. Accept, and deal with your spouse later.

c. Ask your boss and mentor for advice.

d. Go home and negotiate.

7. Your boss has been overlooked for a promotion, and an outsider hired. You:

a. Ask yourself, "Should I look for another job?"

b. Ask "What can I do to lend support?"

c. Make friends with the new person.

d. Ask around to discover the reasons behind the decision.

8. At a job interview the salary mentioned is lower than you expected. You:

a. Ask "Is there room for further negotiation?"

b. Say "I'm disappointed with such a low offer" and wait for a response.

c. Accept the offer and hope they'll give you a promotion when they see how good you are.

d. End the interview and walk out.

9. A few weeks into your new job you notice that everyone in the company seems to be working exceptionally hard and for long hours without necessarily being productive. You:

   a. Ask your boss, "Is this the company norm?"

   b. Start working longer and longer hours.

   c. Keep your normal schedule and refuse to work longer hours.

   d. Complain to your peers and staff.

10. You need help from two other department heads for a project that is running late. You:

    a. Do not impose on them because, after all, they are over-worked too.

    b. Ask "What can I do to help you, if you give me ten hours of help now?"

    c. Ask "Can I have your help for ten hours?"

    d. Decide to work around the clock for two days in order to finish.

11. You've been moved within your company into an area that is particularly volatile and political. You:

    a. Ask yourself, "Who can help me so I don't make too many wrong moves?"

    b. Decide to stay neutral, regardless.

    c. Figure your new boss, even though he's made enemies, should be your mentor.

    d. Ask the present political top banana, "How do you see the situation?"

12. You've been offered a better job for more money and plan to leave your present job. Then your boss matches the new offer in dollars. You:

    a. Stick with your decision; you don't want to appear weak.

    b. Go back to the "better job offer" and ask them to up the ante.

    c. Ask yourself if money is your only reason for leaving.

    d. Ask your boss what else he can offer.

13. When solving a difficult problem regarding increasing overtime costs, you:

   a. Ask your staff to cut back.

   b. Prepare a lengthy in-depth questionnaire and analysis of the situation.

   c. Call a department meeting and ask for input to get to the heart of the problem.

   d. Ask people individually about their problems.

14. When faced with a difficult decision, the first question you ask is:

   a. What are my options?

   b. What are the risks?

   c. What is my objective?

   d. What else do I need to know?

15. You are a new manager in a large computer-programming department. What do you do first:

   a. Nothing but ask a few questions, look, and listen.

   b. Call a staff meeting and ask for introductions.

   c. Ask for a meeting with your boss.

   d. Call a staff meeting to solve current problems.

16. You've been turned down twice by the finance committee for a budget increase request. You:

   a. Decide to wait for next year.

   b. Ask the chair of the committee for advice.

   c. Ask yourself what you've done wrong so far.

   d. Ask a negotiating expert for help.

17. You've been offered the presidency of an industry association, but you think it might conflict with your job and your boss. You:

   a. Accept and hope things will work out.

   b. Ask your boss for support.

   c. Ask your boss how this honor can help your department and the company.

d. Ask board members and former presidents of the association how they worked things out with their employers.

18. Two senior vice presidents are talking together and not paying attention during your presentation. You:

a. Ask questions of other people, and subtly bring them into the discussion.

b. Call a break and privately ask for their support.

c. Ignore them, figuring that you can't expect their attention.

d. Question one of them directly.

19. Two of your peers are talking together and not paying attention during your presentation. You:

a. Stop and wait for their attention.

b. Ask one of them a specific question.

c. Walk over and stand behind them.

d. Ask "Is this a private meeting?"

20. Your creative juices for new ideas have run dry. You:

a. Ask your boss for funds to enroll in a creativity seminar.

b. Ask your staff for their input, rather than solving everything yourself.

c. Ask your boss for two weeks off to go to a retreat and rest.

d. Start reading and getting new input.

21. You are asked to contribute a weekly article for an important industry publication. You:

a. Ask your literary friends, "Do you know a good ghost-writer?"

b. Ask a staff member to write the column, and put your name on it.

c. Ask your entire staff for contributions, and share the credit.

d. Accept and ask personnel to enroll you in a good writing program.

22. Your boss has just locked horns with your mentor over a major policy issue. You:

a. Ask your mentor for advice.

b. Ask yourself, "What is right?"

c. Ask your boss for advice.

d. Ask yourself, "How soon could this situation wear itself out?"

23. Your boss is afraid to let go of any authority. You:

a. Ask for a transfer.

b. Ask him, "What can I do to take over some of the work that you don't like?"

c. Ask "Have you ever felt frustrated by not having all the authority you need to do a good job?"

d. Ask "How could training your replacement make you look good?"

24. You feel your highly regarded boss doesn't trust you. You:

a. Ask for a transfer.

b. Start looking for another job.

c. Ask your boss, "What can I do to gain your trust?"

d. Look for satisfaction in outside activities.

25. In the washroom one day you overhear a rumor from reliable sources that your boss is going to get sacked. You:

a. Tell your boss immediately.

b. Ask the people the source of the rumor.

c. Ask your network if anyone else has heard anything.

d. Start packing your gear for your move into your boss's office.

Answers

1.   a = 0   b = 3   c = 4   d = 5

A smart manager should establish a power base when he or she is first interviewed for a job. This is an opportune time to make demands. In this case, the new manager is told there is a space problem. So asking "Can I have a commitment for more space before I start the job" (*c*) is an excellent tactic. But an even smarter question is "Are there any other major problems?" (*d*). Knowing what the problems are and getting a commitment from your new boss helps you achieve a strong position up front. If you answer (*b*)—"What effect is the small space having on the staff?"—you're asking a good question but not getting any action. And just accepting the fact (*a*) gets you nothing.

2.   a = 3   b = 5   c = 5   d = 0

No busy manager wants to get involved in a difficult, time-consuming presentation. While it's important to be enthusiastic (*a*), it's usually not smart to plunge in when you may get mired in a lengthy project with no payoff. If you want to get ahead, asking "What is the purpose of this presentation?" (*c*) and "Who will be there?" (*b*) will let you judge the potential impact of the project. Wriggling out of it (*d*) before you know the ramifications means that you might lose a great opportunity to make yourself visible.

3.   a = 5   b = 3   c = 4   d = 1

The answer to this question—what to do when a key person asks you a question that you do not understand—depends on who's doing the asking. Each of these answers has some merit, but unless you're a brilliant speaker, falling into double-talk to blur the issue (*d*) spells trouble. You may lose a few points if you admit that you don't know, but make up for it with "When do you need an answer?" (*c*), which shows that you'll find out and get back to the person. Asking the person to see you after the presentation (*b*) is not quite as effective, but can work if the person isn't challenging you head-on. It also suggests to the audience that you know the answer but don't want to take everyone else's time dealing with it. The smartest solution is to ask the person to rephrase the question (*a*). It gives you time to think; you can then come up with an answer or choose one of the other tactics.

4.   a = 5   b = 2   c = 0   d = 3

When you have an opportunity to save time by working with someone you dislike, do you jump to it? You do if you want to get ahead. The best question to ask yourself is "How can I set aside my emotions and make the best of this situation?" (*a*). The next-best response is to accept immediately (*d*). Your boss isn't going to help you solve your personal problems (*b*), although he or she may give you some advice in dealing with the person. Asking "Why should I give myself all this stress?" (*c*) is a useless question. If you're looking to get ahead, stress comes with the territory. You might as well get used to it.

5.   a = 3   b = 0   c = 5   d = 0

How many times do top people say they're going to come to a meeting and then get tied up elsewhere? It can turn a young manager's hair prematurely gray. Asking the two dropouts to commit to a new meeting is not a bad solution if you can get them to write the date in blood. But if you want to get ahead, you must do everything possible to avoid canceling meetings. So the best solution is to have a brief meeting with all three participants and ask if the third person can carry the ball (*c*) Neither (*b*) nor (*d*) is a suitable response. Turning the meeting over to your assistant just to make yourself look more important isn't worthwhile, and asking your boss to talk to the key people is passing the buck.

6.   a = 0   b = 4   c = 2   d = 5

If you want to get ahead, you certainly don't want to refuse the offer (*a*), even though it promises to cause problems with your spouse. The best plan is to go home and negotiate (*d*). People on big career paths need the support of their families, and ideally you can work out a win-win negotiation. The next-best solution, if you are looking to get ahead, is to accept the offer and deal with your spouse later (*b*). It's usually not wise to ask your boss or mentor to help with a personal matter (*c*).

7.   a = 2   b = 3   c = 3   d = 5

When someone is overlooked for a promotion, there's usually a reason. If that overlooked person is your boss, it's in your best interests to find out why. Therefore, asking around to discover the reasons behind the decision (*d*) is the best answer. You can usually lend support to your boss (*b*) and also make friends with the newly promoted person (*c*), and there's no reason not to do both. Immediately casting around for a new job (*a*) isn't intelligent, unless you discover that your company has adopted an "outside hire" philosophy. But don't act before you investigate the situation.

8.   a = 3   b = 5   c = 2   d = 0

If you've sold yourself at a job interview and the salary offer is too low, the best thing you can say is "I'm disappointed with such a low offer" (*b*)—and then *wait for a response*. The first person who talks is going to lose. The next-best response is to ask "Is there room for further negotiation?" (*a*), because it provides an opportunity to talk further. But this isn't nearly as good as (*b*). If you've sold yourself, it doesn't make sense to end the interview and walk out (*d*). And if you accept the offer with the idea that you'll get a raise when they see how good you are (*c*), it probably won't work out. If you're not assertive enough to ask for more money at the job interview, chances are you won't be assertive enough once you're on the job.

9.   a = 5   b = 3   c = 0   d = 1

For this question, the crucial thing to learn is whether long hours and excessive work is a corporate norm (*a*). Only when you know this can you make an intelligent decision. If it is a company norm and you want to get ahead, you will have to commit yourself to longer and longer hours (*b*). If you refuse to work long hours (*c*), you will not advance; it would be better for you to look for another job. (If it isn't a company norm, only a temporary circumstance, you will probably plunge in for the time being.) But you cannot act until you find out. Complaining to your peers and staff (*d*) is fruitless.

10.   a = 0   b = 5   c = 3   d = 2

If you want to get ahead, it's important to learn how to get help and work with other people. And yet powerful people don't want to be in someone's debt. Therefore to retain power when you need help, ask for it, but also negotiate for something you can do in return (*b*). This establishes a standard of give-and-take that will serve you throughout your career. Simply asking for specific help (*c*) isn't a bad solution, but without repaying in some way you're going to be in that person's debt. Being afraid to impose on someone (*a*) and killing yourself to achieve the task by yourself (*d*) are nonproductive solutions.

11.   a = 5   b = 2   c = 3   d = 3

When you're moved into a politically volatile area of the company, it pays to look around for the best advice so you can avoid making too many wrong moves (*a*). You cannot stay neutral too long (*b*); eventually you will have to position yourself. Although the most important person is always your boss, bosses are not necessarily the best mentors. So while (*c*) is not a terrible move, it isn't necessarily the best move. Asking the current top banana for help (*d*) could be the right move, but that person is likely to be biased. The smartest thing to do is stop, think, and ask a few smart questions before making any moves.

12.   a = 1   b = 3   c = 5   d = 3

When you accept a better job offer for more money and your boss makes a counteroffer, there's no reason why you can't change your mind. You're the one who loses if you stick to a decision just to appear strong (*a*). The best thing is to ask yourself an introspective question: "Is money my only reason for leaving?" (*c*). If money is the only reason you're changing jobs, you can negotiate with either the "better job offer" (*b*) or your boss (*d*). If money is not the main issue, if you're leaving because you're not happy in your job, then you have a different set of circumstances.

13.   a = 1   b = 1   c = 5   d = 2

When overtime costs are running your projects into the ground, asking your staff to cut back (*a*) isn't going to get to the root of the problem. And preparing a long in-depth questionnaire (*b*) will just drag the problem out. Asking people individually about their problems (*d*) could help, but it takes too much time. Your best shot is to call a department meeting (*c*) and ask for staff input. You will get to the bottom of the problem and also be able to institute immediate action.

14.   a = 3   b = 2   c = 5   d = 4

When faced with a difficult decision, all of these responses seem helpful. The important thing is to put them in sequence. The single most important question in the decision-making sequence is "What is my objective?" (*c*). Once you're clear about that, everything else falls into place. The next important question is "What else do I need to know?" (*d*). As you fill in these blanks, you automatically weigh options and risks (*a* and *b*).

15.   a = 4   b = 4   c = 5   d = 1

The first thing to do when taking over any large department is to ask for a meeting with your boss (*c*). Almost as good is doing what Edward Finkelstein did when he took over Macy's: nothing but watch, listen, and learn (*a*). It's always good form to call a staff meeting and ask for introductions (*b*). But calling a meeting with the expectation of solving problems (*d*) won't work until you learn what the problems are.

16.   a = 1   b = 5   c = 4   d = 3

When you are repeatedly turned down for budget increases, what can you do? If you wait for next year (*a*) to try again, you're leaving your future in other hands than your own. Asking yourself what you've been doing wrong so far (*c*) is a smart question if you can be objective about the answer. And by all means, if you have a negotiating expert around, ask for his or her advice (*d*). The most productive approach, however, is to ask the chair of the committee for advice (*b*). This is the only person who knows exactly why you're not getting the increases.

17.   a = 1   b = 3   c = 5   d = 3

If you accept the presidency of an industry association for the prestige, the smartest thing you can do is ask your boss how this honor can help your department and the company (*c*). Asking your boss for support (*b*) and asking former presidents how they handled things with their employers (*d*) are good ideas because they give you internal support for the outside work that might take time away from your job. Simply hoping that things will work out (*a*) means that you will be unprepared if conflict does arise between your job and the honorary position.

18.   a = 5   b = 3   c = 2   d = 0

What do you do when senior vice presidents start talking during your presentation? Calling a break and privately asking for their support (*b*) is a weak solution and may not even be possible in companies that have strict rules about how presentations are made. Ignoring them isn't going to help your credibility (*c*); and you're definitely not going to question them directly (*d*). The subtle approach will work best in this case; ask questions of other people at the meeting (*a*), which should generate discussion and gradually involve the vice presidents.

19.   a = 4   b = 5   c = 3   d = 2

The answers change if you're making a presentation to a meeting of your peers. Stopping and waiting for the attention of two talkative people may work (*a*), but if they are engrossed in conversation they may not even notice. Walking over and standing behind them (*c*) is a more subtle approach, but again, they may ignore you. Asking "Is this a private meeting?" is a rude and demeaning question (*d*) and unworthy of a smart manager. The best solution is to ask one of them a specific question (*b*). The question will get their attention, make them feel a twinge of guilt, let them know you want their input, and also get the meeting back on track.

20.   a = 3   b = 4   c = 2   d = 5

All of these solutions can help get the creative juices flowing again after a dry spell. The most helpful would be to start reading to stimulate your mind (*d*). Bringing in your staff can help (*b*), and going to a creativity seminar (*a*) certainly can't hurt. Even taking some time off (*c*), while the least direct method, may also do you some good.

21.   a = 3   b = 1   c = 5   d = 3

If you're asked to contribute a weekly article, you won't have time to do all the work yourself and it's unlikely that you have the money to hire a ghostwriter (*a*). And while it doesn't hurt anyone to become a good writer (*d*), that isn't what managing is all about. I believe that managers should take advantage of every opportunity to help staff people develop. But it's demoralizing to ask a staff member to write the column and then put your name on it (*b*). The best answer is to get the staff involved in the whole process—it will generate their interest and their enthusiasm. Use your name on it, along with theirs. Giving your staff credit makes you look good.

22.   a = 4   b = 5   c = 4   d = 4

When your boss and your mentor are at odds over a major policy issue, you have to look to yourself to discover what you think is right (*b*). This is a tough situation, but you must start with introspective questions about the situation, how you feel about it, and how you'd like things to end up. After you are clear about your own feelings, all of the remaining answers are helpful.

23. a = 1   b = 5   c = 3   d = 4

People who are afraid to let go of authority usually feel insecure. Therefore a smart manager tries to wrestle authority and responsibility from his boss in an unthreatening manner. By taking on jobs he or she doesn't like (*b*) you help rid your boss of a burden, which is a big plus, and ease him into the habit of delegating. Asking about your boss's feelings (*c*) isn't bad, because you're trying to show some empathy, but it's a little too smug. And asking "How could training your replacement make you look good?" (*d*) would work only if your boss has some motivation to move up. Asking for a transfer (*a*) is avoiding the problem, and that's never a good managing solution.

24. a = 4   b = 2   c = 5   d = 1

It is essential that your boss trust you. If he or she doesn't, you might think about asking for a transfer (*a*). But there might be another solution; before you give up, ask "What can I do to gain your trust?" (*c*). If there's something you can do, do it. If the answer is "Nothing," then ask for a transfer, or even start looking for another job (*b*). Looking for satisfaction in outside activities (*d*) doesn't work.

25. a = 2   b = 4   c = 5   d = 1

When you hear a rumor that your boss is about to be fired, don't start dreaming of yourself sitting in his chair (*d*). Before running to your boss to tell him that he's about to get sacked (*a*), use your network to find out what else people have heard (*c*). There may be a lot more going on in the company. Next best is to learn the source of the rumor (*b*); it may be an unfounded bit of gossip. The two best answers both involve asking smart questions.

Scoring

100–125 Points

With a high score you are on target with your thinking as well as your questioning. You have the right balance between confrontation and tact and negotiation. You've done well in developing the Smart Questions approach to most situations, and that ability should be a big help in your career.

85–100 Points

You use questions well but need improvement if you want to move ahead faster. You need to practice the questioning approach until it becomes an integral part of your communication and thinking process. You also need practice in phrasing questions. Once you are emotionally committed, the phrasing should improve.

65–85 Points

You are either avoiding confrontation or making quick decisions and rushing off to the solution. You are not fully convinced that questions can help you. Although it is difficult to let go of an existing pattern, for example avoidance or fast decision making, the Smart Questions system can help you. In every planned situation—calls you make, meetings you initiate—start with questions. Write them out in advance and memorize them. Once you see the improvement for yourself, you'll change your style quickly.

Less than 65 Points

You need to change your style across the board: substitute more questions for statements both verbally and mentally. Try changing your approach. When faced with a new situation, instead of counting to ten and then reacting in your old way, stop and think about a suitable question to explore the situation.

There is no area more important for applying the Smart Questions technique than the advancement of your career. In the following chapters we're going to see the many ways—in getting a top job, seeking promotions and raises, coming up with creative ideas to solve problems—that asking smart questions can make the difference. In the final chapter a select group of leaders of America's major corporations ponder the issue of what distinguishes a rising star from the rest of the management pack. They offer their personal advice on how young managers can stand out in the corporate system, and what they have to say may surprise you.

16
Creative Ideas and Problem Solving

Sam and Rachel, both on the executive committee of a major association, were discussing whom to promote to the position of executive director. They quickly ruled out the present executive director's assistant, the most likely candidate, with "He never comes up with any original ideas." One way to hit a dead end in your career is to be labeled in this way.

Managers need to activate, not merely maintain the status quo, which means that they must come up with new ideas and better solutions to problems. If you are a manager looking to get ahead, generating good ideas and solving problems imaginatively are sure-fire ways to catapult yourself to success.

Most people believe that managers who think quickly and creatively are smarter than others, or have some kind of secret flair for solving problems. In fact, the secret they have is accessible to anyone. Creative thinking involves quiet "cerebration," as one well-known trial lawyer calls it, and the ability to ask smart questions.

Drs. Harold Bloomfield and Leonard Felder, authors of *The Achilles Syndrome*, advise managers to work less and think more. Creative thinking often begins with removing yourself mentally from the day-to-day routine of business. "A brilliant idea, a pivotal decision, a simple solution . . . in those five minutes you can accomplish more than shuffling papers for sixty hours."

Asking questions is a great way to stimulate creative thinking. Assigned to come up with a new product name for dill pickles, the product manager placed a big pickle on the table and asked a group of six people this question: "If you had never seen this object before, what would you call it?"

This one smart question sparked a wealth of imaginative names. Some of their answers: Crisper . . . Canoe . . . Pucker . . . Quencher . . . Greenith . . . Slimy Cuker . . . Cruncher . . .

Marketing strategists use smart questions in many kinds of brainstorming meetings, from inventing new products to naming existing ones, from long-range planning strategies to instant problem solving. The rules of these creative sessions are simple: panel members are encouraged to express any idea that comes into their minds, refrain from negative comments or criticism of any idea, and expand positively upon ideas expressed by other members.

For example, a packaged-goods manufacturer set up a brainstorming session to name a new fruit juice. The panel was comprised of seven people from various walks of life and a market researcher who served as moderator. The moderator asked the panel: "What does fruit juice make you think of?"

Everyone wrote down lists of the words that came to mind, such as:

health	mornings
outdoors	colors
trees	family

"Now," said the moderator, "forget about fruit juice, and let's build on just one word on the lists. What does 'mornings' make you think of?" Again, hundreds of different words popped up:

a.m.	coffee
sunlight	alarm clock
yawns	toothbrush
school	wake up
showers	fresh
cereal	start
eggs	beginning

"Let's try another word," the moderator said. "What do you associate the word 'health' with?"

After building on each word on the original list, the leader picked out a dozen of the most promising words and tested them among a sample of consumers. For example, "A.M." was tried out, and so was "Sunlight," "Wake Up," and "Fresh." In this case, "A.M." topped most people's lists and actually became the name of a product.

Sounds simple, doesn't it? Yet how often do most people, when presented with a new idea, immediately jump to criticize it? We seem to regard ideas as one would a ship—no matter how many good points it has, if there's a hole anywhere in the thinking, the whole thing is doomed to sink.

For some reason the ability to isolate the negatives of an idea—in other words, to criticize—is often more respected in our society than the ability to recognize potential. When faced with a new idea or solution to a problem, managers often struggle to come up with some critical comment that will make them look incisive and intelligent.

People who pounce on the flaws in an idea or seize the chance to play devil's advocate are often seen as quick and discerning. In terms of business, the ability to pick out flaws is undeniably valuable. But if "Can't be done" is your prompt response to anything new and different, you may be nipping your future in the bud. A stubborn resistance to change can only hold you back.

An irate banker once told an inventor to remove "that toy" from his office. That toy was the telephone. A young engineer, bored with laying out computer chips, asked his boss if he could work on designing a personal computer. The answer was no, so the engineer went home, built one on his own, and named it Apple. Many years ago, a young clerk working in a hardware store suggested to his boss that they set up a table in the middle of the store and sell off obsolete inventory items for a dime each. The sale was a success, and the clerk then suggested that they open a store that sold only nickel and dime items. His boss said he was crazy; they could never find enough items to sell at a nickel or a dime. Years later the boss lamented, "I figure every word I used in turning down Woolworth has cost me about a million dollars."

The ability to see the kernel of a great idea and build on it is much more profitable than the ability to criticize and discover the flaws in every idea. People who respond to the positive are rare, and refreshing to be around. Other people are eager to present their ideas to them because they'll be examined in the best light. People love to share their thoughts with those who see the good things.

That doesn't mean that everything you think of, or your staff thinks of, will pan out. On the contrary, only a few ideas are ultimately worthwhile. But to get one sensational idea, you have to welcome all ideas, no matter how bizarre. And to get one idea to the top, you have to be willing to push all ideas as far as they can go.

Most good ideas that succeed have been shaped and restructured to become workable; they don't just pop out of the air in perfect form. Inventors and innovators often seek out broad new concepts and original ways to meet unsatisfied needs, then work out the details of how to implement or execute them later. If you've got something worthwhile, you can usually iron out the problems and make it work.

Accent the Positive

The essence of modern creative thinking techniques is to build on the positive. As mentioned earlier, in brainstorming or think tanks, negative comments of any kind are usually forbidden because of their counterproductive effect. Negative comments inhibit people and often choke off valuable thoughts before they are explored. All ideas, however improbable, are assumed to be worthy of consideration. Participants are asked to build on ideas, not tear them down. What appears to be a wild and impractical approach often turns out to be the key to finding an imaginative and effective solution.

Use Your Team to Generate New Ideas

Creativity often derives from special knowledge. Ken Blanchard was in the field of management consulting for years before he wrote *The One Minute Manager* with Spencer Johnson. He knew the field thoroughly. Jonas Salk spent years in the research laboratory before discovering the vaccine for polio. New ideas may fester for years in the minds of the engineers who see the same products manufactured day in, day out. They are in a position to know what's practical and what's out of the question. Bookkeepers stuck with the same system for months on end may be dying to tell someone—anyone who would listen—about a better way.

If you are a manager looking for new ideas, doesn't it make sense to talk to the people involved, the people who know the most about your business, or about the idea or the problem?

Often creativity has been squelched for so long that the manager feels he needs a stick of dynamite to enliven things again. Smart managers find ways of encouraging their people to come up with creative innovations. If you are a manager looking towards the future, always let your people know that you are open, receptive, and positive. Tell them you're interested in their constructive input, since you know that no one knows the business—whatever business it is—better than the people who keep it running smoothly day after day.

Smart Questions Help Create Ideas

As we've seen, questions are a great device for coming up with new ideas. The next step is to evaluate that idea. Again, questions provide the best way to pinpoint the positives and systematically determine the value of the idea. When considering any new idea, ask yourself or your staff these smart questions:

"What specifically are the positive aspects of this idea?"

"What specifically are the negatives?"

"What is interesting about this idea?"

"What makes this idea unique or valuable?"

"In what ways can I build on the idea's advantages?"

"Are the possible advantages so great that it must be considered further?"

"Are the negatives so dominant that further thinking is a waste of time?"

"Can the basic concept be applied to different areas? Different products? Different departments?"

"Does this idea suggest any others that might work better?"

Smart Questions for Problem Solving

Creative thinking may also prove to be the key to solving some of your toughest on-the-job problems.

One newly hired executive in a growing pharmaceutical firm observed that various groups within the company were at loggerheads. Numerous major and minor mistakes were being made—on quantity and quality checks, in proofreading, and in other areas—costing the company possible lawsuits, poor publicity, and time and money. Department heads blamed each other and morale sagged across the board. Productivity declined.

The executive pondered this situation and came up with a series of solutions by asking herself some smart questions.

"What is the history of this problem?"

"When did it start?"

"What could be the source of the problem?"

"Who is involved?"

"What has been done about this in the past?"

As she tried to answer these questions, she realized that this was a relatively new problem that originated when the company began its expansion. Here was a large company with virtually no communication among its senior managers. In fact, no one had ever been out to the manufacturing plant. Once she recognized the problem for what it was, a solution was readily at hand.

As a result of her thinking, the executive came up with a program where everyone met as a group for one hour every month. At each meeting, members of one department gave a short presentation: how they fit into the big picture; what they needed from other departments—from manufacturing, advertising, marketing, and so on. Then they asked for feedback from the other groups. Every session concluded with questions from the floor. Speakers also gave out some written material so that anyone unable to attend the meeting could catch up on it. Tours were also developed, so every employee got to see how products were manufactured and packaged.

After a year, the program was reevaluated and it was discovered that many persistent, serious problems no longer existed. The executive who had come up with the plan received an important promotion.

When faced with a problem that seems to defy positive solution, smart questions can help you set a decisive course of action. Ask yourself:

"What is the source of the problem?"

"Who is involved?" (If the situation involves a problem with a specific individual, always examine the other person's point of view. Until you understand the problem as the other person sees it, you can't deal effectively with the problem itself.)

"What aspects of the problem are controllable?" (Managers often have more control over situations than they think. Don't assume anything until you know for certain.)

"What aspects about this situation require outside help?"

"What has been done in the past?"

"What worked? What didn't work?"

What Are Your Objectives?

When it comes to solving a problem, many people don't know what it is they're after. Sometimes the best way to discover what you want is to ask yourself what you don't want.

"What don't I want to happen?"

"What is the worst thing that could happen?"

"What is the best thing that could happen?"

Planning Strategy

"What are all the possible ways to approach this problem?" (Go for quantity at first, not quality.)

"What obstacles are we going to face?" (Be realistic, not negative. For example, if you will have to fight for approval, think of a creative way to do it.)

"What are the options?"

"What is the backup plan?" (Have at least one.)

"What are the trade-offs?"

"What's the bottom bottom line?" (Remember the story of the authoritative stranger who came into the office and asked, "Who's the Main Man around here?" The boss proudly stepped out and introduced himself. The man said, "I'm with the IRS." The boss quickly added, "Oh, you want the Main Main Man.")

"What help do I need to carry out the strategy?"

"From whom do I need support to put over the strategy?"

Personal Goals

"Did I choose this solution only because my associate or boss wants it?"

"Did I choose it because others expect it of me?"

"Did I choose it because it's the fashion?"

"Because it's easy?"

"Because it's hard?"

If you answer yes to any of the above, you should rethink your choice. Ask yourself one more smart question: "Is this the solution I really want?"

Using Your Team to Solve Problems

It is common today for companies to hire outside consultants to solve a variety of problems, from managerial to marketing to personnel-related difficulties. Frequently, one of the first things these consultants do is carefully interview the client firm's staff. Many companies, it seems, don't take the time or trouble to listen to their own people.

Many creative solutions do not involve a single decision or directive. More often, problem solving is a matter of discussion, cooperation, and an ongoing process of change. When you let your people actively participate in creative problem solving, you gain in two important ways: you are more likely to discover a solution that strikes directly at the heart of the problem, and you build the cooperation and loyalty of your staff.

People are often reluctant to come to a boss with problems, unless the boss has established an atmosphere where the bearer of bad news isn't shot on the spot. William S. Lee, Chairman and CEO of Duke Power Company, says that this is a sure sign of a poor manager: "Managers must build the right sort of climate where people can speak up and report unpleasant news upward."

You may find it valuable to hold regular team or staff meetings to discuss problems. Make it clear up front that these are not griping sessions or an excuse for mudslinging, but serious updates on serious business. At the same time, such meetings are worthless if people do not feel free to speak honestly without fear of disapproval. A good manager should be able to hear problems or suggestions without taking personal offense.

These sessions serve another purpose: potential problems may be cleared up before they become full-grown ones. The managers I know who have meaty problem-solving sessions never operate under crisis management.

How can a manager use staff people to solve problems imaginatively? Ask a few smart questions:

"How long have you been aware of this situation?"

"From your perspective, when and why did it start?"

"What factors do you think have contributed to the problem?"

"Is this particular problem part of a larger problem?"

"What ideas do you have to improve the situation on a day-to-day basis?"

"What steps might we take to solve the problem for the long term?"

"Can you point out any related problems?"

"What does this problem tell us about the larger picture and the way we are currently approaching our work?"

Of course, the ultimate responsibility for choosing any solution remains with the manager. And there will be problems that no outside input can help you solve.

The sign of an outstanding manager—a manager destined to move ahead and succeed within the organization—is the ability to make a decision and carry it out. The crucial part of any new brilliant idea or any imaginative solution is actually making the decision to go forward—and giving your brainchild every opportunity to succeed.

17

Dare to Decide

Nothing is valued more in organizations than a good decision. And nothing is criticized more—and remembered longer—than a poor one.

Lou, an executive vice president of a major insurance company, was promoted to run the West Coast office. As a result, he was asked to name his own replacement, a choice to be made from three of his best people. Each candidate had good qualities and all had been with the company for several years. Lou's final choice came down to which one could make the best decisions.

Before making his selection, Lou gave each candidate one important decision to make:

Candidate A was asked to choose the best marketing consultant for a new product line. "A" called up his cronies on the old boy network, found out whom they used, and went with their advice. Lou eliminated Candidate A because he did not interview and investigate on his own, and therefore had no assurance that he had gotten the best available consultant for the job. This wasn't the way Lou wanted his replacement to operate.

Candidate B was asked to select the best computer system for programming the new products. "B" methodically gathered the facts and made a thorough investigation. But as much as Lou pressed him, "B" put off making a decision. There were always more and more "essential bits of information that were still needed." Lou felt that no amount of prodding could help solve Candidate B's intense insecurity and fear of making a mistake. He eliminated Candidate B.

Candidate C had a reputation as an eager beaver. He was so energetic that he often rushed his decisions and failed to look at all sides of an issue. Lou asked "C" to develop the advertising plan and budget for the new line. Candidate C realized how much was at stake. Instead of following his usual pattern of jumping the gun, he went to Lou and asked for help. And this was the deciding factor for Lou. While none of the candidates was a first-class decision maker, Candidate C had the most potential because he was highly motivated and was willing to learn. Jim chose him as his replacement.

If I had to sum up the quality that's most essential for effective management, I'd say that it all comes down to decisiveness. You can use the most sophisticated computer in the world and you can gather all the charts and numbers available, but in the end you have to bring the information together, set up a timetable, and act.

Some people work their way up to the decision step, then are reluctant to act. Why? Because it's with the action—not the idea, not the analysis—that you win or lose. Every decision involves a risk. But each risk can be minimized.

Getting any idea off the ground involves two basic steps. First, you have to make a decision. Second, and equally important, you have to take action on what you've decided.

Step One: Making the Decision

It's important to understand the decision-making process to learn where you might go wrong. For example, do you tend to be overly conservative or to cave in under pressure?

Many managers let themselves get bogged down by the confusion of having to make rapid choices. And few businesses can afford the luxury of slow decision making. Obviously, you're responsible for gathering as many relevant facts and projections as you possibly can. But at some point you've got to make a decision based on your own instincts. Have confidence in your past successes. After all, decision making is a skill and if you did it right in the past, you're likely to do it right again.

Timing is everything. Even the right decision is wrong if it's made too late. A young designer I know took much longer than anticipated to bring out her important first line because she felt compelled to make it perfect. By the time the clothes were completed to her satisfaction, the fashion scene had found a new set of styles, and she had to start all over from scratch.

The fashion business, like so many businesses, is rooted in trends. Some trends move faster than others. Similarly, many products and services are seasonal, or dependent on shifting demographics or other factors. A manager must move heaven and earth to deliver the product to the marketplace before the marketplace shifts or even disappears. Whenever you make a decision—regardless of the nature of your business—you have to be aware of the clock ticking.

It's natural to want to see all the facts set out before you and to hold out for research that puts risk at a minimum or guarantees that a particular program will work. If you're going to invest money and resources, you want to be absolutely sure you're on the right track. But not every business problem can be solved by research. At some point, someone—some decisive manager—has to dare to decide.

How much information is enough? It's impossible to put a figure on it, but clearly when you move ahead with only 50 percent of the facts, the odds are stacked against you. At the same time, you'll never know 100 percent of what you need. When you must act with less than complete information—as all sharp managers must be able to do—there are things you can do to minimize the gamble.

First, make sure the information you do have is reliable. Know your people: your experience should tell you what sources are trustworthy and whose judgment is most sound and consistent. Encourage debate. This is just when you need feedback the most.

Make sure that whatever specific information you have makes sense. Don't take for granted that the list of figures you've been handed is accurate. As much as possible, check things out yourself.

It's important to recognize your own decision-making style. If you tend to be a Commander or Convincer decision maker, ask some caring team players or Calculating quality controllers in your group or organization for their opinion, to act as a balance and prevent a rash decision.

Listen to what others have to say, but listen more to your own instincts. Do you have any lurking doubts or feelings of uncertainty? Taking action often helps relieve nagging feelings of ambivalence and doubt, but don't act quickly merely to alleviate tension. A certain amount of uneasiness and uncertainty goes with the territory, and your subconscious may know something you don't know. Try to pin down what's bothering you.

Last, and most crucial, always monitor the success or failure of your decisions. One reason decisions are risky is that a manager never knows until afterwards—sometimes not until much later—whether it was a good decision. An example is hiring someone or deciding on a new product. And yet, short of making the decision to order a firing squad to shoot, most decisions are not irrevocable.

Research shows that once people make a decision, they do everything in their power to convince themselves it was the right one. Don't fall into this trap. Make it your business to get feedback. Make sure the decision is having the desired impact. If it's not, figure out why and help it along. Or if you realize that your first decision was a bad one, have the strength to change direction and cut your losses. This doesn't mean that you shouldn't stand by your decisions or that you should give up on a project the minute something goes wrong. It means that in certain situations, insisting that you're right when you've clearly made a mistake is much more costly in the long run. If you're digging a hole in the wrong place, digging it deeper or wider won't make it any better.

If you discover you've made an error, the most valuable thing you can do for yourself is to learn from the experience. All successful people use failure as a valuable teacher. It's a given that everyone makes mistakes, but only those who can analyze past failure to improve future performance emerge as winners.

So, making good decisions depends on knowing how to take calculated risks. When you don't have all the facts—which is most of the time—asking smart questions can give you a specific technique to speed decision making and help reduce the risk. When faced with choices, what kind of questions can you ask yourself in order to make the best decision? Realistically, most business decisions are not based on one clear-cut preference but on the lesser of several evils.

Exploring Your Options

Smart questions can help you explore the advantages of various options. List all your realistic alternatives and pose these questions about each one:

"What are the benefits of making this decision?"
"What are the risks?"

"What's the best possible result I can hope for?"

"What can I do to maximize the possibility of this happening?"

"Can I achieve this end in any other way?"

"What is the most probable result?" (Both positive and negative.)

"Does this satisfy my objectives? Will I be happy with this result?"

"What's the worst possible result?"

"Can I handle it?"

"If it's the wrong decision, how can I retrieve the situation and my self-esteem?"

"Should I alter my plans to avoid this possibility altogether?"

"Is there a way I can or should compromise?"

"If I'm a Commander, whom should I consult?"

Here's another issue to consider:

"Will my action go against the interest of some other part of the company?"

"Or of a colleague or team member?"

"Or against my own interests?"

"Is it worth this price?"

The Three Questions That Lead to a Winning Decision

Ultimately it takes only three very smart questions to reach a winning decision. Before you make *any* decision, be sure you know the answers:

1. "What will it cost—in money and resources?"
2. "What impact will this decision have?"
3. "What happens if we don't do it?"

Step Two: Taking Action

Taking the time to make a good decision and then failing to put the results into practice is like spending all your money on a beautiful house and failing to move in. Good decisions are worthless unless they're acted upon.

Once you have your decision, make the decision to *act*. Carrying out a plan or idea that has hitherto existed only abstractly can be a traumatic experience, but it's one that managers live with every day. It's like the author I know who finished a manuscript and locked it in his desk drawer. He couldn't face sending it out to publishers and risking the possibility of rejection. Or the would-be restaurateur who devised a fabulous thematic restaurant, spent months laboring over the plan, then dropped the whole idea when it came time to actually lease the property and open the doors. Or the speaker who developed scripts for a videocassette and couldn't decide which producer to go with.

The same thing happens frequently in all sorts of businesses. People spend time working up ideas, doing research, devising and planning innovations, and then let the whole thing slide away from them, just when they're ready to put it over the top. Why?

Perhaps because the closer you are to achievement the harder it all seems. There are also more subtle psychological reasons. When ideas and plans have taken a long time to evolve, people get attached to working on them. They hate to let the project go and send it on its way. For perfectionists, the work is never quite finished enough to turn loose. And if it's a particularly big plan, they might dread the actual implementation, which can be strenuous.

It's also hard to take the risk of testing your hard-won decisions, especially in a corporate world where putting yourself on the line is perceived as dangerous to your career. Many companies function on the principle of inertia, and in these organizations it's risky to rock the boat by promoting even a small change. But this means that the manager's career path will remain equally static.

Managers who succeed in making their ideas move have determination. Behind every enormous skyscraper that goes up there is a person determined to turn drawings into buildings. Donald Trump, the flamboyant real estate baron who has already made his mark on Manhattan's skyline, has said, "I never think of the negative. All obstacles can be overcome."

People who get ahead keep their eyes fixed on the end result—on what they want to achieve. And that end result is never the idea itself but the implementation of the idea. You can have the best ideas in the world, but upper management values and recognizes the person who turns ideas into actions.

Self Questions Create Successful Action

In some of my training programs I use an exercise called the Desert Survival Exercise. In this theoretical exercise, people are stranded in the desert with their gear. From the supplies on hand each person must arrange the items in order of their importance to his survival. Here's the important part of the exercise: If the person fails to set his objective first, he will make the wrong choices for survival. That is, he must first decide whether he will go forward or stay where he is. Every other decision is based on that objective.

Some managers are so eager to make a decision and get moving that they forget to set their objectives. So, every action you take should be preceded by this question: "What are my specific objectives? Short term? Long term?"

Then you can go on to the active part of the questioning:

"What specifically has to be done to carry them out?"

"How many people will this involve?"

"Who are the best people for the job(s)?"

"What information do they need?"

"How will they need my help?"

"Who else should be briefed to ensure success and cooperation?"

"How much time should I allot for each phase of the action?"

"What are the target due dates for each phase? What are the actual deadlines?"

"How will I get feedback on the ongoing progress?"

"How will I monitor long-term results?"

"Do I have any hidden resistance to seeing this project through?"

There is no such thing as a wishy-washy, insecure leader. Decisiveness is the essential element of success. The managers who get ahead make sound decisions and act on them. That doesn't mean they are perfect—every decision involves some risk, and you can't make the right choice every time. But asking the right questions in advance can reduce the risk and turn the odds in your favor.

Making your own decisions is one thing. Reaching a compromise with other people is another, equally important, sign of the manager with a future. How well and how smoothly you negotiate can affect your advancement.

18

Sharpen Your Negotiating Skills

Over lunch I asked one of the dynamic speaking agents I work with what she liked most about her job. She answered without hesitation and with a gleam in her eye: "Negotiating." Negotiating is a specialized form of problem solving. By definition, problem solving becomes negotiating when two people or groups start from opposing positions and attempt to reach a satisfactory middle ground, with each side hoping to give up as little as possible. It might more pointedly be described as the art of getting what you want with as little bloodshed as possible. Not all of us love it, but we all have to do it.

Negotiating and compromise are a fact of daily life and daily survival. Negotiating may involve money, power, and control. Or you can negotiate over who takes out the garbage, or who gets up to change the diapers on a crying baby. As a part of daily human interaction, negotiating is a tool that we all understand very well.

In the workplace negotiating may be relaxed and friendly, as it is when colleagues need to solve some relatively minor problem that's interfering with work. Or it may be complicated and emotional, as in situations involving unions and contracts. In business, the person who can negotiate in a variety of circumstances and conclude with everyone feeling satisfied about the outcome is worth his or her weight in gold to any organization. One of my clients is known as a masterful negotiator.

Her customers always say, "She can get me to say yes to anything and be happy about it."

The objective of negotiation is to reach some compromise acceptable to both parties; it should not be a game of win or lose. Compromise means the willingness to bargain, change, and keep an open mind. That's why the word "opponent" is not constructive. I prefer "counterpart." This makes it clear that you are in this together. You stand a better chance of negotiating successfully if your counterpart trusts you and respects you.

At the heart of all good negotiating is knowing how, and when, to ask questions. A good negotiator uses smart questions to gather information, and then to control the direction the negotiation takes.

I once watched a little girl playing with a small, flimsy sand pail on the beach. She saw a younger child playing with a larger, heftier pail. Instead of going over and grabbing the pail she wanted (which is a popular negotiating style, not only among children), she sized up the situation and went over to the younger kid and sweetly said, "That pail must be heavy for you. Wouldn't you like a pail that you could lift up easily?" The little girl happily walked away with the coveted pail, and the younger child was thrilled! That's a win-win negotiation.

Your Negotiating Style

As you can see, anyone can be a good negotiator. But to develop your skill it's important to recognize your own style and learn to accommodate it. You should know your own strengths and weaknesses. Your counterpart may know them well, and will not hesitate to take advantage of them. Are there certain issues or attitudes that tend to make you emotional and might cloud your judgment? In your heart, are you afraid you are a pushover? The time to bring these concerns to the surface is before you begin a negotiation, not during or after. The more in touch you are with yourself, the more confident you can be—and the better your results.

For example, Commanders are good hard-line negotiators—they are direct and self-contained, and are not apt to give out too much information. Because they thrive on confrontation, they are well suited for confrontational negotiations. They gather all the information they can, and they use it. On the down side, Commanders tend to be impatient and competitive. In any negotiation, patience is a virtue. To be more effective, Commander managers need to develop patience. They also need to damp down their competitive edge so they don't automatically approach others as combatants.

Convincers, because of their ability to express ideas well, can be adept at getting both sides to compromise in a negotiation. However, many Convincers are not organized enough to do all the preparation necessary to be a sharp negotiator. Convincers also may lose out on a deal because they care too much about social approval and don't want to be disliked even temporarily.

Carers are usually skillful at building the support and trust that serves as a base for the deal. But they are not confrontational and may give in under pressure. However, the fact that they are not direct communicators can be an advantage, especially when the counterparts in the negotiation are less direct.

C's, the Calculators, can really dig in their heels and be inflexible, but they'll have all the necessary facts and they'll stick at it. And this persistence may serve them well when it comes to pulling off a successful negotiation. They also may withdraw under pressure. Although Calculators are not direct communicators, their sensitivity and intuition can be a big help in negotiations. Creators are not strong negotiators and like to leave the negotiations to others. Material things don't matter too much to them, but when it's related to their "baby" they will fight for it like a tiger.

Confidence

A confident negotiating style goes a long way towards giving you the psychological advantage you need to win. Regardless of your style, all successful negotiators have one thing in common: they exude confidence. It can be a quiet confidence or a dominant presence. If you seem convinced that what you're asking for is the best choice, others will be too. If you waver, you send a signal that you're either unsure of what you want or unsure of how to get it.

I remember a lawsuit in which a public figure was suing a newspaper for libel. The newspaper corporation maintained its powerful image of integrity and honesty, even as it grew more and more doubtful that its case could be proved in court. The individual who was suing, despite the fact that things seemed to be going his way legally, appeared defensive and insecure. The power of the newspaper frightened him. As the pressure mounted, he backed down and withdrew the suit before a judgment could be reached.

A confident attitude should sink all the way into your bones. As Herb Cohen, negotiating expert and author of *You Can Negotiate Anything*, succinctly points out: "Power is based upon perception—if you think you've got it then you've got it. If you think you don't have it, even if you've got it, then you don't have it." Or as Sophia Loren likes to say, "Sex appeal is what the public thinks you've got."

Know Your Counterpart

To know your own negotiating style—your strengths and weaknesses—is one thing. It's equally, and sometimes more, important to recognize the negotiating style of your counterpart. Consider this axiom: "If I know more about you than you know about me, I can control the negotiation. And if I know more about you than *you* know about you, I can control you."

You must do as much research as possible on your counterpart. Remember the old saying "Know thine enemy"? Enemy or not, it pays to know the other side. You can't outmaneuver an unknown quantity.

If your counterpart is a Commander, give it to him fast and straight. If he is a Convincer, don't let yourself become sidetracked by extraneous issues. Nudge things along and keep bringing him back to the essential points.

If your counterpart is a Carer, constantly testing you, never show impatience. You can get him to agree because it's safe, secure, and good for his team. Never push a Stabilizer.

With Calculators you sometimes have to know when to push. I was once in a negotiation with a client for a series of seminars. He had agreed to twenty specific programs and then backed down to two. I sent him detailed background information on hundreds of previously successful programs and called frequently to see if he needed more. Finally, when we were face to face, I remembered his desire for perfection and his fear of criticism. I said, "You thought this was the right way to go two months ago and I know you make logical, sound decisions. Why change your mind now?" He made the decision on the spot to go with the whole program. So, if your counterpart is a stickler for details, wear him down with facts, logic, and information. And then make your move.

With Creators, let them feel you understand their ideas and concepts. Let them know that the deal under negotiation will free them from future worries over money, details, and people. Creators can often give in to get you off their backs, especially if they are in the midst of the creative process.

Reason vs. Emotion

Negotiation is above all an exercise in logic and clear thinking. Whenever emotion supercedes your reasoning power, for all intents and purposes you have lost. Negotiating requires a clear view of all the issues, all the shifting pros and cons, at all times. Getting angry or frustrated not only doesn't help; you are giving the advantage to your opponent.

A corollary to clear thinking is the ability to express yourself clearly. Negotiating is a specialized form of problem solving. If you fail to communicate your specific problems, needs, and bottom-line positions, you will probably not get what you want.

The Psychological Edge

You should always enter a negotiation armed with a list of concessions that you can make without any great sacrifice. But when you *do* give up something you consider minimal, create the impression that it's a significant compromise on your part. When a negotiator wins a major concession by giving up something insignificant, he gains a tremendous psychological boost. It's like trading a five-dollar bill for a ten.

Also, remember that the more time invested, the more the other party has at stake. When we were buying our computer we spent hours with each salesperson and at the end they kept giving us more and more concessions to get us to close the deal and make their time count.

If you are a Commander, remember that when it comes to negotiation, patience is indeed a virtue. I remember a line said by Oscar Homolka, playing a Russian general, in the film *War and Peace*. When news was brought to him that the French had won a victory in the field, Homolka smiled craftily and said, "That's all right. We can wait."

A negotiator who is anxious and impatient for a quick outcome cripples his chances of getting the best deal. Nobody wants a negotiation to go on for hours or days, but if you insist on pushing for an immediate resolution you're apt to give up much more than you have to. In fact, knowing that your counterpart is in a time bind may be a major advantage for your side. If you want something badly, holding back may turn out to be the best way to get it. Also, it's important to recognize the impact of the negotiation beyond the deal at hand. Could you actually be giving up something by winning? You might find yourself in the proverbial situation of winning the battle only to lose the war.

A manager I know recently spent several hours negotiating a simple misunderstanding with an outside consultant. "It was a trivial matter," she said, "and the problem would never have arisen if we had clearly understood the terms of our agreement before we started the job. As it was, we were at a standstill."

It seems that the consultant sent in a bill that reflected many more hours on the job than the manager had contracted for. "He said that with our various requests we had used up much more of his time than originally stated," the manager recalled. "Our position was that he didn't mention this extra time until he submitted his bill, which didn't leave us any options—that is, we were not given the opportunity to rethink our objectives and decide whether the extra hours were worth the price."

The manager and the consultant spent several hours on two different days working out a mutually satisfactory compromise. Why did the manager bother?

"Because I liked his work and hoped to continue working with him," she said. "Also, we wanted to avoid a more severe situation where we might wind up in a lawsuit. In the end, by taking time with the problem we both felt good about it. I appreciated all the extra effort he had put into the job, and we traded off some of that time for future jobs."

Smart Questions Negotiating

Good negotiating skills depend on your ability to ask smart questions and listen carefully to the answers. A negotiator's success depends on constantly "reading" his counterpart and responding with the proper strategy.

Big talkers, only interested in touting their point of view, are poor negotiators. Skillful negotiating means giving away as little as possible up front. Your first step in a negotiation is to gather information. Before you play your cards you should be getting a sense of your counterpart— his personality, his mind set, his attitudes, his weaknesses. The best way to accomplish this is to ask questions. Asking questions lets you listen more and reveal less.

Negotiating typically has three phases: preparation, opening bids, discussion and compromise.

Preparation

It is virtually impossible to be a good negotiator if you don't do your homework. If you're involved in a business negotiation with another company, for instance, it's vital to know the size and scope of the firm, their history, the resources at their disposal, their financial status, their corporate style and philosophy. All these elements will help you tune in to their point of view, their strengths and weaknesses, their bottom lines. As much as possible, have a grasp of whom you're dealing with before you start.

The more you know about the issues to be discussed, the better chance you will have of overcoming the objections and showing how you can both benefit. Try to find out as much as possible about the issues before going into negotiation. That may mean asking your counterpart for information, or you may want to go to others in the organization. Sometimes inside information can be the wild card you need.

Part of your preparation is to set your goals. Before the negotiation, make sure you know the answers to these smart questions:

"What do I want to accomplish?"

"What are my real needs?"

"What is the most I could get?"

"What do I absolutely need?"

"Where specifically can I compromise?"

"What insignificant concessions can I make?"

"What concessions can I make that would hurt, but are still possible?"

"Do I have a clear understanding of what's at stake, what issues are involved, and all my bottom-line limitations?"

"What are my strengths?"

"What are my areas of vulnerability?"

"How can I deal with these?"

It is equally important for you to discover and fully understand what your counterpart is looking for. Do you know the answers to these two smart questions?

"What does my counterpart want?"

"Do I know why he wants it?"

You may think you know why someone wants something, and you may be completely off track. Warren, a vice president of a computer manufacturing firm, got into a head-to-head conflict with Jill, one of several fast-track managers on a planning committee to reorganize a production unit. Jill, an energetic, hardworking manager with her eye on advancement, did the research, developed the ideas with the team, and wrote the final version of the planning report. She insisted that she receive full credit for the task and that her name appear on the report cover. Warren, although appreciative of her work, wanted to submit the report under his name. It was company precedent for vice presidents to sign all reports emanating from their department.

"I did the work, I wrote the report," said Jill. "I deserve to have my name on it."

"To give credibility to the report and have influence with upper management, the report must be submitted under my umbrella and that of the planning committee," Warren argued.

Jill was dissatisfied and angry. Warren felt there was a danger that he might lose her, and she was the best of several managers who reported to him. Warren stewed over the problem and finally asked Jill to come in to see him, with the hope of smoothing over the problem.

"For some reason, when she walked in the office, a question popped into my mind," Warren recalled. "I asked her, 'Can you tell me a little more about why you want your name on the report?' "

"It's important to me to become more visible to upper management. I'm the first woman to produce such a report and it's important for me to set a precedent. I want them to know about my contribution."

Immediately, Warren had a different handle on the problem. "I'm not sure that putting your name on the cover is the best way to accomplish that," he said.

The solution they arrived at—the answer that satisfied them both—was to submit the report to top management with a cover letter describing Jill's contribution. In addition, when the report was presented orally, Jill would be the manager to deliver the presentation.

The point is this: Do not assume that you know the reason behind someone's demands. This amicable agreement was reached because one person took the trouble to discover the real reason—the "why"—behind the demands.

Questions for Opening Bids

It would be ideal if in all negotiations, you could both say simultaneously: "This is what I'd like, and this is what I'm willing to settle for." But in most cases the person who reveals this information first loses, unless he or she has the counterpart in a squeeze.

Formal and definite statements of position, especially at the start of a negotiation, sometimes polarize the negotiators. But if you ask your counterpart a few smart questions, informally, you can learn a lot of valuable information and at the same time open up the negotiation:

"What would you like to see happen here?"

"What are your goals?"

"What in your mind is really the crux of the matter?"

Questions That Lead to Discussion and Compromise

The golden rule of negotiating is "Make yourself ask for more than you want, and then be quiet and wait." But sooner or later you're going to have to say something. Smart questions allow you to find out all you need to know and guide the discussion in the way you want. Ask your counterpart:

"What do you see as areas of common ground or common interest?"

"Is there anything about my position that I haven't made clear?"

"Perhaps I can explain my position more fully. Are there specific areas where you feel I'm being inflexible or unreasonable?"

"Is there a more constructive way that we can approach this problem together?"

"Is there anything about your position that you'd like to clarify or expand on?"

"What sort of answers can we come up with that will be better for each of us?"

A good negotiator stays flexible. While patience is valuable, you may also need to be quick—quick to alter your strategy, quick to pick up on a new factor or pounce on an advantage, quick to change direction if necessary. On a moment's notice good negotiators can decide to forfeit certain prizes in order to get different ones.

The way to be alert to shifting opportunities is to constantly ask yourself certain key questions throughout the negotiation:

"What is my counterpart's stated reason for this particular demand?"

"What could be his underlying reason?"

"What is really going on?"

"What is my bottom line?"

"What is my bottom bottom line?"

"If my counterpart makes this particular concession, how can I help him save face?"

Throughout the negotiation, pay attention to eye contact and shifts in body stance. Ask yourself, "Is my counterpart sending any nonverbal signals? If so, what do they mean?"

Such a signal can tell you when to hold the line and when to push forward. I was once able to score a lucrative contract because I witnessed a change in my counterpart's stance. Throughout the negotiation he appeared nonchalant and casual. Then I noticed him checking his watch when he thought I wasn't looking. He started fidgeting. His body language gave away the fact that he was running out of time. I held to my bottom line and he gave in.

So, whether you're negotiating the price of a car, a deal with your landlord, or a labor contract for your company, watch for the unconscious signals the counterpart sends out.

Closing Negotiations

When you close a negotiation, make it firm. Sign, shake on it, whatever. But when it's done, it's done. End the negotiation with civility. Don't slip away as though you've taken your counterpart for a ride, because that's enough to make him feel that way. You and your counterpart should feel comfortable and confident with the results. One good, mutually beneficial deal paves the way for others.

Afterwards look for a way to follow up. Make an effort to speak to or write to your counterpart. Invite him or her out for a drink to celebrate. Or set a date for a future meeting. But don't just offer a token invitation. You must carry it out. You have everything to gain from establishing this kind of continuity. The next time you do business together you'll have a platform of mutual respect and understanding to begin from.

Negotiations are a fact of life. They take place in every business, in every circumstance. And managers who get ahead know how to make the most of each negotiating opportunity. But there's one special kind of negotiation that stands out in every successful manager's life. This particular negotiation has a tremendous personal impact on your present life and an even greater influence on your future: negotiating for a raise.

19

Negotiating a Raise

Do you feel you're paid as much as you're worth? Funny, I've never met anyone who answered "Yes" to that question. There's only one way to get more money: ask for it. It's not an unreasonable demand, and it's not asking for a favor. Raises are a normal part of business life. Everyone, including your boss, would like to take home a bigger slice of the pie.

In certain situations, it's actually more harmful *not* to ask. People in the corporate world are often judged by the size of their paycheck more than by their ability—even within the company. Also, if you don't request an increase after a certain amount of time, your boss may think you're crazy, or at least unambitious.

While annual or semiannual raises might be standard in the firm, your chances of securing a large sum are greater if you bring it up. During a debate with Sandra, a second-line supervisor for an airline, I reiterated that she would get ahead faster if she asked for a raise rather than waiting for review time. She countered, "It's never done in my company." But since she was ambitious, she decided to give it a try. Not only did she get the raise, and another at review time, but her boss (who had never thought her assertive enough to get ahead) began to groom her for future promotions. For the most part, bosses are proud of the go-getters in their departments.

*   *   *

Managers destined to get ahead always keep trying to increase their salary. If you allow yourself to be underpaid, you lose respect. Ironically, even your boss will probably value you more if he's paying you more. And you'll naturally be more motivated when you feel your talents are appreciated—especially when that appreciation is reflected in financial terms.

In other words, no raise or promotion is achieved in a vacuum. Both are functions of your value to your boss and to the company, and of your political position within the firm.

Timing Your Request

The most important element of asking for a raise is to time your request so that you (not your boss or your company) are in the strongest position possible. It may help if your boss is in a good mood and not particularly pressured or harried. But this will not get you your raise. What *will* get you a raise is if you've just brilliantly completed an important project, pulled off a major financial coup, or otherwise proved or underlined your special worth.

Recently I observed a young MBA graduate, hardworking and ambitious, get herself a $10,000 raise. Lesley works for a giant real estate development firm in Florida. She had done a phenomenal job in the year she had been with the company, and they wanted her to become their divisional manager in the Orlando area, with a salary increase of $2,500 a year. She knew she was needed and she also knew that she was much better at her job that other managers in the firm. Lesley surveyed the territory and accurately assessed that there were not enough good managers to match the company's rapid growth. She replied, "I feel the job is worth $10,000." That's all she said. She waited, and eventually received the full amount.

If you've got a very visible success story or some attention-getting ideas to show off, now is the time to pull them out of the hat. And stay alert for opportunities. If your boss has just lost two good people, that is an especially good time to ask. Or if several people in your department have just left, your experience and willingness to take on added responsibility could be priceless to your superiors at this time.

Self Questions to Evaluate Your Timing

Asking for a raise is usually a difficult and emotionally charged situation, but asking yourself some smart questions in advance can lessen anxiety and help you smoothly achieve your goal. Like any other negotiation, asking for a raise requires some homework. And the best way to do this is ask yourself some very smart questions.

Take a good look at corporate policy as well as the financial health of your company and even your industry. Periods of economic depression or widespread financial losses, for example, do not bode well for your chances, unless you are perceived as invaluable in solving the current problem.

To get an overall view of your company's status, ask yourself these smart questions:

"What had been the pattern of raises managers in my position have received in the past?"

"To what extent is compensation a fixed part of the budget process?"

"How much freedom does my boss have in deciding on raises?"

"What are the current conditions of business within the company? Within the industry?"

"What are the company's plans for the immediate future?"

"What is my role in those plans?"

The next step is to evaluate your position *vis à vis* your boss. How does your boss—and *her* boss—look upon raises in general, and how are they likely to feel about you when you make this particular request? To get an overall picture, ask yourself these questions:

"How does my boss treat me?"

"Does she seem to trust and value me?"

"Does she praise or criticize specific parts of my performance?"

"What is my boss's position in the firm? What are her ambitions for growth?"

"Does my boss take me for granted?"

"How well does she understand what I do?"

"How much does she know about my bottom-line value and contributions?"

"How does my boss talk about me to her peers and to upper management?"

The answers to these questions will point out the strengths and weaknesses of your position. For example, if your boss takes you for granted, it's up to you to change her attitude before asking for a raise. If she seems unaware of your contributions, you will have to make your bottom-line value obvious.

When considering your boss and your relationship with her, try to anticipate any criticisms that she might bring up so you can counter or negotiate around these points. Remember that no individual's performance is so flawless that it can't be legitimately criticized. You should never become offended or defensive in a negotiation, and the best way to keep your cool is to be prepared.

Ask yourself some tough questions in advance:

"Has my boss indicated dissatisfaction with any aspects of my performance in the past?"

"Have I followed up on her suggestions? Can I point to improvement?"

"Where else have I shown improved performance or increased productivity in the recent past?"

"In what areas might my boss say I could do better?"

"How can I respond in a positive way to these comments?"

"What special strengths or achievements can I bring up to counter weaker areas?"

Establishing Your Value

The best way to move ahead in any company is to establish your value to the organization and make your contributions visible. One way to establish your value is to keep adding to your Career and Confidence Inventory (discussed in the following chapter). Another is to interview for other jobs at least once a year. (Don't let anyone—including your boss—get too complacent.)

But the most important aspect of preparing for either a promotion or salary negotiations is pinning down your value to your firm. You're in the best position when you can prove your worth impressively in dollars, growth percentages, or other concrete terms.

Ed Weihenmayer, Vice President of Human Resources at Kidder, Peabody & Co., emphasizes this point: "No matter what task you're working on, always ask yourself, 'How does what I'm doing impact on the bottom line?' "

If you're in sales it's fairly simple to identify your bottom-line contribution to the company. But all employees should try to look for a bottom-line connection when getting ready to negotiate for a raise. If you're a copywriter in an advertising agency, for example, and you wrote a successful slogan that helped your agency keep an account that bills $2 million annually, that's a dollar value that's tough to refute.

You can also look for other ways to assess your corporate worth. What is your reputation within your department? Within your company? Within your industry?

And what is the value of someone in your position on the open market? You should always be aware of competitive salaries within your firm as well as outside it. If you can show that your firm is paying 10 percent less than its competition for the same level of job, you have a strong case. When other companies are willing to hire you for more money (or your company thinks they are), you will always appear more desirable. That's why I advise managers to go out and look once or twice a year. Occasional job interviewing keeps things in perspective. (You might also discover you're not worth as much as you think.) Going to professional conferences is another way to network within your industry and stay abreast of what's going on in terms of job openings and salaries.

Another smart question for you to ask yourself: "How easily can I be replaced?" If you have special talents or skills or experience, if it would be hard to replace you, you are in an excellent negotiating position.

But this strategy has been known to backfire. A company may be uncomfortable with someone who thinks he is "irreplaceable" and always has the firm over a barrel. Your assistant probably knows more about the job than you think —and when you come right down to it, no one is irreplaceable (only expensive). Know your worth, yes, but don't get carried away.

It's good strategy to demonstrate your value as often as you can. If you've saved hundred of hours by reorganizing department systems, be ready to say so. Or if you've been able to reduce overtime, shout it out.

Choose Your Strategy

Once you've defined your overall value, it's time to select a strategy. When you ask for either a raise or a promotion, you must have a specific approach planned out ahead of time. Given your particular circumstances, what is the best way to present your case to your boss?

The Straightforward Approach

If you have a long string of accomplishments, you may want to approach your boss in a fairly straightforward manner. You matter-of-factly point to your achievements and to documented evidence of increased profits, and ask for your well-deserved reward and recognition. You show confidence and control; there is no need to be demanding or emotional in any way.

The Ultimatum Strategy

The straightforward approach works well in many corporations. However, after examining your boss's attitudes and those of your company, you may decide that a stronger power play is necessary. Attempt this only when you have a lot of ammunition on your side—you feel you are indeed of great value and your firm is well aware of it—and you feel secure enough to take the risk. Ultimatums work best when you have an ace up your sleeve or some special knowledge that your boss needs. Your boss may not realize just how much he needs you until you force the issue. Perhaps you have a handle on the company's five major accounts and the client wants to deal only with you. Or an audit is coming up and you have the figures.

If you threaten to leave if your terms are not met, you must be fully prepared to pack up. If you wave another job offer in their faces, you should be quite willing to take it. This is not a good time to bluff; your job and your career could be at stake. When you play for high stakes, risk is part and parcel of the game.

Craig, a Commander, full of self-confidence and with an overinflated ego, was sure his company, a small public relations firm, couldn't do without him. Without preparation or a backup offer, he stormed into the president's office and demanded a large increase and a promotion to vice president of marketing, or else. The president, although valuing him, knew that Craig had serious flaws in his ability to deal with staff and decided that this was a good time to let him go. He refused the ultimatum and Craig had nowhere to go but out.

Even when you win with your ultimatum strategy, however, there could be other drawbacks. No one likes being painted into a corner, especially not your superiors. When you consider the ultimatum approach, take into account the ill will you may create. But also keep in mind that nice guys don't always make the most money, and that many people respect someone who drives a hard bargain. A subtle ultimatum, a veiled implication, can be very effective without spelling it out.

The Education Strategy

What if, after answering all the self questions about your performance and your boss's attitude, you reach the conclusion that you're not a superstar? What if you do good, steady work but have no startling figures to report? What if you have an adequate relationship with your boss, but he seems to take your work for granted? Are you still entitled to a raise? You bet you are. You simple need to employ a more subtle approach.

You must begin a campaign to educate your boss as to your true value long before the salary question is broached. Look for opportunities to clarify the skills and nuances necessary to performing well at your job. Let your boss know the strategies you've worked out that make his or her job easier and the operation run more smoothly. Your boss can't appreciate you fully when he doesn't know exactly what it is you do. While you're implementing this strategy, don't be overly self-congratulatory, and don't make it seem as if you're complaining about being overworked. Your attitude should remain positive and cooperative as you gradually make the powers-that-be aware of your difficulties and your successes.

The Promotion Strategy

The most obvious way to justify a raise is to first get a promotion, a new title, or increased job duties. To a certain extent, being promoted is the logical result of doing your job well and playing your political cards right. But sometimes you have to take things into your own hands.

Analyze the range of your job responsibilities. Then ask yourself two smart questions:

"Are there more visible, complicated, or sophisticated tasks that I can concentrate on?"

"Are there less important or more routine items that I can safely delegate?"

By answering fully these two questions, you can begin to carve out a promotional path for yourself. You may be able to subtly shift your job responsibilities to a higher level and gradually change the perimeters of the job itself. It's not uncommon for a hard worker hired as an office clerk to eventually run the office. Who hasn't heard of the secretary who became CEO? And once your job has changed, it's easy to prove your increased responsibilities and show that your salary should be adjusted accordingly.

The Attitude to Take

Whatever strategy you choose, a positive attitude is vital. Remember that you are entitled to a raise because of the good work and extra effort you put in. When you go in to make your claim, go with the assumption that you're going to win.

You should be confident and natural. Don't change your personality just because the issue is money!

Be pleasant. Accusing your boss of failing to appreciate you is not a good way to get him on your bandwagon. You might even begin by telling your boss that you value his support and fairness and that you know you can count on him in this instance too.

Reassure your boss that he's doing the right thing by raising your salary and that you will respond with renewed loyalty and enthusiasm.

And don't make it seem that money is your sole motivation for doing a good job. A fair salary should be just one way of compensating you for loyalty and hard work.

It is also a good idea to avoid the obvious statement "I want a raise," with its demanding and poutish feeling. Try something a little more sophisticated—"an adjustment in salary," "increased compensation," or "more monetary recognition."

A List of Don'ts

While you're rehearsing your positive attitude, it's helpful to examine this list of negatives:

Do not: plead (remember, you are not asking for a favor)
          apologize
          complain or whine
          pester (unless your boss is a Commander or a Convincer)
          get defensive
          get angry or emotional

Setting Up the Meeting

In terms of actually setting a time for the initial meeting, some experts suggest that you schedule a formal appointment with your boss, specifically to deal with this topic. In my experience, however, this can lead to unnecessary tension and anxiety because of the negative implications surrounding the subject. If you refuse to explain in advance why you want to meet, this can also cause concern since it is automatically assumed that the topic must be serious and urgent.

In most cases, I feel it works better to tie your raise request in with some other private discussion you're having with your boss, whether it's a regular update meeting or a project review. This approach tends to be more successful since it reduces the need for a formal and perhaps awkward pronouncement and makes it clear (especially in your own mind) that your asking for a raise naturally evolves from your day-to-day work. But don't make the mistake of thinking that an informal approach means that you can be any less prepared.

Naming Your Figure

Whatever your strategy, you should always be the first to state the figure you had in mind. If your boss has the first word, he or she will undoubtedly name an amount that's too low, and you will be in the awkward position of having to say that's not enough.

Figure out what you think is a fair and realistic amount and then inflate it somewhat (if you'd settle for 15 percent, go for 20) so you will be in a position to negotiate down. Don't go wild and ask for the moon (unless you really and truly have a shot at it). Remember that you want to emerge from the negotiation in a winning position, so don't stack the odds against yourself. Aim for something you can realistically accomplish.

Smart Questions That Get Raises

How can you use questions to generate a positive response from your boss? Try these:

"I've been doing two jobs for three months. Don't you think it's fair that I get paid for them?"

"Do you believe that managers should be paid what they're worth?"

"You don't want me to work without the reward, do you?"

"I will be more productive and feel better about my position. Don't you think that would be best for both of us?"

"Money is a symbol of what we think something is worth. Don't you agree?"

"What would make you see me as more valuable?"

"How can we both come out ahead here?"

"What happens when a valued employee is paid less than he's worth?"

"What about the $30,000 I saved the company last week?"

"I increased my worth on the open market about $10,000 when I went from account executive to senior account executive. What compensation can you offer?"

Countering Your Boss's Strategies

There are several typical ways in which bosses try to evade the issue and thus avoid increasing your paycheck. I remember the first time I tried to get a raise. My boss was the champion guilt-producer in the company.

He cried "Poor ... No budget ... I'm harried by other problems ... Come back later." But I was well rehearsed and calmly kept coming back to the point: I had tripled my sales goals and wanted compensation. Although I did not get the raise, I was promoted to senior account executive; three months later, after two other "raise interviews," I got the compensation. Preparation, persistence, and patience are the keys to any negotiation.

So, if your boss tells you in confidence that the company or department is losing money, do not be angry, unbelieving, or unsympathetic— and do not feel guilty. Simply say that you fully understand, but you have your own financial needs to deal with. Fairness dictates that you be paid a proper amount for the work you do. Does the company charge less for its products or services when a consumer or client is in financial straits?

If the company is truly in trouble but you decide to stick it out, you might suggest stock options, profit sharing, or guaranteed bonuses when the financial outlook improves (get it in writing).

When an employer tells you that you deserve a raise but his hands are tied by company policy, there are several ways you can go. Ask these smart questions:

"Have there been no exceptions?" (Make sure you've investigated in advance.)

"Who can bend the rules?"

You may decide to go over your boss's head (with your boss's full knowledge), although this can create some bad blood. If you decide this is your best course of action, tell your boss that you completely understand his position and realize that he does not have the proper authority to fly in the face of company policy; then politely ask a smart question: "Who does?"

Smart Questions Can Get You Promoted

Even if your raise request is turned down flat, don't go away empty-handed. If there's a cap to what someone in your position can be paid, for example, it's a good time to negotiate for a promotion. Try these questions:

"If I can't get a raise right now, what else can you offer?" (Give your boss time to think it over; come back later for his answer.)

"As you know, I've been getting extra responsibility. How about a new title?"

"How can you increase my responsibilities?"

"Can I work more closely with you on the new departmental reorganization?"

"When can I receive more education?"

"Can I make the proposals to the management committee?"

"Can I work with upper management?"

"Will you send me to the industry's next top managerial conference?"

If you gain any of these concessions, you may get a direct promotion, or at least put yourself in line for a future promotion, greater opportunities, and ultimately more money. You've created the expectation, and your boss, if you do a good job, will want to help you.

When you negotiate for a raise, be strong, be confident. Never hesitate. Above all, do everything you can to perform your job with excellence. No boss wants to lose a winner. Think how you would feel if one of your key performers said he was leaving. You know how tough it is to recruit, select, and train a top achiever. You will do everything in your power, and more, to keep that person. If you're good—especially if you're great—at your job, your boss feels the same way about you. Believe in yourself and keep asking.

But what happens if your career path seems blocked in your company? What if the direction open to you is not the direction you choose? Can you change jobs, or even change careers, and win?

20
Finding a Job with a Future

Managers on the fast track look for ways to move up—and sometimes moving up means moving out. Can you hopscotch from company to company and come out on top? You certainly can, and if you're bogged down in your present organization you should calculate a career move.

Finding a job you love, and a job that will pull you ahead speedily, is a challenge. Don't dread it; look for ways to have fun with the experience. After all, if you work up until you are sixty-five you'll be working some 96,000 hours. You might as well make them count.

Two fundamental tasks take much of the guesswork out of getting ahead: deciding which job you want, and then marketing yourself to get it. The first part can actually be harder than the second. Choosing what you want to do involves a great deal of self-questioning. Once you choose the field, you need to select the companies that might be right for you and to figure out what specific jobs lie on your career path. From there, you must arrange an interview with the individual in each company who has the power to hire you. And sell yourself to that person.

Figuring Out the Path

While most companies do not have direct, rigid lines of ascent—that is, specific rules about promotions from one job to the next—it's usually pretty clear where the opportunities for advancement lie within a company. For example, in pharmaceutical companies top management is promoted from product managers, who frequently were promoted from the sales force. In automobile companies, plant managers usually come from production and related areas of plant operation, rather than from personnel or sales. In the steel industry, managers with ambition should not head for the advertising or marketing department. But in a company devoted to cosmetics or other consumer goods, advertising and marketing are in the front line, and these jobs tend to be positions with great potential for growth.

The key is to recognize that the exposure to top management depends upon the type of company you work for, and to select the most probable path of opportunity. The following method for finding a top job with a future has been developed over a long period of time and is based on my experience as a consultant to numerous corporations. I have sat through hundreds of job interviews and reviewed thousands of resumes. What you read here is a distillation of that experience—how to make it work for you. If you are thinking of changing jobs to jackrabbit your way to the top, or if you are looking to alter your career path in your present organization, here is the basic technique that will send you on your way. The process is so sound that it can work in either situation.

Five Steps to a Top Job

Finding the right job requires a targeted marketing approach. This is not an effort in mass marketing, but a highly selective undertaking. Your quest is comprised of five specific steps, each with a specific purpose. Although the overall goal is to secure a job, if you focus only on the end result you stand to miss out. Every step must receive your complete attention, and each must be fulfilled before going on to the next. In brief, the five steps are:

1.   Develop a "Career and Confidence Inventory." A Career Inventory lists assignments you've had in the past, the actions you took for each one, and what you achieved with each. Ideally, when you finish your career inventory you will have a list of ten to twenty Assignments, Actions, and Achievements (AAA's). The object of this step is to define the offer you will ultimately make in Step 3.

2. Draw up a list of at least twenty targeted companies, each with the name of the person who might hire you. The objective is to compile or refine a workable mailing list. If you're looking within your present organization, make a list of the divisions and division heads whom you want to work for.

3. Send a carefully drafted letter targeted to the special interests of each person on your mailing list. The objective is to get their attention, and the letter will include your offer.

4. Establish a persistent phone call strategy to follow up the letters. The objective is to get an appointment for an interview.

5. Go to the interview. Your goals are to gather information about the company and to get a job offer.

Your Career and Confidence Inventory

Modesty, says renowned economist John Kenneth Galbraith, is a much overrated virtue. Looking for a job is no time to play shrinking violet. You have to sell yourself, and before you can do that you must believe in yourself. Creating your Career and Confidence Inventory is a way to build your self-esteem and also to define what you have to offer.

You deserve to have a good job and be well paid for it. Choosing the right sort of career involves delving into who you are, what you want, and where you are going with your life. And this is the hard part. Before you can sell yourself, you have to know what you're selling and why. To give yourself a start, answer these smart questions:

"What am I best at?"

"What do I like most?"

"Who's willing to pay me the most?"

"What exactly do I want to do?"

"Where do I want to do it?"

"Are there other departments or divisions in my own company where I would have these opportunities?"

"If not, which organizations interest me?"

"What are my long-term goals?"

"What price am I willing to pay for success?"

With your answers in mind, invest your time in developing your Career and Confidence Inventory. Employers are looking for people with skills in three basic areas: technical, human relations, or conceptual. Which category—or categories—do you want to fall into?

"What are my strongest technical talents?"

"What about my sales abilities and sales performance?"

"Do I seem to handle other people well?"

"Do I get along with most people?"

"How do I rate myself when it comes to thinking up new ideas?"

"How much money have I saved or made for my company?"

When you have selected one or two general categories that interest you, start to compile a list of ten to twenty Assignments, Actions, and Achievements (AAA's) that relate to those broad categories. To make the list you may need to work backwards. Begin by asking yourself some smart questions that will help you remember your accomplishments.

"Have I ever saved money or time?"

"What projects have I organized?"

"What excellent people have I hired?"

"How have I been innovative?"

"What difficult problems have I solved?"

"Have I made some tough decisions?"

These questions will help you remember all the impressive accomplishments that you may have forgotten. Once you've remembered the Accomplishment, go back and tie in the Assignment and the Action that led to the Accomplishment. Now, write out a complete list of your AAA's. Here's an example of one I used when I was looking for a job in sales and marketing:

Assignment: "My job was to open up the West Coast market for my company."

Action: "I achieved this by mobilizing a strategic marketing system."

Accomplishment: "At the end of the year the West Coast market accounted for 40 percent of my company's gross volume, which was 25 percent over our projections."

Your Mailing List

The approach I advocate is to make a list of twenty companies you want to work for and the job you might be interested in. If you're looking within your own organization, make a list of the division you want to work for and the job you want. Then send a specific letter to each person who is in a position to give it to you. Your best bets for finding this information are people you already know in the business or sources at the public library. The more specific your marketing approach, the better. Direct-mail marketers say the better the mailing list and the better the offer you make to the list, the more responses you get.

Forget about preparing a resume. Resumes are used primarily to screen people out. I've sat in on so many hiring sessions where we plowed through a pile of resumes, elimiating most of them. Why bother? Resumes are primarily for mass marketing or for lower-level jobs.

The Letter

The purpose of the letter is to get the attention of the prospective interviewer and make that person want to see you. Send your letter only to the people you have researched, who you know have the power to hire you. You don't need to know whether there is an actual job opening. People are always leaving, moving up or out or sideways, leaving vacant slots.

Your letter should be brief but packed with information, confidence, and benefits for your prospective employer. Start by telling about your experience—what you've done for others. Do this in one short, punchy opening line: "If you are looking for a dynamic results-oriented sales manager with a proven track record, look no further." Concentrate on what *you* can do for him and the company.

Include two AAA's, targeted to a specific job. The AAA's you describe must be something that could be applied to the company. For example, the Assignment and Accomplishment described earlier could be used for any marketing or sales job but would not be appropriate for a design job.

The Action step that you describe should be short and not too specific. You don't want to give them a blow-by-blow account of what you did; you want to tantalize the reader.

Above all, your letter must contain an irresistible offer. And that's what the AAA's give you. By concisely giving two AAA's you offer a track record—your past performance—which is the best indicator of what you can do for the reader. If your offer isn't tempting, everything else is irrelevant. Concentrate on how your AAA's might benefit this new company.

Don't tell the reader what he can do for you or what you are looking for. No one's looking for anyone to do favors for.

Conclude with "I will call you on _____ to make an appointment at your earliest convenience."

A resume can never do the job that this kind of letter can do. A resume is only an outline; the letter described here contains an irresistible offer. When you're going for a growth job, a letter, plus an interview, can be enough. In this kind of job search, you bypass personnel and appeal directly to the person you will work for. By definition, this will be a busy person who probably would ignore a resume but might read a short and enticing letter.

The Telephone Call

The follow-up telephone call has only one objective: to get the person to grant you an interview. Be persistent, but agreeably so. Keep asking for the appointment. Do not allow yourself to be screened out or interviewed over the telephone. The more you say on the phone, the less the person needs to see you. If you are asked a question, you might reply, "I can answer that much better in person. When can I come in to see you?" Once when I was trying to get an interview for an important job I rented a limousine and took the person to the airport. If you really want to see someone you will find a way.

Interview Goals

Once you've got the appointment, you have two objectives. The first goal is to find out as much as possible about the job, your potential boss, and the company. The second is to sell yourself. Whether or not to accept the job should always be *your* decision. Even if you don't want it, secure a job offer. You'll need all the selling practice you can get.

When you go for an offer, to get a "yes" you come into an interview with a different attitude. It's the difference between a dress rehearsal and an opening night. Show them that you want the job, not that you're desperate for it.

One reason to make sure that you interview well, no matter what, is that other possibilities may arise. A friend of mine applied for a position as production manager at an advertising agency. There was no opening, but because she seemed too good to lose they offered her a job as an account executive. She took it and is now a vice president.

Your main goal is to find out what the interviewer's problem is (the work he or she needs done), then to demonstrate how you can help solve it. Remember: you're doctor, he's the patient.

Beatrice Buckler, the former publisher and editor of *Working Woman*, told Jane Trahey how she felt about hiring staff for her magazine: "I want people who can convince me they are interested in my needs. I don't want to hear about their psyches. . . . I don't want to hear what her needs are. I want her to tell me how she will help me."

Even though you want a job that furthers your career, your attitude should be focused squarely on the present. Ask not so much where you can go as what you can do with the job available. And let that attitude show in the interview.

This is the usual scenario before a manager begins interviewing: "I'm desperate for a good person. My boss is furious that I've put off looking for so long, and my staff is overworked and dissatisfied. I've got so much pressure, so little time, and I've got five people to interview today." Never underestimate the anxiety of the person interviewing you—especially when that person is your future boss. (Personnel interviewers don't feel as anxious, since they are always interviewing.)

As unbelievable as it seems to a harried job-seeker, the interviewer has more at stake than you do. His or her job is on the line in a real way. Smart companies evaluate their managers by the people they hire, and too many poor hiring choices weaken the reputation of even the best managers. Knowing this fact when you are being interviewed gives you a distinct advantage. Remember that you are there to reassure them that you are the best person for the job. Anything you can do to reduce the interviewer's risks and anxieties will make it easier for him to say yes.

You have two important subtexts in the interview: "What's your problem? What can I do to help?" This is the attitude you make obvious to the interviewer. The second attitude is your secret agenda: "Is this the right job for me?"

Every question you ask should come out of these two contexts. An attitude of confidence and control should be evident from the first moments of the interview, especially if you are up for a responsible executive position. It takes an interviewer less than ten seconds to get a first impression of a candidate. Long before you have a chance to say anything intelligent, your attitude and your body language have conveyed volumes.

Positioning Yourself

The impression you make on the interviewer—your future boss—carries over into the job itself. If you position yourself as strong, capable, and ambitious in the interview, you begin to establish your position and reputation—your power base—for the future.

Most people do not realize it, but once someone has gambled on you and offered you a job you are in a powerful position. That person wants you to succeed. You must recognize this, and get all that you can up front in the way of equipment, money, staff, and resources to make a strong start.

You can shave years off your upward career path if you are wise to this idea. Leonard was offered a job as manager of an electronic data processing unit. Two things stood out at his job interview: the area he was to head had a long-standing complaint of being short-staffed and short on space. Before he took the job, Leonard got a commitment that he could hire necessary staff and get additional space. As a result, he started off in a strong position with his staff, since their previous two bosses had done nothing. At the same time, upper management respected him because of his astute bargaining. Down the line, Leonard was able to accomplish twice as much as other managers because of his fast start, and he continued to expand his power base.

To recapitulate: When you get the interview you're after, you have two goals. In the first part of the interview, get information. In the second part, actively sell yourself. In between, decide if you want the job. Smart questions can carry you through each of these phases with flying colors.

The Smart Questions Interview

You never know exactly how an interview will be conducted until you get there—which doesn't mean that you should wing it. On the contrary, you should be thoroughly prepared for anything. Do your homework.

You should already know a great deal about the company, and something about your potential boss. Sketch out a list of at least ten questions that you would like to have answered sometime during the course of the interview. Carry this list with you, and if your mind goes blank take it out of your briefcase and read it over. Or bring it out at the beginning and keep it in front of you. Remember that one of the ways smart interviewers evaluate you is by the quality of the questions you ask, so be prepared with good ones.

Nowadays there are some standard questions you can expect to be asked, and you should prepare in advance your answers concerning your own strengths and weaknesses. Some pointers: only reveal your strengths, even if you disguise some of them as weaknesses. For example, a positive weak point might be that you tend to be a bulldog—you never let go of a problem until it's solved. Another: you're too much of a perfectionist, but you're working on it. With these kinds of weaknesses, who needs strengths? But don't invent desirable qualities out of the blue; really examine yourself and select your most saleable strengths, and then make sure you communicate them. Don't just answer the questions you're asked—use them as an opportunity to tell the interviewer everything that you want him to know.

The interviewer should set the style and tone of the interview. If he's a skilled and experienced interviewer, which few people are, he's likely to suggest that you ask questions as the interview progresses. If he's insecure or inexperienced he may say, "I'll start off with some questions. If you have anything you want to ask, reserve your questions for the end. I'll allow plenty of time to answer." Or if the interviewer is a real game-player, he may say, "This is strictly a fact-gathering expedition. Our purpose right now is to find out something about you and if you will fit in with Continental Widgets. I hope you will answer freely. If you seem to be the right candidate, there will be time to discuss the job and any questions you have in a follow-up session."

Any of these scenarios is possible, and it's up to you to decide what you want to do about them. You may play by the rules the interviewer establishes, or you may object. But don't merely react blindly; tackle the situation with your eyes open.

The fact is, you cannot make a sound decision and sell yourself as the "doctor" until you get enough information. It's a given that the interviewer has more control over the situation than you do, and all of your preparation is based on trying to get some of that control for yourself.

The more questions you ask, the more control you have. Participate actively in the interview. Do not sit back and let the interviewer pick you over to see if you have the goods. What does he or she have to offer? What's this job all about? Whom would you report to? What are the department's greatest concerns?

Opening Gambits

Let's say that this is a normal interview situation, an exchange of questions and answers. Try to ask the first question—pleasantly. Take control smoothly and comfortably. Your objective is to find out as much as possible about the particular job, the people you'll be working with, and the potential for growth. You can begin by expressing interest in your interviewer. What is one serious mistake that many high-level job candidates make? They hesitate to ask questions that get their potential boss talking.

Every situation is different, but show in your questions that you have done some research about the company and are interested in learning how your interviewer fits in or contributes to the organization. If you can find out something about the person ahead of time, it gives you a distinct advantage: "I recently saw your name mentioned in the 'Business Today' section of the paper in relation to your upcoming union negotiations." Or "What are the things you feel have contributed to your success here?"

Suppose you've come through a recommendation. "John Smith has gotten us together because he thought there might be something mutually beneficial for us. What has he told you about me?" Or more casually, "How do you and John Smith know each other?"

Staying with the Interview

Questions can keep you in control and ensure that you reach your objectives:

"Your company is definitely on the move. What are the things you find most satisfying?"

"How did you come into your present position?" (You want to get a feeling for how career paths form in the company.)

"How many managers report to you?" (Seven is the magic number.

More than seven and the boss isn't going to have time for you.)

"How are managers cross-trained in your department?"

"Can you tell me what things you are most likely to delegate?"

"Are there certain things you don't like to delegate?"

"How often will you meet with me to discuss problems and issues?"

"What are your primary needs and concerns at the present time?"

Build questions as if *you* were hiring someone, but in reverse. Ask "How will I relate to the specific job, the team, the organization as a whole?"

As in other situations where control is vital, most of your time should be spent in asking smart questions and listening carefully to the answers—not in talking endlessly about yourself without a clue to what the other person actually needs to hear. Further, you will be judged by the quality of the questions you ask.

My own most challenging job interview was with a sharp sales manager at Bell and Howell. He saw that I had had a varied background and asked me: "Do you think this job could satisfy you because of your many interests?"

I realized that denying it wouldn't help, so I asked a smart question instead: "Does your job satisfy all of your talents?"

I was subsequently offered the job, and I believe that one question was the turning point.

Specific Job-Related Questions

During the course of the interview, make sure you learn the answers to these questions:

"What do you foresee as possible obstacles or problems I might have?"

"In terms of my major responsibilities, how much actual authority do I have?" ("How much money can I spend? How many people do I supervise? Do I have full power to hire and fire?")

"Do you have performance standards for my key job responsibilities?"

"If you hire me, what would your expectations be?"

The two smartest questions you can ask during any interview are these:

"If in the past someone has not fulfilled your expectations in this job, what were the main problems?"

"What do you think is the one major thing that would contribute to my excelling at this job?"

Team-Related Questions

"Is there some reason why you're not promoting someone within the company for this job?"

"How many people held this job within the last five years?"

"Are any of them still with the company? Would it be possible for me to talk with them?"

"With whom would I be working and may I talk with them?"

Company-Related Questions

"Since corporate fit is so important, how would you describe the ideal manager in your company?"

"How is job performance evaluated here?" ("How is it rewarded?")

"Since each corporation is unique, how would you describe the corporate climate here?"

"How are decisions made here?"

"What kind of decisions will I have to make?"

"How much time will I have to make them?"

"What kind of support will I get?"

"What happens if I make a mistake?"

"What happens if I win?"

If you are a woman or a member of a minority group, ask, "How many women [or minorities] are working in middle and upper management?"

Only when you have asked these or similar questions about the specific job, the team, and corporate fit should you ask questions about the potential for growth.

Questions for Your Future

Even though you're dealing with the present situation and the present job, the job interview is an appropriate time to consider your future with the company. Because you don't want to give the impression that your only interest is to get on the fast track, these questions are best asked towards the end of the interview.

Most companies today are concerned with succession and training people for the future. You should ask questions that probe for company policy in this area.

> "I see that your company is expanding in the Northeast—where do you see the company moving?"

> "What are you doing in terms of human resources planning to make that happen?"

> "What about career paths for new employees, as well as employees within the company?"

You must also interview your potential boss and find out whom he has promoted and what his career goals are. A dead-end boss can be a dead end for you, too. The most important question you can ask for your future is: "What can someone coming in at this level and performing in an outstanding way hope to achieve?"

Countering Questions During the Interview

The more information you get in the beginning of the interview, the better you can answer questions the interviewer puts to you.

Listen closely to questions you're asked. The less you're thinking about yourself and what you're going to say next, the better the interview will go. This is worth repeating: Nowhere is listening more important than in the job interview. Listen for the content and the intent all the time.

Only answer the question that's asked. Answer simply, directly, and briefly. Don't elaborate. If you're not 100 percent sure of what you're being asked, ask a clarifying question:

Interviewer: Tell me about yourself.

Candidate: What specifically do you want to know?

Interviewers typically ask questions that you should not or cannot answer properly without more information. Don't hesitate to ask for it.

Interviewer: What accomplishments make you most proud?

Candidate: I've done many things which please me. What areas are you interested in?

Tough Questions to Answer

Some interviewers enjoy trying to make you feel uncomfortable. Your best counter-move is to remain calm, never lose your cool, and use humor as much as possible. Don't be grim. It just *seems* like a matter of life and death.

You can be almost anything—aggressive, charming, funny—but never be defensive or angry.

Interviewer: What makes you think you're qualified to work for this company?

Defensive response: I've done . . . [You rattle off a list of reasons why you are qualified.]

Nondefensive answer: That's an interesting question. You're in a better position to answer than I am. What do you feel is the one thing that would make me qualified?

Or: That's an interesting question. I could answer that better if I knew more about the job, and more about the company.

If you think someone is deliberately trying to manipulate you, the best answer, said with humor, might be "What makes you think I'm not?"

Here's a tough one: "Tell me why you were fired from your last job." That's a damned if you do, damned if you don't kind of question. If you weren't fired, quickly say so. Otherwise, explain calmly that it was a mutually agreed-upon parting of the ways, and immediately ask another prepared question.

Interviewer: Do you like working with people or things?

This is a loaded question unless you know what the job is. As Dustin Hoffman said to the director in *Tootsie*, "Which answer will get me the job?"

Interviewer: What are several of your recurring problems?
Candidate: My definition of a professional is a person who recovers fast and seldom makes the same mistake twice. Do you agree?

By holding a nondefensive position you can consider the interview a challenging experience and enjoy it.

Talking Money

Never talk money until you know there's a job offer. This is a different tactic than negotiating for a raise. Wait until the interviewer is sold on you. No matter what. If you must, wait for the second or third interview. The more time they invest in you, the more they have at stake.

If the interviewer asks you early in the interview: "How much money are you looking for?" you counter, "Is this a job offer?"

Or if that seems too direct, ask another question: "I think it's more important that we talk about your needs first, and if I'm the right person we can talk about salary a little later." Then ask another question: "What would you say is the primary skill needed to succeed at this job?" Think of it as a game. Once you deflect a question or refuse to answer, you must throw the ball back in the other person's court by asking another question.

If the interviewer asks you about money at the right time, and you're ready to negotiate, your immediate task is to avoid naming the first figure. There are three levels of interviewers: people who can offer you any amount of money, people who can offer you a range, and people who can only offer you a fixed salary based on company policy. You need to know the authority of the person who's interviewing you.

Interviewer: How much money are you looking for?

Candidate: I know a manager can negotiate basically three types of salaries—unlimited, ranges, fixed salary. Which category does this job fit into, and what are you offering me?

Interviewer: What are you looking for?

Candidate: What I think I'm worth and what you think I'm worth may be very different. What are you offering? [Stick with it. If you mention salary first, you've lost the advantage.]

Finding the job of your choice takes belief in yourself. A specific marketing approach is the key. You can handle the most difficult job interviews if you have the techniques. Knowing how to ask smart questions can help you discover where and with whom you'll spend those 96,000 hours.

Getting started in the right job, however, is only one step in moving ahead. You may be in the slot, but you now have to maneuver your way through the corporate maze—all the way to the top.

21

Tuning In to the Corporate Culture

Jeffrey is a witty, stylish vice president of operations for a well-known brokerage firm. He is respected by his colleagues and knowledgeable in his field. He loves his job, but he also loves his own time. Jeffrey comes in to work at 9 A.M. and leaves between 5 and 6. Because Jeffrey is an excellent manager, and because he has fewer people in his area than the other vice presidents, his group functions perfectly within Jeffrey's time span. Twice Jeffrey's been passed over for senior vice president of operations. Why? Because the corporate norm is 7 to 10, not 9 to 5.

It's not enough to do your job well. You must find a way to tune in to the vibrations of the corporation, read the hidden messages, and pick up both obvious and faint signals that unerringly point the way to success.

If there are 500 managers in your corporation, 450 of them are anxious to move up. Unfortunately, a corporation seldom has clear rules about how to get ahead. Managers are not provided with a road map that they can use to pick out the fastest and most efficient way to get from here to there.

Frequently the corporation itself isn't even aware of its many paths to the top. It may have some vague mile markers but does not outline specific roads for its managers to reach them. Corporations are always moving—fluctuating, changing.

A jogging friend of mine recently left her hectic, demanding job as an account executive in advertising, where she was on call evenings and weekends. She had recently married and had taken up skiing and wind-surfing. She wanted time on the weekends for her family and leisure activities. She was no longer willing to be part of a corporate culture which made such time-consuming demands. Fortunately she was able to go into her family's successful retail operation. Not everyone has such a viable alternative. But executives who want to move up must be aware of and compatible with the corporate culture, or find one that suits them.

One way *not* to get ahead is to ignore the corporate signals that do exist and set your own path. As William Granville, Manager of Technology Transfer at Mobil Oil Corporation, has pointed out: "Corporate fit is important. You must perceive the norms within the corporation. Either you must be flexible enough to adjust to them or you must find a corporation that matches your style perfectly. Corporations tend to promote people who fit the corporate structure, and then hire a team around those people."

Corporate Style

Even though many corporations today have some room for individual style, they still emphasize comformity. When you're looking to get ahead, it's important to know the culture of your organization. You needn't be a carbon copy of what you think the company wants, but your own personal style should be at least complementary to the company's ideals.

To quote human resources consultant Alan Barratt, "Managers tend to support people in their own image." Mavericks sometimes do succeed, but for the most part, if you behave differently from those who are respected and admired in your organization, you'll be slowing your own career momentum.

It's within your power to improve your image and your situation. Corporations are political institutions, with a lot of action and power shifts going on behind the scenes. So many people are in competition that getting close to the top isn't a matter of luck, it's largely a matter of honing your image so you can position yourself intelligently within your particular corporate culture.

When you examine behavior that is highly prized and rewarded in your organization, you may be surprised to find that much of it has little or nothing to do with getting the work done. Sometimes *how* you do something is more important than what actually gets accomplished.

Something as irrelevant as where people eat can turn out to be critical. In some companies, for example, executives are expected to lunch in the company dining room, and in others it's considered bad form. I know an account manager who recently went to work for an insurance firm with offices in the World Trade Center. During her first week on the job she was spotted lunching in the luxurious cafeteria in the lobby of the tower and was, fortunately, told the next day, "Our executives don't eat there."

Consider these seemingly innocuous factors: dress, manners, working hours, vacations, expense accounts, smoking, drinking, and the location, decor, and neatness of your office. Now, consider the executives in the upper reaches of management in your organization. How do they handle such things as dress and manners? Ask yourself:

"How well does my behavior fit?"

"Am I acting the way a successful person in my company is expected to act?"

"In what ways could my behavior be hurting my image and my career?"

Notice what leads to promotion and success in your organization. Corporations vary in terms of the styles of behavior that are rewarded. Take Ford and General Motors: from the beginning they represented two extremes of corporate styles. GM has always been clubby and genteel, with dozens of committees and multiple levels of management. Ford, by contrast, has a more competitive environment, with less staff review and more of an entrepreneurial spirit. The person who flourishes in the slow, well-ordered world of GM would undoubtedly founder in Ford waters—unless he tuned in to the difference and adapted his style.

At Mobil Oil, flexibility in relocating is deeply woven into the corporate culture. Only those executives willing to put time in at refineries in less glamorous parts of the world get a shot at the top.

Culture is often the result of a company's early needs and the personal style of its founders. Many brokerage and garment industry firms, for example, began as small family businesses and clung to this style long after they became large-scale corporations. They arrived late to the concepts of enlightened personnel development. Entrepreneurial in origin, they remain primarily interested in bottom-line objectives. According to these traditions, social skill, prudence, and loyalty to employees are qualities that come in second. Banks and utilities, on the other hand, possibly because they are traditionally concerned with an image of public service, pay more attention to the development of human resources.

To a certain extent culture is reflected across the spectrum of an industry, but within that image corporations often have varying styles. One of my clients manufactures a high-ticket item and the managers most valued within that corporation are polished, soft-spoken, and well dressed. Another manufacturing client, this one of novelties, couldn't care less how people dress as long as they can deal with the frenetic pace.

Corporate culture can be subtle. I knew a product manager who got fired because he used to walk into his boss's office without knocking. Although perceptive in other areas, his corporate antennae weren't hooked up. He failed to pick up the signal from his boss and other superiors that his behavior came across as too intimate. In that corporation the culture was formal, and executives were judged by the deference they inspired in their subordinates. The key to success in this case was to keep a polite distance.

Smart Self Questions for Getting Ahead

The concept that there is a corporate culture unique to every firm is not a new one. Nor is the notion that there are rebels who succeed in spite of the rules. But identifying the varied and individual factors that define a particular corporate culture can give you a definite advantage. The best way to isolate the corporate culture is to ask the right questions.

The answers will give you an overall view of all the little pieces that make up a company's corporate culture. Ask yourself these smart questions:

"How would I describe the type of person who is most successful in our corporation?"

"What is the company norm regarding working hours? Strictly 9 to 5?"

"Do important executives work late? On weekends?"

"Do they arrive at 7 A.M.?"

"Are they expected to wine and dine visiting clients?"

"What is the unstated dress code?"

"Are the company's leaders creative geniuses or buttoned-up administrative types?"

"Is the ambiance high-tech or high-touch?"

"Entrepreneurial or old-boy network?"

"Does the firm seek out academic degrees or street smarts?"

"Is getting the job done the thing that counts most—no matter what?"

"How fast do people move up the corporate ladder?"

"How many women and minorities are in middle to upper management? Line jobs or staff?"

"How often does the company promote from within?"

"Exactly who and what are being rewarded in the company? Who is really getting ahead?"

As you ask each question, apply the answer to your own temperament. Are you able to adapt yourself to suit this company? For example, if you're in a bottom-line-oriented company you could have a problem if your own priorities are people development and growth.

One of my clients is a computer support company performing all the programming and automated functions for several manufacturing firms. Executives who are valued are either highly creative programmers or calm, diplomatic individuals who can deal with the frustrations inherent in a support-type organization. An aggressive, pushing type of individual would not get far in this outfit.

Clothes, working hours, attitudes, can always be changed if you are willing to put in the effort. But a company culture that goes against the grain of your own personality and temperament is much tougher to come to terms with. Maybe the operation you're in will never make you happy and you should face that now. You may decide that rather than try to change yourself you should switch companies.

There are many different kinds of corporations. Many firms look for creative minds, while others seek out loyal, consistent individuals who will get along well with their colleagues and work hard. IBM, for example, is known for rewarding loyalty and service by taking care of its employees, offering excellent benefits and career security.

Hidden Messages

Sometimes it's hard to nail down the corporate culture. Firms frequently pay lip service to policies that have little to do with the realities of corporate life. Many companies send mixed messages. One overt message may be: "We want you to develop your people, bring them along, work with them, and focus on participative management." However, a penetrating look around will tell you that the people who get ahead are the steely-eyed, unyielding, bottom-line producers.

I work with a small manufacturing firm where the vice president of personnel earns over $100,000 a year, suggesting that the company is committed to developing its human resources. Yet the corporation does not spend any money at all throughout the year on professional seminars or training.

I'm also familiar with a large brokerage firm that proclaims it's out for quick profits. Yet top management is so conservative that it's hard to push anything through. In this corporate culture they do things very slowly, step by step. How they get the job done—safely and securely— is actually their biggest concern.

Perhaps your organization publicizes the fact that it's an equal-opportunity employer. When you take a good look, however, all top-level people are white male graduates of Ivy League schools. If you're a fast-track minority, you'll have to move mountains to change the culture. You may decide to switch to a company where there's greater opportunity.

Smart people recognize hidden messages. For example, suppose you receive a directive from your boss: "We assume that you'll take vacations and that your people will too."

You ask yourself, "Who gets ahead around here?" You observe that the CEO works around the clock and hasn't been on a vacation for the last five years. And that the managers who work for him are totally glued to their work and don't take vacations either. Those who actually take the time off that they're entitled to, on the other hand, rarely get promoted and don't stay around too long. Conclusion: If you want to get ahead, don't take vacations.

Some corporations tout reducing customer complaints and even give rewards for it. One customer-service manager in a large bank believed the overt corporate directive and concentrated on solving customer complaints. She was so successful at reaching this goal that she received an award at the end of the year. But her colleague, who ignored the directive, was promoted to vice president of customer relations. Why? This manager was responsible for bringing in a consultant who made the company $25 million with an innovative computerized direct-mail program.

Smart Questions for Tuning In

Developing a managerial style that fits with what's promotable in your company is important to your success. It's unlikely that you will ever find the ideal corporate culture to suit all your preferences. Nothing's perfect. Every new job and every new situation requires some adjustment on your part. You can't walk into a corporation and assume that the same norms you've been acting on in a previous organization will work in this one too. You may change the style of your dress, for example, if you switch from the fashion industry into banking.

Even as your job and level of responsibilities within your own company change, it's almost inevitable that you will need to make some changes in your style. Bosses and managers come and go; you join a new department or are promoted to a different area. Many such situations call for sensitivity and minor adjustments.

Successful managers know how to ignore meaningless objectives and tune in to the real corporate culture. It is especially important to answer these practical questions during the first couple of weeks on a new job. Take a good look around and ask yourself:

"Which corporate objectives are really going to help me get ahead, and which are just there for show?"

"How are decisions made in this organization?" ("By consensus? By individuals?")

"Are quick-decision-makers considered valuable?"

"How do I get support for my projects?"

"How do I get to the top people?"

"How do I get on the best committees?"

"Whom do I need to know?"

"Who makes the decisions?"

One company executive told me he discovered something during his first weeks on the job that proved invaluable for his later success: "In my company if you do something wrong, you can't win if you dig your heels in and get defensive. But if you throw yourself on the mercy of the court, they tend to be forgiving."

So here are some more smart questions to ask yourself:

"What happens in this corporation when something goes wrong?"

"If I make a mistake, how do I get another chance?"

"What happens if a manager refuses an assignment?"

Adjusting Your Style

"Corporations will bring in an oddball if they feel it will save a particular situation, but that person might not fit afterwards," says J. Sheldon Caras, Senior Vice President of Marketing at The New England (formerly New England Life Insurance Co.).

The go-getter who charges in to solve a major problem and does so successfully may have to change drastically once his initial task is accomplished if he hopes to move up in the company.

Not everyone can do what Thomas Jefferson did after he finished all of his courses at William and Mary University in two years. The college insisted that if young Jefferson wanted to graduate he must stay for four years, no matter how many courses he had completed. Jefferson left and eventually started the University of Virginia, which from its founding was based on less rigid principles.

Can you change your style? Certainly. Tuning in to what's going on in your company is worthless unless you also analyze your own style and figure out what you need to do to adjust.

Ideally, adjusting your image to fit the corporate culture should be a matter of polishing up the fine points. If your company has a style and a culture that makes you uncomfortable, rather than torturing yourself you should look for another company. On the other hand, if your company has a style and a culture that appeals to you but you don't fit in, then look for ways to develop your image along company lines.

Louise, a talented and experienced operations manager in a large brokerage firm, was virtually unpromotable because she was overweight, spoke poorly, and lacked a college degree. Several times her vice president had suggested she "get her act together." Louise promised to improve but never did. Fortunately for her, the vice president was eager to maximize her potential and engaged in a little smart questioning: "Where would you like to go in the company?" he asked.

"To vice president of operations," Louise replied.

"How do you expect to get there?"

"As usual—working hard. Wheeling and dealing with the right people."

"Have you noticed who gets ahead in this company?"

"The well-dressed, smooth-talking MBAs."

"If that's so, what do you think you'll need to do?"

"After I shoot myself . . . I could lose some weight and go back to school."

"What's first?"

"I'd better start with school—it takes longest."

"Let's get the catalogs and sign you up for the next semester."

Louise was lucky. I also remember a lively junior account executive in a large advertising agency. John had the energy and the hustle to make a good account executive, but not the style. He dressed in polyester suits and wore clip-on ties. His shoes were run down at the heels. A senior account executive thought enough of him to tell him about the dress code that he had failed to observe for himself.

Now, you may not be lucky enough to have a boss who cares enough to help you out in this way. Most managers have to take themselves in hand. Like Louise and John, many people feel that hard work will gain them recognition. This simply is not always the case. Conveying an easily recognized, dynamic impression is often the key that unlocks the door to success. Whatever your career choice, a solid, believable image can help you reach your ultimate goal.

Tuning Up Your Image

Showing your awareness of the image expected by your corporation reflects professional savvy and dedication. Those who control your career development will recognize that you're paying attention to the details and to the overall picture of the corporation. In short, your image serves as a vehicle for communicating your competence. It is a reflection that bears long-lasting influence in your bid for success.

Another important point is that any image should be consistent. It doesn't work if you get yourself together on some days of the week, and then on others—say, when you don't have any important meetings—just let yourself go. If you're consistent in your style, your bosses feel secure; they know they can count on you to present a positive image at any given moment. If you're erratic they'll feel insecure, always a little worried, never quite sure that you'll be on target in front of a client or supplier.

A question I often hear is "Isn't it dishonest to present some sort of image, when that really isn't me?" The answer to that is, what shows *is* the reality. Your image is an expression of your best self. It is not something you put on like a dress or a suit. Your image should reinforce all of your best qualities. For example, if you continue to show confidence even when inside you feel unsure, you eventually will feel confident.

Personal styles can vary within an organization, but a strong image almost always reflects certain constants: self-confidence, reliability, the unmistakable aura of success.

Self Questions about Your Image

To get your image together, ask yourself these smart questions:

"How am I perceived now?"

"If I were my own boss (peer, employee), how would I describe me?"

"How do I feel about those perceptions?"

"How do those perceptions fit my corporation's culture?"

"What do I have to offer my company that is unique and special?"

"How can I make the most of my uniqueness and still fit in?"

"What are the most attractive points of my current image?"

"Which aspects detract?"

"What can I do to enhance my best qualities?"

The Courage to Change

How can you use smart questions directly to help you find the right corporate fit? Do a little undercover research; ask around. Your self-perception could conceivably be very different from how others see you.

One brave executive in a large department store used the Smart Questions system this way: Katherine, a sportswear buyer, passed out an anonymous questionnaire to all the divisional merchandising managers and to the firm's senior executives, asking what they thought of her. Here are the questions she asked:

"What are my chances for promotion?"

"Could I become CEO?"

"Why? Or why not?"

"How would you describe my corporate image?"

"What would you do to change it if you were me?"

Katherine was surprised to receive neatly typed, but unsigned, replies from almost every executive. She was more than surprised when she read them. There was a definite consensus among the respondents. Katherine discovered that she was perceived as abrasive (she thought she was people oriented). They didn't like her staff. Overall, the respondents did not think she was "part of the team." No one felt she could become CEO unless she radically changed her style.

Katherine was determined. At last count she had not made it to CEO, but through her nondefensive reaction to the feedback she has begun to alter her style. She was recently promoted to divisional merchandising manager and has her eye on the next rung. The questionnaire told her that the hidden corporate culture valued a team approach. Simply sending out the questionnaire indicated to top management that she wanted to be part of the team. Her story supports the idea that people—especially important people—like to be asked for their opinions.

If you do decide to do an image makeover, do it subtly and gradually. Like dyeing gray hair, if you do it a little at a time, you'll eventually end up with a major change but people won't suddenly be taken aback.

Remember that a good image cannot work unless you back it up with self-confidence. Henry C. Rogers, public relations expert and author of *Rogers' Rules for Success*, says, "Self-esteem and self-image are all important. The beginning of any success story comes when a person begins to feel good about himself."

One of the most important jobs you'll ever have is to tap into your strengths and express the most positive parts of your personality—for the sake of your happiness as well as for your corporate success. You may change your clothes to suit the corporate climate, but the intelligence and enthusiasm and personality—all integral parts of your image—are yours. Images can grow with you.

Tuning in to the corporate culture is step one on the path to success.

Your corporate fit is important, but only a piece of the giant corporate road map. You can't sit in your office all day looking good and expect to get to the top. You'll be glad to know that although image is important, it isn't everything. There's plenty of evidence that brains and hard work still count the most. To get ahead today, you must be very very good at your job.

22

Rising Stars and Powerful People

Who does get ahead in today's complex corporate jungle? It's both a tricky question and a fascinating one. I interviewed a number of CEOs of major corporations, as well as top executives from a wide variety of industries, and their answers may surprise you. The responses were highly individualistic and varied; yet I heard the same fundamental themes expressed again and again. In this chapter I will use their answers to define the basic principles of getting ahead and to suggest questions that will send you on your way.

From Harvey Schein, the Executive Vice President of News America Publishing, Inc.: "The very very able, and the very very smooth, inherit the world." I begin with this piece of wisdom because it clearly isolates the two main factors that go into making a corporate "star": ability and image. Let's start with ability, in itself a complicated concept.

Ability

What does ability really mean in business terms? For a corporation, ability is valuable only when it translates into high-quality performance. And high-quality performance includes many factors: hard work, dedication, loyalty, and results are the essential elements that make your ability abundantly clear. Personal talents and abilities that are not used to fulfill corporate goals are talents and abilities wasted. Your dedication and enthusiasm must help your company first, if they are to help you in the long run.

William S. Lee, Chairman and CEO of Duke Power Company, makes this comment: "To get ahead takes a combination of sensitivity and inner courage. You can't be defensive or afraid of change. You must be able to put your personal aspirations aside and do your best for the company."

William Granville, Manager of Technology Transfer for Mobil Oil, agrees that the company should come first: "To get ahead," says Granville, "you must support the principles of your organization. If your principles clash with your company's you're not going anywhere. Highest marks go to loyalty and competence."

Gerard A. Miller, Vice President, Director of Finance, Merrill Lynch and Co., Inc., adds that hard work is vital: "The person who gets ahead has the ability to get things done. He has a vision of where he's going and where the organization is going. A strong work ethic, coupled with commitment. You must be willing to pay the price—long work hours, and dedication."

And Alan Barratt, a human resources consultant and former Mobil executive, agrees: "You must have political and organizational sensitivity and a devotion to duty. You must be hardworking, self-starting, someone who's not going to put his foot in it."

Several corporate authorities say that they can spot a "comer" by his or her dedication and enthusiasm. "If the person always delivers on time," says J. Sheldon Caras, Senior Vice President of Marketing for The New England, formerly New England Life Insurance Co., "it tells you one thing. But if that person beats a timetable it tells you something else—that he's an eager beaver, and somebody to watch."

Supporting the company is also essential. The sure sign of a rising star, according to Helen Galland, President of Helen Galland Associates and former President and CEO of Bonwit Teller, is the person "who shows enthusiasm for projects—and endorses projects even if he or she isn't 100 percent in agreement."

It's clear that applying your capabilities to your firm by virtue of loyalty and hard work can turn your ability into star quality.

Always Say Yes?

Another aspect of having a lot of ability is deciding when to use it. Lois Wyse, president of the New York office of Wyse Advertising, was interviewed recently by *Success* magazine and advocated a policy of enthusiastic acceptance:

"I tell my daughter, 'Always say yes, because nothing ever happens to girls who say no.' It's true in business and it's true in life. 'Will you stay late and work?' If you say no, nothing good is going to happen to you. 'Can you take this extra assignment?' If you say no, *nothing* is going to happen to you. You have to learn to say yes."

Alan Barratt also advises that you take on a wide range of tasks in order to learn all you can: "Get a variety of jobs before age 35; if you're in a small company, move. If you're in a large organization, work in different divisions."

Film producer David Brown also credits his success with a "do-everything approach." "I was always willing to take on more than one job," he said in a recent magazine interview. "When magazine staffs were being cut back and organizations were being decimated by the Depression, I would do everything: I'd even be on the switchboard if necessary."

As a result, Brown learned everything about the publishing business. When a major reshuffling came about at his magazine, *Liberty*, Brown was the only person on the staff who had experience in all editorial departments and was the only person qualified to be editor-in-chief. It was this position that led him to a job with Darryl F. Zanuck, and eventually to the board of directors at Twentieth Century Fox.

The enthusiastic and adventurous attitude that these authorities suggest is clearly a plus for anyone looking to broaden his range of opportunities and gain attention as well as experience. But I would advise some caution. Saying yes to everything is fine in theory, but in the real world you have neither the time nor the energy to accomplish everything. Your time is valuable. In a corporate situation, when you're asked to volunteer, ask yourself if it's a project that you, your company, or your boss really values. If the project is a low priority with the company, or something that upper management really wouldn't pay attention to, it's foolish to devote weeks of energy to it. There are scores of other areas where your efforts would be appreciated.

It's great to get out there and handle the switchboard if your office runs into a crisis. But to let yourself get stuck doing double duty indefinitely because of some sense of idealism or martyrdom is a waste of your talents and energy. Overall, do volunteer, do the job—any job—but put your priorities and energy where they will count most.

"... And the Very Very Smooth"

As Harvey Schein pointed out, ability alone is not sufficient for success. You must cultivate an image of power and success in order to distinguish yourself from the group. Alan Barratt says: "You need to be a visionary, to have a magical aura."

William Granville makes an attempt to address this elusive magic. "The fact that you are worthy of respect travels along the grapevine; it is never officially granted or acknowledged." Says Granville, "Present yourself so people want to be associated with you. Dress the part, assume control, forget about being part of the crowd. Stay out front. And when you ask a question, ask a good one."

The smart question to ask yourself is: "How can I get positive attention without violating the prevailing corporate culture?"

J. Sheldon Caras told me, "In a dynamic organization, you need to show more difference than sameness to rise to the top. You must be a little bit of an iconoclast."

There's a fine line, yet a big difference, between the oddball and the star performer. For example, in certain large brokerage firms a top producer can be a little unconventional and still move up. You can wear a striking color or carry a flashy briefcase and get away with it, especially if it's not the dominant part of your image.

Herman Kahn, of think-tank fame, used to wear sneakers with his business suits when he made client presentations. In the early days of Doyle Dane Bernbach, when that original and creative agency was beginning to gain national recognition, one copywriter sent in his copy on cocktail napkins.

I knew a manager in a large textile plant who had clocks that went off and played a tune every hour. Because he was such a fine executive and his plant was a top producer, the firm used to joke that perhaps every manager should play the same tune. As Abraham Lincoln said when told that General Grant was drinking too much whiskey, "Get me the brand, and I'll send a barrel to my other generals."

On the other hand, the eccentricities of an average or poor performer would be looked upon with considerably less humor. The corporate culture will dictate the allowable degree of deviation.

Visibility

The main point, of course, is that you must be highly visible if you're going to rise to the top—but you have to be visible for the right reasons. There's a fine line to walk between being visible and being arrogant. Every company has its share of prima donnas; I'm sure you've run into someone who will do anything to draw attention to himself. If he's got the talent, he may be tolerated. He will certainly never become a trusted leader, however, and it's more likely that his showing off will get him shown to the door.

I know an extreme case where a top executive was hired by a cosmetics firm to help straighten out the marketing department. He went full steam ahead—and then ran right off the rails when he hired his own personal publicity agent. Theoretically the PR person was paid as a consultant to the company, but it soon became evident that his major concern was touting this one executive to the newspapers. This was a fatal error on the executive's part, and not surprisingly, he was fired.

On the other hand, a certain degree of self-promotion is natural and even necessary. If there's an opportunity to deal with the press or to comment publicly on something you've achieved, grab it. You don't want to hang back and stub your toe in the dirt. No one goes around checking to see if any wallflowers are in bloom. Ego, drive, and pride in self are all important for success.

But of course there's a world of difference between a strong ego—essential to any success—and an overblown one, which is destructive as well as offensive. The person with an overblown ego is always climbing over someone else to gain recognition and needs to be continually patted on the back. He thinks he's a cut above the others. And he typically talks down to the people who work for him, which immediately disqualifies him from being an effective manager or leader. The worst part about overblown egos, from a corporate viewpoint, is that they are easily manipulated. All anyone has to do to get the right response from them is to apply a little flattery.

The person with a strong ego, on the other hand, knows his own strengths. He's confident. He has a realistic idea of what he can accomplish, and he moves purposefully toward his goals.

How can you get visibility in your company without looking like an egomaniac? How can you be appreciated for your strengths and get the credit you deserve without spending all your time at it? You want to be visible—but you want to be visible in the right way.

The first thing you have to do is to develop a strategy for increasing your visibility. If your aim is the top, you have to start very early with a well-chiseled image that you will present to the world. Your image should be a common thread that runs through everything you do. It should be apparent in your letters, memos, clothes, relationships, every aspect of who you are.

Having this focus on yourself and your role will help you in all your responsibilities and job functions. It will help you do your job with more imagination, flair, and effectiveness. Start by asking yourself:

"How do I want to be perceived?"

"How do I want people to perceive my role in the company?"

"How do I want individuals (my boss, my peers, my staff) to perceive my relationship with them?"

"When I write a letter, a speech, a memo, or a presentation, what do I want the receiver to know (feel) about me?"

"How can my image help me to communicate and excel?"

Visibility and Power

Power, resources, and opportunity always flow to the visible high achiever. In fact, power and visibility go hand in hand. Whatever the fine points of your image, being a person of power has to be uppermost and consistent. As William Granville stated, you must "assume control."

You know when power is yours—and it always shows. You are listened to when you speak. People solicit your opinions. No phone calls go unreturned. You're invited to sit in on important meetings.

Power is sometimes acquired in the simplest ways. Inventory your verbal and nonverbal signals. Monitor your speech and manner. Stand and sit alertly. Walk briskly into a room as if you're in command of yourself.

Most important, ask the right questions and answer questions briefly and vigorously. Smart questions allow you to exhibit your competence and confidence. That sense of self-esteem will send out signals that others can't miss.

Allen E. Murray, Chairman of the Mobil Corporation, cautions that the misuse of questions can be devastating: "Questions that reveal that the other person hasn't been listening or hasn't studied a proposal are annoying and cast the questioner in an unfavorable light. I believe listening is a critical communication skill that should be mastered."

William Granville says this about questioning: "Questions give you power. Ask questions—but not a lot, and only the right ones."

When you do your homework and use your head, questions are by far your most valuable tool for gaining positive attention and respect at all times, whatever your strategy for visibility and success.

Increasing Your Visibility

Meetings are one perfect arena for you to show yourself. Every company has them—all the time. Surprisingly many executives overlook the opportunities meetings offer for increased visibility simply because there are so many of them that they take them for granted. It takes leadership abilities to run meetings or give talks, lectures, or seminars. But they are all good ways to build your visibility.

Speaking at a meeting is entirely different from private conversation. It requires thought and preparation. A speaker may be well informed, but if he hasn't thought out exactly what he wants to say today, and to this audience, he won't stand out.

It's imperative that you make the effort to learn how to speak effectively. Many fine speakers were shrinking violets when they started out. There are a lot of people out there with terrific ideas who have trouble explaining them to other people, but this needn't be the case. It's always a shame when a person with great talent can't tell the board or a committee what's in his head.

Self Questions to Enhance Your Performance

Examining how you perform at meetings, and then continually refining your technique, is a good way to boost your campaign for greater visibility and success. Try these self questions after every big meeting:

"How well planned was my presentation and contribution?"

"Did I have the right people there?"

"Whose support could add clout to my next meeting?"

"How did I perform in the leadership role?"

"Did I exhibit power and control in a charismatic way?"

"If the CEO of the company had been there, how would he have evaluated this meeting?"

"Did I enhance my image?"

"Did I ask smart questions?"

"Did I listen to the answers?"

And don't get discouraged if the responses you come up with are negative—just get better.

In addition to becoming a good public speaker and running results-oriented meetings, there are other ways to make yourself visible. For one thing, you can set out to become an expert in a particular area, and make yourself stand out in this way. Knowledge is power. Vera was an average manufacturing executive in a textile firm. She had studied the Asian markets in college and spoke some Chinese and Korean. Hence, when her company got involved in the Asian market, she became the expert and her career skyrocketed.

This can work in any field; the business world will always need its computer specialists, design kings, research whizzes. It takes talent and certain skills, yes, but like everything else, in most cases it's 99 percent determination and perspiration.

Publicity

Publicity is a terrific way to gain visibility. If you have an opportunity to be interviewed for a newspaper, magazine, or news program, say yes. But never, under any circumstances, allow yourself to be interviewed without first being prepared (unless it's on something you've talked about many times before). An interview can feel like a battle between you and the interviewer, and it's a battle you can win if you know what you want to get across. No matter what the interviewer says or asks, you answer with the points you want to emphasize. Observe politicians and others being interviewed on television and watch how they answer questions with their own answers, regardless of what the question was:

"Mr. So and So, is it true your company is planning to build an eighty-story building on the site of the old mill pond?"

"You know the wonderful thing about that, Bill? This new building will bring so much new vitality to this area. . . ." You get the idea.

Maintain the momentum of a locomotive. Whatever happens, you keep barreling along. Know your material inside and out. And before any interview, think of all the rotten questions an interviewer might throw at you, and figure out a maneuver to deflect each one.

Whatever you do, when you are interviewed, be brief. Thirty seconds should be enough for any answer.

Filling the Vacuum

Many executives I spoke to advocated this particular method of getting ahead, and it's among the most challenging and creative of all. "Organizations pay attention to vacuum-fillers," says Harvey Schein, "the people who can identify and grasp opportunities."

J. Sheldon Caras has this to add: "The person who gets ahead is able to think beyond the horizon—beyond the narrow furrow of his or her job."

And Ed Weihenmayer says, "Keep your eyes open for opportunities. There should be no boxes—no limits—on your imagination."

What are these high achievers suggesting? Simply that you do more than get your own job done and wait to be promoted through the regular channels. They are advocating that you take your career advancement into your own two hands and create a promotion track for yourself.

As an ambitious person today you can't simply wait for desirable jobs to open. Take the less conventional route: carve out your own position.

Identifying the Opportunities

Exactly how do you find these "vacuums" to fill? J. Sheldon Caras says that people who succeed know their organization's goals and expectations: "They stand back and ask themselves: 'What is the general direction of this organization? What has to be done to steer it that way? What is not being done now?' Then they come up with an answer and follow it through."

Harvey Schein adds that asking smart questions can help you spot any niche waiting to be filled:

"What problems does my company have?"

"What problems does my department have?"

"What are the issues involved?"

"Is upper management concerned about this problem?" (If the answer is no, forget the problem. If the answer if yes, then that's the one to try to solve.)

Harvey Schein's questions lead to others: "What does my company need? A new product line? A cost-cutting system? Another marketing approach?"

Take a good long look at the marketplace, as well as your industry and your competitors. Which way is the wind blowing? Ask yourself:

"Is the industry getting more high-tech? More high-touch?"

"Is the public demanding expanded services? More specialization?"

"Is the company keeping tabs on modern developments and trends?"

"Are there new ways to cut costs or overhead? Are we operating efficiently?"

Are you a manager who can anticipate the future and take advantage of it? When you have a vacuum-filling idea, do all the research you can. Figure out the potential ramifications for your company, yourself, and your job. Your final step is to write a thorough, practical, and well-documented proposal. Show it to your boss.

If he or she is uncooperative and unresponsive, try your boss's boss. In extreme situations, if your vision warrants such a drastic measure, go to the top.

Remember, nobody will be anxious to implement an idea for you simply to advance your career. Your suggestions must clearly benefit the company in a significant way.

A personnel director at a hospital developed a series of workshops that the hospital could offer to women in the evenings as part of a community service program. In her proposal, she showed the hospital administrator how they could exploit the wasted nighttime space that they paid rent and utilities for anyway, and gain public recognition in the process. Her program was a great success in the community, and as an additional benefit it ultimately brought new patients into the hospital.

An operations manager at a company that manufactured bedspreads—a slowly declining industry—came up with a way the company could convert their looms to make draperies and wall hangings.

A vice president of sales promotion in a retail manufacturer thoroughly researched and developed a program to create a mail-order department for his company, expanding their business by 37 percent in a single year.

All of these projects took vision, insight, research, and hard work—and all of them were successful.

Help from Powerful People

An entirely different approach to getting ahead involves enlisting the aid of powerful people. In other words, finding a mentor.

Victor Kiam, CEO of Remington Products in Connecticut, said in a recent interview, "Never be associated with someone you can't be proud of, whether you work for him or he works for you."

But don't just latch onto someone because they wield power. William S. Lee suggests asking yourself this important question first: 'What do I need a mentor for?' If you need a mentor to learn from, then choose the person who can teach you the most in your field. Go with the best; whatever reason you need a mentor for, attach yourself to a fine example and learn from him or her. The value of a mentor is not getting ahead, but to develop and stretch yourself." And that, of course, is what ultimately leads you to success.

Make sure you consider what that particular mentor means to you. According to Ed Weihenmayer, "A mentor is usually not a kindly person being nice to you. It's someone who is interested enough to tell it to you straight. The mentor relationship relies on being candid. If you're the recipient, you must have the confidence and maturity to listen to what the mentor tells you."

In almost all of my interviews, everyone agreed that mentors are important. Everyone uses mentors in some way, shape, or form. But finding the right mentor might not be easy. Forget about the traditional form of mentoring, where a powerful person picks you out and guides you up the success path; it's great, but it's like winning the lottery—one chance in a million. If you're going to find the right mentor, you'll have to do it yourself.

Self Questions for Choosing a Mentor

Advice is a commodity seldom in short supply. Your challenge lies in identifying the person who can offer advice that's worthwhile. It's a good idea to begin your quest by asking yourself a few smart questions:

"What do I need mentoring in?"

"Who would be the best person to give it to me?"

"Do I respect the person enough to listen to him—and take his advice?"

When these questions are answered, you can go to the next step: "What is the best way to approach this person?"

Suppose you come up with the perfect mentor. You're going to ask him or her to do something for you, to give up time and energy and information. Working in your favor is his instinct to express his ideas. The desire to be helpful may also encourage him to share information. Make the process enjoyable for the person of your choice: ask him interesting questions, display your interest. Many people enjoy having a protégé and nurturing a career, turning their knowledge over to another. A mentor also may get satisfaction from exercising subtle power in order to help your career.

Look for ways you can meet the mentor's needs. Say a top-level executive has a strong personal interest in a charity. Offer your help and support. Freely give your time to help him do his thing—but you must make it your thing, too. You must sincerely and generously give of yourself, with no strings attached. This is not a business deal or a fair exchange. Give loyalty and respect if you want to get any in return.

A young performer I know has worked his way to the top of the nightclub circuit with the aid of a famous Broadway composer. The performer has a history of gaining the sponsorship of well-known show business personalities. How did he do it?

He's a genuinely giving and talented young man who offered his services to organize and catalog musical memorabilia and materials solely for the privilege of helping some of the older, currently less prominent names in the music business. He spent months in dusty basements going through boxes of disorganized and abandoned files, put them in order, and then typed out catalogs of everything he had found for the use of music scholars.

True, he was in the right place at the right time. But I'm convinced that he never used his connections in a calculated attempt to get a leg up in the world. When he met someone he respected, he looked for a way to offer help. If deep down he was conscious of every move he made, it certainly never showed.

A mentor is not something you go and fill out an application for.

When asked how to get a mentor, J. Sheldon Caras could only offer: "Natural affinity. Social friendship is unnecessary, but there must be mutual liking and respect. Work for a trusting relationship that works both ways." The mentor must trust you. If he feels you're looking out only for yourself, why should be help? And he added, "If you have one, and he or she is the right one, you're fortunate."

Having a Mentor

Gerard A. Miller says, "Mentors are vital for the creation of history in a corporation. They pass on to individuals the goals and aspirations of the organization. One important value of a mentor is to guide you in decision making. He can tell you what the norm is in your organization, tell you what top-level management takes into account when they make decisions."

And Helen Galland suggests that once you have a mentor there are certain things you should do, and certain things you should not do: "Never say 'no'—always try whatever your mentor suggests, or at least say you will. Even if the task seems difficult or impossible, always make an effort and show that you tried. But don't be a 'yes' man and jump at every request your mentor makes."

She continues, "Although many successful people don't have them, mentors do give you an advantage. There are many different kinds— passive mentors, someone just to talk to; active mentors, those who give you specific help by introducing you, making moves for you, generally paving the way."

William Granville agrees that having one powerful mentor may not always be the best way to get ahead and nurture a career. "You have to seek new sponsors at different levels and get different sponsors for different purposes, different components of your work. You may need a professional sponsor for one thing and a personal sponsor for another."

Alan Barratt explains how different mentors may be appropriate at different stages: "In the beginning of your career a mentor can help you identify who's got the power in the corporation structure. Later in your career a mentor can support you when you are trying to make moves in the organization. Still later, as you get toward the top, the best help a mentor can give you is to be your confidant."

Certainly mentors come in many different stripes, but three of the most basic are the mentor who offers technical training and information; the mentor who can help you politically, and the mentor who serves as a role model, someone you watch and emulate in terms of how they dress, think, or handle themselves. (In this case, your role models may not even know that they're your mentors.)

One last suggestion: When you ask for advice or mentoring, be sure you're looking in the right places. Power can be dispensed only by those who have it. Power is transitory; it shifts from hand to hand, from year to year. The question uppermost in your mind should be: "Does the person from whom I'm seeking power and help actually have it to give?"

To conclude this chapter on getting ahead I'd like to make a distinction between the specific goal of getting to the top and the broader concept of achieving success. Fran Tarkenton, former NFL quarterback and chairman of The Tarkenton Productivity Group, had this to say in a recent newspaper interview: "Success, in my view, is the willingness to strive for something you really want. The person not reaching the top is no less a success than the one who achieved it, if they both sweated blood and tears and overcame obstacles and fear. The failure to be perfect does not mean you are not a success.

"The people part of management is the hardest part," says Tarkenton, "but it's the most important part—making people feel like human beings, with a purpose in life."

If the future belongs to the very very good and the very very smooth, it also belongs to those perceptive and flexible human beings who can anticipate and recognize technological and social changes around them, and in the process still maintain a strong professional and personal image. This is the challenge managers face today. Those who can cope best with change, who can help their people adapt more quickly and comfortably, are the successful leaders of the future. One way to start is with smart questions.

The underlying advantages of developing a smart-questioning approach go far beyond the ability to handle specific job situations well. Once you have mastered a natural questioning response, you have disciplined your mind to think clearly and to respond creatively in almost any situation. And clear thinking has a positive effect not only on your job, but on your life.

People who think and ask smart questions before they act make fewer mistakes. All of us have made blunders that we wish we could take back. But when you're in the habit of asking good questions—getting all the angles and relevant information before taking action—you have a better chance of making a decision you can live with.

Smart questions let you make a major change in your life with relatively little effort. Getting in the habit of using your head to question yourself and then question others is not difficult. The most important step is to fully accept the power and value of asking smart questions and start putting them into practice whenever you can. It becomes easier as you gradually feel more and more in control of your situation and eventually your career.

Asking questions is obviously important in life, but it's essential in a successful manager. With all the responsibilities and stress a manager has to deal with, smart questions are the ideal way to break out of the running-in-place mode managers often find themselves in and to give your career a forward thrust. Only when you begin to ask the right questions do you begin to find the right answers.

Index

A

Ability, 270–273
Achilles Syndrome, The (Bloomfield and Felder), 202
Am I Getting Paid for This? (Rollin), 42
Answering question with another question, 51
Anxiety, questions to reduce, 33
Appraisal (*see* Performance appraisal)
Authority, delegation of, 141–142
Awards, merit, 134–136

B

Barratt, Alan, 259, 271–273, 282
Bennis, Warren, 132
Blanchard, Ken, 205
Bloomfield, Harold, 202
Brainstorming, 203–204

Brown, David, 272
Buckler, Beatrice, 248

C

Calculator type personality, 63–65
    asking questions of, 65
    characteristics of, 63–65, 68
    managing, 65
    negotiating style of, 221, 222
    working for, 65
Caras, J. Sheldon, 265, 271, 273, 278, 282
Career and Confidence Inventory, 244–246
Career planning, 242–243
Carer type personality, 62–63
    asking questions of, 63
    characteristics of, 62–63, 68
    negotiating style of, 221, 222
Carnegie, Dale, 3

285